THE UNITED STATES AND IRAN

Also by James F. Goode

THE UNITED STATES AND IRAN, 1946–51: The Diplomacy of
Neglect

The United States and Iran

In the Shadow of Musaddiq

James F. Goode
Professor of History
Grand Valley State University
Michigan

St. Martin's Press
New York

THE UNITED STATES AND IRAN
Copyright © 1997 by James F. Goode

St. Martin's Press, Scholarly and Reference Division,
175 Fifth Avenue, New York, N.Y. 10010

First published in the United States of America in 1997

This book is printed on paper suitable for recycling and made from fully managed and sustained forest sources.

Printed in Great Britain

ISBN 0–312–17272–9

Library of Congress Cataloging-in-Publication Data
Goode, James F., 1944–
The United States and Iran : in the shadow of Musaddiq / James F. Goode.
p.   cm.
Includes bibliographical references and index.
ISBN 0–312–17272–9
1. United States—Foreign relations—Iran.   2. Iran—Foreign relations—United States.   3. United States—Foreign relations—1945–1989.   4. Musaddiq, Mohammad, 1880–1967.   I. Title.
E183.8.I7G66 1997
327.73055'09'045—dc21

96–50912
CIP

To Robert H. Ferrell and David M. Pletcher
In admiration and friendship

Contents

Preface

In the early years of the cold war, the government of the United States found its time almost consumed with concerns about the Soviet Union, but in what little time remained it often discerned communist conspiracies against third world countries – with the purpose of discomfiting the United States. Such proved the case notably in relations with Iran, where there was some Russian activity but not nearly as much as Washington officialdom espied.

In those early years of involvement in Iran the United States was not alone. Great Britain had a major economic stake there, the Anglo-Iranian Oil Company, and did all it could – both in Washington and in Tehran – to push the Iranian government into what it considered good behavior.

Some of the tale that follows may seem familiar. But when one analyzes British and American contacts with Prime Minister Muhammad Musaddiq and his officials, one finds a remarkable series of misunderstandings. How wonderful if, somehow, they could have been allayed. They originated in the very different cultural backgrounds of the principal players, who brought their biases to whatever they sat down to negotiate. Often one side seems not to have heard what the other was saying, basing responses on preconceived ideas. This happened repeatedly during the oil crisis in Iran, with fateful consequences. To be sure, Musaddiq was by no means free from such thinking – almost to the end he believed the world could not do without Iranian oil. But US and British failure in this regard was notable. Representatives of the two Western nations held the whip hand, their nations having arrogated positions of power; it was incumbent on them to make a greater effort at understanding.[1]

The saga of the United States versus Musaddiq did not end with the coup of 19 August 1953 that removed the Iranian leader from power. For Musaddiq personally little was left. He seemed no longer to count. He spent three years in prison and passed his final years under house arrest outside Tehran. His health deteriorated – he always had been fragile physically. He died in 1967. But he in no sense was apart from the scene.

For long years his memory haunted the West. And it assuredly should have. We study him today because what happened in his time dramatically affected American policy for years thereafter, and not only in Iran but throughout much of the so-called third world.

Decades have passed since the initial errors, and it is time to look back, even though the world's equations of power have changed drastically with the collapse of the Soviet Union. From what one can now adjudge, looking at the world of the late 1990s, the future problems of international relations – and, because of the intertwining of economic fortunes these days, the problems of domestic politics – are going to arise in connection with developments in the smaller and sometimes the smallest nations. The third world has fragmented into a congeries of national groups, each vying for attention. It is no longer possible to ignore the newly independent peoples, however small their geographical confines, however parochial their outlooks. Which is to say that the Iranian experience of the early years of the cold war is going to be repeated, unless officials of the major governments, and now notably those of the United States, face up to those experiences, look carefully at the errors of the past, and determine not to repeat them.

Acknowledgements

To the librarians and archivists of the Franklin D. Roosevelt Library, the Harry S. Truman Library, the Dwight D. Eisenhower Library, the John F. Kennedy Library, the Bennett Library and the Gerald R. Ford Library, Ann Arbor, the Library of Congress, the National Archives Diplomatic and Modern Military Branches, the National Archives Pacific Southwest Region, the Naval Historical Center, the Public Record Office, Kew, the Australian Archives, the University of Georgia, Grand Valley State University, the Houghton Library Harvard University, the Lilly Library Indiana University, the Seeley G. Mudd Manuscript Library Princeton University, the Foundation for Iranian Studies, Bethesda, MD, the Bodleian Library, and the London School of Economics, I extend my sincere thanks for their assistance and many kindnesses, without which I could not have written this book. Special appreciation also to Professor Geoffrey Warner of the Open University for access to the diary of Kenneth Younger.

I would like to thank also the diplomats and officials who willingly shared their memories with me. These included John Bowling, Henry Byroade, Richard Cottam, Robert Komer, George McGhee, George Middleton, Mehdi Sami'i, Peter Ramsbotham, Dean Rusk, Phillips Talbot, and Denis Wright. For their financial support of my research, I am grateful to Grand Valley State University, the University of Georgia and the National Endowment for the Humanities.

To those scholars who read all or part of this manuscript and offered helpful suggestions, including Ervand Abrahamian, Richard Frye, Mark Lytle, Afaf Lutfi Al-Sayyid Marsot, Linda Qaimmaqami, David Pletcher, and William Stueck, I extend my sincere thanks. As always, Robert Ferrell has been especially generous in this regard.

My family, Virginia, Matthew and Zachary, have supported this project with their patience, interest, and understanding, for all of which I am truly grateful.

Chapter 13 appeared earlier in slightly different form in James F. Goode, 'Reforming Iran During the Kennedy Years,' *Diplomatic History* 15 (Winter 1991): 13–29, and is reproduced here by permission of Scholarly Resources.

List of Abbreviations

AID	Agency for International Development
AIOC	Anglo-Iranian Oil Company
CENTO	Central Treaty Organization
CIA	Central Intelligence Agency
EDC	European Defense Community
IBRD	International Bank for Reconstruction and Development
IMF	International Monetary Fund
MEC	Middle East Command
NSC	National Security Council
NIOC	National Iranian Oil Company
OCI	Overseas Consultants Incorporated
OPEC	Organization of Petroleum Exporting Countries

Prime Minister [Shahpour] Bakhtiar visited ex-Prime Minister Mossadeq's grave and made brief speech saying Mossadeq's ideals were now being implemented and promised reburial of Mossadeq's body where he originally wanted to be buried near Rey with others who were killed during Mossadeq era.

Ambassador Sullivan, 26 January 1979

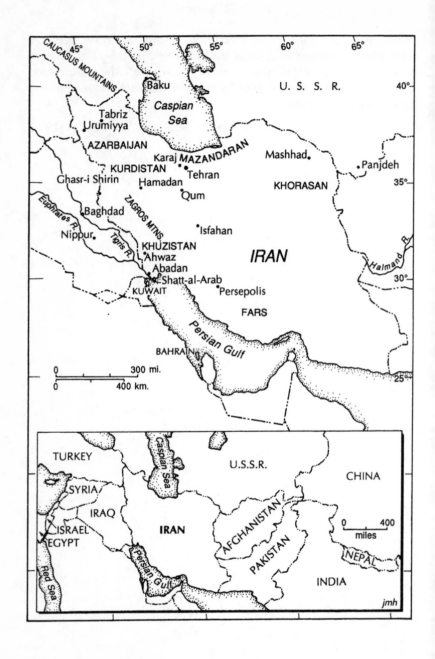

1 The American Experience

Iran and indeed the entire Middle East attracted little attention in the United States prior to World War II. To be sure, there were bursts of concern, such as the Perdicaris affair in Morocco during President Theodore Roosevelt's first term, or the scheme to establish a mandate over Armenia in 1919. But such events were spasmodic and only confirmed in American minds stereotypes of Middle Easterners as uncivilized, even barbaric, hardly capable of managing their own affairs. Such notions developed out of centuries of Christian–Muslim conflict on the borders of Europe, which left a legacy of mistrust. European expansion into the region in the nineteenth century exacerbated these animosities.

Reports from American travelers to the Holy Land often strengthened prejudice. Authors such as Herman Melville, John Ross Browne and Mark Twain wrote disparagingly of the land and people. Melville, the least critical, noted that 'No country will more quickly dissipate romantic expectations than Palestine – particularly Jerusalem. To some the disappointment is heart sickening.' Browne first met Arabs at Zanzibar, years before he traveled to the Middle East, and concluded they were 'second to no people in the art of loafing . . . of all the shameless libertines I ever saw the Arabs are preeminent.' At Damascus he 'saw nothing but . . . lazy dogs and lazier Arabs, basking by the roadside "showing mutually the luxuries of dust and flies."' All this led him to conclude 'how much better are American ways than those found abroad.' He neatly forgot that American cities in the nineteenth century were hardly places of scenery worth remembering – for years pigs rooted in the streets, and even in the century's last years the smell of manure from the horses hung over everything. From Twain, of course, criticism of 'foreign' places abounded. He poked fun at them. Of the scene between Damascus and Tiberias, he wrote, 'the people of this region in the Bible were just as they are now – ignorant, depraved, superstitious, dirty, lousy, thieving vagabonds.' In Samaria he slept with 'lice, fleas, horses, jackasses, chickens, and, worse than all, Arabs for company all night.' As for Jerusalem: 'Rags, wretchedness, poverty and dirt, those signs and symbols that indicate the presence of Moslem rule more surely than the crescent-flag itself.' What most impressed him was 'a combination of Mohammedan stenches,' (oddly, considering the primeval stench at home) leading him to observe that 'such is Oriental luxury – such is Oriental splendor!'[1]

The Middle East remained far removed from American concern – it might, to use a popular phrase, have been on another planet. Whether for travel or intellectual curiosity, not to mention business, US interest centered on Western Europe and some select parts of Central and South America and, to be sure, the islands of the Caribbean.

In the unformed, uncivilized, smelly Middle East, so far as Americans measured the area, the US government naturally had little reason to interfere, and such impressions as the nation's people made upon the area were largely by what one might describe as unofficial personages, who were usually missionaries or archeologists. In a real sense they were chosen instruments for what little diplomacy existed. They chose themselves. Their personal interests brought them to the area and then, once they were in residence, affected their outlooks and actions.[2]

Missionaries proved the most important national presence. They had come out of the early nineteenth-century revivals to establish missions in the Ottoman Empire at Smyrna, Constantinople, Beirut and lesser cities in eastern Anatolia, and later in Iran at Urumiyya (1835), Tehran (1871), Tabriz (1873), and Hamadan (1881). They may have exercised as much influence as their better-known colleagues in faraway China. Forbidden to proselytize Muslims, they worked among the isolated Christian minorities – Armenians, Nestorians and Orthodox – and Jews. Their schools fostered local nationalisms. In Anatolia fear aroused by missionary activity may have contributed to the Armenian massacres. Creation of a Maronite-led Lebanon under French tutelage in 1920 owed something to missionary schools. It is easy to exaggerate, for Muslims avoided missionary institutions, believing 'a Muslim who sent his sons to a Christian school was equivalent to a man who commits adultery in public.' Nonetheless the influence of the schools was there.[3]

If the missionaries contributed less to Middle East national-ism than was previously assumed, there is little reason to doubt their impact on popular views in the United States. To attract financial support, missionaries on leave presented lantern slides to eager audiences in towns and cities across the land. They used these opportunities to speak of the baneful influence of Islam, which, they contended, worked against progress and enlightenment.

The US government sometimes called on missionaries to represent the country, as was the case with the Reverend Henry Jessup and Iran in 1882, and in times of trouble missionaries always turned for succor to powerful political friends at home.[4]

Another source of involvement came via archeological ex-peditions and digs, which began in the 1880s. The University of Pennsylvania organized the earliest, but other institutions, among them the University of Chicago, the University of Michi-gan, and Yale University, soon joined in. If their presence was intermittent, their influence was profound. They, too, were sources of lantern slides, on such fabled subjects as Persepolis, Luxor and Nippur. The very names caught attention. In such a country as the United States where almost everything was new, at least as compared to the Middle East, it was fascinating to hear of places where life had gone on for ages as opposed to the rawness of even the largest cities in the United States, a land where the frontier itself only came to a nominal end (there remained huge expanses of virtually unsettled land) in the year 1890.

Archeologists, too, had tales to tell at home that did not reflect well on Middle Easterners. The noted Egyptologist and founder of Chicago's Oriental Institute, James H. Breasted, attributed the uprisings he witnessed in Egypt and Iraq (1919–20) to the Arab predilection for violence, and wrote approv-ingly of the mission there of the mandate powers under the new League of Nations. Another, responding to incessant foot-dragging by authorities in Ankara, urged the necessity of cuffing Turkish ears; reflecting on earlier times, he thought 'Roosevelt and Curzon would make the right combination.' Thus archeo-logists added to the store of confusion, not to say prejudice, coming to the public through slides, lectures and publications. The halls of Congress echoed the refrain as senators debated the Armenian mandate and doubted the courage of Armenian men who could not protect their women and children against malevolent Muslims.[5]

Not all Americans reported negatively on the region. Lew Wallace, author of *Ben Hur*, minister at the Ottoman Porte (1881–5), toured the United States on his return, extolling Turkish virtues of 'sobriety, piety, and tolerance.' But when he persisted during the Armenian massacres of the mid-1890s, audiences hissed him. Samuel G.W. Benjamin, minister to Persia (1883–5), found much to praise in Islam and within Persian society, but audiences preferred his books on art and sailing. Dismissing Benjamin's insightful *Persia and the Persians*, one reviewer observed that the author was, after all, 'not an Orientalist.' One wonders, to be sure, if the reviewer was an orientalist – and, if so, if he had managed to get to Western Europe, not to mention what was known a century ago as the Near East.[6]

Benjamin represented a small group of US diplomats – among them E. Spencer Pratt, Morgan Shuster and Wallace Murray – who over the decades came to know and admire Iran and Iranians, and did what they could to extend, improve and, when necessary, smooth relations. But they busied themselves almost exclusively with disputes between missionaries, archeologists, an occasional businessman, and the Iranian authorities.

Prejudice prevailed. Americans seemed unpersuaded by arguments that ran counter to notions built up over years of religious controversy. Increasing disparities in wealth and power between East and West reinforced the belief that the Christian, democratic, and progressive West was superior in all respects to the Islamic, autocratic, and stagnant East. Benjamin faced a difficult assignment when he joined the missionaries in Tehran. It was to protect those 60 or so Americans in Iran that relations were established. The minister did not always approve their methods, but he served ably for two years until a change of party in the Executive Mansion led to his recall.[7]

More numerous and influential were diplomats who conjured a less flattering image of Iran, a land, they said, of ignorance, corruption and disorder. Arthur C. Millspaugh, would-be financial savior of Iran in the 1920s, returned during World War II to redeem his failed program, only to be forced to withdraw a second time. Resenting his double defeat, he attacked Iranians in his *Americans in Persia*, attributing failure to flaws in their character. Burton Y. Berry, diplomat, connoisseur, collector of

Near Eastern art, found Tehran unbearable. Although he had served happily in neighboring Turkey, from the day he crossed the frontier at Ghasr-i-Shirin in October 1934, he found fault. After six months he discovered not a single virtue. He no longer feared Judgment Day, he declared, for even if assigned to hell it could not be worse than Tehran. In a trip north to Mazanderan on the Caspian shore, he admitted 'the people of that province are a lot more like people than the humans that inhabit the other provinces of Iran I have visited.' He departed Iran on Thanksgiving Day 1935.[8]

Berry's colleagues shared many of his sentiments. Tehran offered fewer refinements than Istanbul and points west, and yet one is puzzled by the criticisms leveled by so many who served there. Foreigners have accused Iranians of xenophobia and to the extent that this assessment is accurate it can be attributed to local history, most of which foreigners were blissfully ignorant. Iran had struggled over the centuries to maintain cultural identity. Wave after wave of invaders – Greeks, Romans, Arabs, Turks, Mongols, Russians, Britons, Americans – tried to mold the land and people. Each left their mark, none succeeded. In Egypt one encountered a warmth and openness toward strangers that might startle an arrival from Tehran, where one had to work to penetrate the culture. Iranians resented criticism. In the 1930s, Riza Shah broke diplomatic relations with the United States because newspaper stories offended him. What might have seemed trivial rankled. He reestablished relations only on the eve of World War II.

Meanwhile, Britain became the dominant power at Tehran. For decades Britain and Russia had vied for influence at the shah's court. In 1907 they agreed to divide Iran into spheres to lessen confrontation such as that at Panjdeh on the Afghan border in the mid-1880s, where British and Russian surveying parties almost came to blows. Iran was nominally independent, but representatives of king-emperor and tsar could exercise much influence. Then in 1917 came the Russian Revolution and the Soviets withdrew, leaving the field to Britain. London negotiated the Anglo-Persian Agreement, which aroused fear that Britain wanted to turn Iran into a protectorate. A storm of protest, including a blast from Washington, contributed to its defeat. This setback did not discourage General Edmund Ironsides from using his influence as commander of British

forces in northern Iran to advance the career of Colonel
Riza Khan of the Cossack Brigade, who established the Pahlavi
dynasty. Ironically, Riza, a reformer and a nationalist, opposed
foreign influence, and for this reason attracted support from
politically active Iranians.

Unlike the Americans in these years, the British had a substantial economic interest in Iran. The Anglo-Persian Oil Company in the southwest represented one of the country's most
profitable overseas investments. Under Winston Churchill, First
Lord of the Admiralty, the government became a majority
shareholder just before 1914. In the depression of the 1930s,
Iranian oil represented one of the few bright spots in Britain's
ailing economy.

The years passed, everything seemed the same (save for the
oil), and yet it was not the same. The curtailment of foreign
influence had been one of the major goals of the Iranian
Constitutional Revolution that began in 1906. It drew support
from the ulama, the body of Muslim scholars and jurists, who
resented the spread of Western ideas at the shah's court.
Muzaffar al-Din Shah (1896–1907) was pressed into signing a
constitution, which called for an elected parliament, the Majlis,
and restricted royal prerogative, limiting the monarch's power
to mortgage the nation's assets. Such action had provided rulers
of the Qajar dynasty (1794–1925) with a favorite method to
pay for lavish trips to Europe, and as a consequence foreigners
had obtained increasing control over Iran's resources.

Meanwhile, liberal nationalists – only a small minority after
1918 – had become frustrated in their attempts to establish a
constitutional monarchy. The rapid rise of Riza Khan saw the
establishment of a regime that although reformist and nationalistic was increasingly despotic. Riza Shah, as he became after
1925, coopted many constitutionalists, who approved his steps
to strengthen the army, put down rebellion in the provinces,
and end the treaty rights enjoyed by Westerners. They took
pride in the 'new' Iran, ignoring the shah's ruthless domination of parliament.

It is a curious fact, however, that not every constitutionalist
made peace with the new regime, and chief among those who
held out was Muhammad Musaddiq. In the changing schemes
of things in twentieth-century Iran, Musaddiq represented a
small sign of encouragement, if representatives of the Western

powers had had the wit to see what he stood for. He supported
Riza Khan until it became apparent that Riza intended to seize
absolute power. Musaddiq was one of only five deputies in
1925 who voted against establishment of the Pahlavi dynasty.
For his opposition the shah sentenced him to many years of
imprisonment and internal exile.[9]

In the present century nationalism was rising, and after the
World War of 1914–18 Iran felt its effect, at the same time that
its oil was becoming important to the world economy. In many
ways politics in Iran seemed much as always – a business, virtually, of influence. But now, as the hold of Riza Shah became
ever more obvious, there was the very interesting spectacle of
Musaddiq rising in opposition, and suffering for it.

Musaddiq came from a prominent family of landholders; he
was related to the previous dynasty through his mother. His
father, who died when he was a boy, had held high positions
during the reign of Nasir al-Din Shah (1848–96).

The future leader was really a remarkable personage. As a
young man he pursued his intellectual interests in France and
Switzerland, receiving a doctorate in law from the University
of Neuchâtel in 1914. Following his return he gained respect
for his honesty and patriotism as provincial governor of Fars
and Azarbaijan. He often recalled his mother's advice that the
importance of an individual in society was equivalent to the
hardship he or she suffered on behalf of the people. This
principle guided him throughout his long political career. He
loathed corruption and made enemies in a system where it was
endemic. His memoirs recount numerous incidents while in
government service of confrontations with colleagues, even with
superiors. His high standards and reputation for integrity
helped limit his tenure in office.[10]

Musaddiq admired some reforms that Riza Khan introduced
as minister of war and later as prime minister, but refused to
accept him as a ruling monarch, for that, he believed, would
violate the constitution. In parliamentary debate he spoke out
against the dynasty:

Today, in the twentieth century, is it possible that anyone
can accept that a constitutional country can have a govern-
ing king? . . . if you wanted such a person, why was the blood
of so many spilt on the road to freedom? . . . You could have

spared many lives by coming out on the first day and saying that we do not want a constitution, we do not want freedom, we are an ignorant people and have to be ruled by the sword. . . . Even if they cut my head off . . . I will not accept such words.[11]

He failed to embolden his fellow deputies, who voted overwhelmingly to make Riza Khan shah. Nevertheless, his refusal to embrace the regime in the interwar years enhanced his reputation.

Musaddiq respected the constitutional monarchies of Western Europe, none more than that of Britain, which he considered a model for Iran. He respected European culture and once considered becoming a Swiss citizen. But he opposed the wholesale adoption of Western ways. Useful ideas and methods needed to be adapted to suit the Iranian way of life, otherwise they would prove unworkable. He opposed the use of foreign advisers, who had little or no experience in Iran; they rushed to introduce alien laws and methods.[12]

Furthermore, he considered these advisers agents of foreign governments, threats to Iran's independence. From earliest days in government service he had opposed the influence of foreign powers, especially Britain, which he had witnessed in the provinces. Drawing on those experiences, he rarely missed an opportunity to point out their harmful effect. The British, who possessed the greatest economic and hence political interest in Iran, received his harshest criticism. To limit foreign influence he espoused a policy of negative equilibrium. Rather than siding with one power, Iran should remain neutral, freeing the nation to pursue its interests.[13]

Musaddiq's political formation was largely complete by the end of the 1920s. He was no ideologue, but until the end of his life he remained firmly attached to the fundamental principles of freedom for his people and independence for his country.[14]

The outbreak of World War II in September 1939 raised several sensitive issues that eventually affected the United States. At that time, to be sure, few Americans were bothering themselves with Iran, which to use the phrase of Neville Chamberlain in regard to Czechoslovakia, was a faraway place. For

Americans, having barely survived the Great Depression, and looking forward to more normal ways of life after a decade of what seemed the worst tribulations, the Middle East was one of the last places on which they conferred their attention.

Not so the British, whose representatives in Iran had become suspicious of the shah's increasingly cordial relations with Germany. The Soviet Union had sought to reestablish the influence in Tehran which it had abandoned in the early years of the revolution. The shah was looking for a third power as an alternative to Britain and the USSR. When the United States showed no interest, Riza Shah turned to Germany, obtaining military and technical advisers and purchasing goods not manufactured in Iran. Two years after the opening of war, the abortive anti-British uprising in Iraq in May 1941, followed by the German attack on Russia, convinced the British and Soviet governments that they could not risk a German breakthrough in the Caucasus, which would bring Hitler's troops to the borders of a friendly Iran. They decided to act. Riza Shah failed to heed warnings from London and Moscow that he should expel the several hundred German nationals in his country, and on the morning of 25 August Iranians awoke to leaflets fluttering down on city streets, announcing an Anglo-Soviet invasion:

IRANIANS!

There are thousands of Germans on your soil; according to important plans they hold key positions in your industry, and they are only waiting for one word from Hitler to disrupt your principal source of wealth [oil]. The German embassy has organized all this and each one has his special assignment. You know how German instigations caused such uprising and revolution in Iraq. The failure there had no effect in keeping them from doing the same thing in Iran. This is the same method followed in many small European countries before the Germans overcame them.

Those gentlemen in control of Iran paid no attention to our repeated warnings and feigned ignorance of Germans on your territory. This is not just a danger for you but also for the English and the Russians. We have decided that the Germans must go and if Iranians will not deport them then the English and Russians will and our forces will not

welcome resistance. Iranians! We have no quarrel with you
nor designs upon your nation nor upon your property or
your lives, we only want to expel the accursed Germans
because they have no motive except to involve your country
also in the circle of war and bloodletting and to punish you.
If you help us now, we will help you now and in the future.[15]

Iranian resistance quickly collapsed. The shah abdicated and
went into exile, leaving the throne to the 21-year-old crown
prince, Muhammad Riza. Overnight the political situation
changed. Political prisoners went free, censorship ended,
political groupings appeared. Although nationalists criticized
foreign intervention, theirs was no more than a pro forma
declaration; the overwhelming mood was one of euphoria over
the shah's departure.

A few months later the Japanese attack on Pearl Harbor
brought the United States into the war. Britain's forces were
spread too thinly around the world, and London invited Washington to send troops to Iran to operate the supply lines from
the Persian Gulf to the hard-pressed Soviets. So began the
Persian Gulf Command, 30 000 American soldiers to man the
Bridge to Victory over which passed tens of thousands of trucks
and airplanes, and millions of tons of supplies to blunt the
German offensive.

It is of considerable interest that an American presence in
Iran – which would necessarily be followed by far more interest in Washington than ever had been evident before – had
little to do with Iran itself, but with Iranian territory, which
one might describe as Iranian facilities. The people and government were incidental. The Persian Gulf Command appeared
in Iran without any formal agreement with the government
in Tehran; only later did diplomats attend to the niceties. The
young shah, whose power was negligible, did not oppose the
arrival of US troops, thinking they might provide a counter-
poise to British and Soviet forces. Suddenly, Washington found
new interest in Iran. President Franklin D. Roosevelt off-
handedly suggested to his roving emissary, Brigadier General
Patrick J. Hurley, that Iran might become a model for development after the war, providing an example to the world of what
American expertise and initiative could achieve. One could not
take Roosevelt's passing suggestion seriously. Nothing came of it.

On a more substantial note, the United States, at the request of Iran, sent two military missions, one to the Iranian army, the other to the gendarmerie. The army mission under General Clarence Ridley had a decidedly minor role. It came without adequate personnel but managed to reorganize the quartermaster corps and to run a few training schools. Brigadier General H. Norman Schwarzkopf, father of 'Stormin'' Norman' of Gulf War fame, did much to rehabilitate the corps of gendarmes. Unfortunately he became entangled in local politics, antagonizing the shah and the Iranian chief of staff, and eventually had to leave.

After Riza Shah's hurried departure, the Majlis once again became the focus of national political life as the constitution of 1906 had intended. Although the thirteenth Majlis, organized prior to August 1941, represented continuity, the fourteenth, elected between November 1943 and February 1944, revealed how far change had proceeded. Over 800 candidates vied for 136 seats, and numerous factions struggled for power. Almost half the deputies elected were newcomers, which indicated that the body would be difficult to manipulate. Important landowners dominated – in numbers – but many deputies came out of the urban intelligentsia, and from the first session in March 1944 debated issues with unusual passion.

Musaddiq took the lead in several debates. He advocated a policy of negative equilibrium, which would deny favors to any power, rather than positive equilibrium, which had sought to attract one or another power by offering it special advantages in Iran. Pursuing this policy, he successfully opposed a Soviet oil concession in the north in 1944 and then all oil concessions.[16]

Exploiting their expanding power during the war, the Soviets pressed Iran for a northern oil concession. Although officials opposed the idea, no one dared speak out. Musaddiq, recently returned to parliament after years of imprisonment and house arrest, did not hesitate to defend the national interest. He feared that a Soviet oil concession would trap Iran between the common oil interests of Britain and the USSR and that Iran would never be able to rid itself of their baneful influence. Deputies responded to his speeches, refusing any concessions during the war and requiring postwar governments to obtain Majlis approval before entering into oil agreements.[17]

With somewhat less success he argued for governmental

rather than royal control over the military, which he saw as the prop for Riza Shah's despotism. He sought disfranchisement of illiterate Iranians, whom he believed were too easily manipulated by corrupt officials and landlords. He would pursue these two issues after he became prime minister in 1951.[18]

Iranian politics confused Westerners. Unable to fathom the shifting alliances among the deputies, and within the court, they easily concluded that Iranians were 'irrational . . . undisciplined, unprincipled and erratic.' Or, as British Ambassador Sir Reader Bullard (1941–6) opined, Iranians were psychologically immature.[19]

In Western chancelleries Musaddiq came to represent all that diplomats disliked most about Iranian politics. They considered him old-fashioned, narrow-minded, xenophobic, and even 'a hysterical and demented demagogue.' He earned opprobrium for opposition to foreign oil concessions in the fourteenth Majlis, and reports to Washington had little that was good to say about him. Generally they just ignored him.[20]

It is not surprising that Musaddiq received so little attention from the Americans during the years 1944–51, for to those who knew little about the complex Iranian political scene this elderly nationalist (63 years old in 1944) seemed to operate at the margins of political life. He consorted, they charged, with extremists of the left such as the Iranian communist party, the Tudeh, and those of the right, such as Mulla Abulqasim Kashani and perhaps through him with the terrorist Feda'iyan-i Islam (Devotees of Islam) as well.

Musaddiq espoused causes that if successful could weaken containment of the Soviet Union, a serious consideration as the cold war intensified in the early postwar years. He wanted Iran to pursue a neutral course, adhering to neither East nor West. He spoke of the need to maintain good relations with the Soviets even though he would not tolerate attacks on Iran's sovereignty from them or from anyone else. His call for neutralism and negative equilibrium found much support. 'No Iranians are madly in love with Uncle Sam or John Bull,' wrote one editor, 'only friendship and respect [for them] and the same can be said for the USSR.' According to another, 'Iran is not a colony and has no need of guardians.' Others called for Iran to become the Switzerland of Asia. Whether or not such sentiments were realistic, most politically active Iranians

– including the shah – were initially reluctant to join a power bloc.[21]

These Musaddiq sentiments fell on deaf ears in Washington, where officials considered them defeatist and naive and those who espoused them became suspect. When an occasional diplomat suggested that what really mattered to Iranians was not communism but rather imperialism and the standard of living, such comments passed unnoticed.[22]

Musaddiq continued to oppose the employment of foreign advisers, whom he considered detrimental because they took from Iran, giving little. Moreover, if they came from one of the major powers, their employment would violate the principle of negative equilibrium. He remembered the failed missions of Millspaugh, who had become embittered and painted Iranians as weak, inefficient, corrupt, faithless and therefore not entitled to run their affairs.[23]

Washington looked askance at such heretical views, for civilian and military advisers figured prominently in the American plan to contain the Soviets. The two military missions continued to expand after 1945 in conjunction with the supply of surplus US materiel for the Iranian army. Then came Overseas Consultants Incorporated (OCI), a private consortium of mostly American firms designed to develop Iran economically. And finally the US government's own Point Four began operation at the grassroots level, digging wells and improving livestock-breeding in Iranian villages. Washington expected these advisers would help stabilize Iran and make it more resistant to Soviet intrigue. Musaddiq worried that American advisers, representing their own nation's interests, would do all they could to align Iran with the West, a policy he thought disastrous. Thus, he preferred to use Iranian experts whenever possible and only if absolutely necessary would he condone the use of foreigners – and then he tried to recruit from such nations as Italy, Mexico or the Netherlands, states that had no strategic interests in Iran.[24]

Finally, Musaddiq continued his crusade to limit the shah, to turn him into a constitutional monarch. To accomplish this he needed to cut the tie that bound the military to the Pahlavis. Despite his deep suspicions of British policies in Iran, Musaddiq had great respect for Britain's constitutional system, and he repeatedly urged the shah 'to stand above politics' and 'to

avoid the dirty business of appointing and dismissing ministers, deputies and governors.' In that way he would gain the
respect of the whole nation.[25]

This argument, too, ran counter to American policy in Iran.
At first the United States had considered Muhammad Riza
Pahlavi weak and inexperienced, but as the nation staggered
from crisis to crisis, and as the Soviet menace grew, policymakers
put aside concerns about the shah's limitations and embraced
him as the only source of stability in that chaotic land. Officials quickly understood that the monarch's chief support would
come not from an adoring people, most of whom were indif-
ferent, but from the army. Hence it was crucial to bolster the
shah's powers and to maintain his ultimate control over the
military. Ambassador John C. Wiley (1948–50) encouraged
them with reports of the childlike simplicity of the Iranians.
'The paucity of competent public men in Iran is appalling,'
said he. 'Like the story of the ten little nigger boys, the roll
call in Iran ends, "and then there was one." He is the shah.
When the shah is eliminated, Iran will disintegrate. Iran is ripe
fruit on the tree of Soviet appetites.' Wiley never considered
Musaddiq or any of the National Front leaders, who represented a loose coalition of middle-class interests, potential prime
ministers.[26]

If US diplomats in Iran came to rely almost exclusively on
pro-American officials and politicians, they were not impressed
with the caliber of the material. Most of them seemed politically inept and even the shah, they concluded, was emotionally
and psychologically unable to do all that the Americans would
have liked. This led to an audacious conclusion. 'Iran,' wrote
the second secretary, 'can continue to exist only as a free nation
because of our will that that be so.' Behind this bold, confident statement lay the longstanding and often-repeated view
that Iranians were incapable of taking care of themselves.
This notion had infected American thinking on Iran – and
the Middle East – for decades; and it seemed impervious to
change.[27]

Many Westerners needed to spend only a short time in Iran
to become 'experts' on the weaknesses of the national character and then to prescribe remedies. Iranians, like their Muslim
brothers elsewhere, were intellectually dishonest. They lacked
faith in themselves due to a real spirit of inferiority, showed

resignation to the will of Allah, evinced no loyalties except selfish personal ones, lived day to day, made no effort unless there was an immediate return. The litany went on and on. Rarely did observers – especially diplomats – note a single redeeming virtue. How, one wonders, had such an unfortunate and poorly endowed people maintained its political and cultural identity for millenia?[28]

Observers disagreed whether it would be better to reform Iranians or to control them. Commiserating with the ruler of this forlorn land, Second Secretary Joseph Wagner wrote: 'If nature had worked things out correctly, the shah would have been born a good, middle-class Christian, in a Christian land.'[29]

The point is not that Iranians were without faults, nor that Americans working in Iran were not frustrated in their relations with Iranian colleagues and counterparts, but rather that Americans and Europeans surrendered to a thinly veiled chauvinism, which repeatedly undercut opportunities for understanding, led Iranians to become skeptical about the supposed benefits of contact with the West, and ultimately worsened relations.

And so Americans ignored Musaddiq and the National Front, whose opposition to royal power ran counter to policy. Almost no one seemed to ask whether a popular leader such as Musaddiq might not provide more stability in the long term than a regime propped up by the army.

In late 1947, Musaddiq had strong support for the prime ministership, for as one editor noted, 'No one is his equal in patriotism and love of freedom.' But the shah intervened to defeat him. The Americans did not know this freedom-loving Musaddiq, for what little information filtered through to Washington provided only negative views. The British, of course, seldom missed an opportunity to belittle him. The US embassy in Tehran, in one of its rare references to him, inaccurately characterized the National Front as a coalition ranging from extreme right to extreme left, inclining toward support of Tudeh party policies, and led by Musaddiq, 'the apostle of a strange political creed called "negative equilibrium".' Two months later the embassy reported National Front deputies opposed to branding North Korea the aggressor in the Korean War, showing their true colors by attending Soviet and Polish receptions while avoiding Fourth of July celebrations at the

American embassy. The shah helped sow the seeds of doubt in American minds when, in early 1949, he justified not having consulted Musaddiq regarding the calling of a constitutional convention because he seemed 'not to be in full possession of his senses.'[30]

A crisis loomed at the end of 1950. Embassy officers continued to meet with the shah, court politicians and members of the traditional elite; all those who had come to support alliance with the West. Moreover, as the shah's power grew, the Americans became more reluctant to risk offending the very suspicious monarch.[31]

Often in history one can tell as much from what did not happen as from what did. When we examine reports on Iran between September 1950 and April 1951, critical months when the oil crisis was intensifying, Musaddiq's name is conspicuously absent. An embassy document of 25 September 1950 mentions him once; a Central Intelligence Agency (CIA) report of 16 March 1951 refers to 'ultra-nationalists' and to 'Mulla' Kashani but is silent on Musaddiq; notes from the undersecretary's meeting of 25 April – less than a week before Musaddiq became prime minister – with both Secretary of State Dean Acheson and the special assistant to the president, Averell Harriman, in attendance, make no mention of the leading Iranian personality.[32]

It should come as little surprise that US officials were unprepared for the rapidly changing events in Iran after Musaddiq came to power. Ambassador Henry F. Grady, who had earlier entertained many royalist politicians, scheduled his first meeting with Musaddiq for 2 May, the day *after* he became prime minister. Here one cannot resist an analogy to events years later, in the late 1970s, when the regime was crumbling and even the shah urged US officials to contact Ayatollah Khomaini at his headquarters outside Paris asking, 'How can you expect to have any influence with these people if you won't meet with them?' *Plus ça change.*[33]

2 Background to Crisis

When World War II ended in August 1945, Iran was in a pitiable state. Tens of thousands of Soviet, British and American troops occupied its territory; autonomy movements in Kurdistan and Azarbaijan, the breadbasket of Iran, threatened national unity; and inflation and chronic shortages of food and other consumer goods presented a bleak prospect for the months ahead.

After the withdrawal of British and American soldiers in the autumn of 1945, international attention focused on northwestern Iran where Soviet forces remained in apparent violation of the Tripartite Agreement signed at the Tehran Conference in December 1943, pledging that all foreign troops would leave within six months of the end of hostilities. The Americans became increasingly suspicious of Soviet motives, and with US support Iran brought a formal complaint – the first – to the newly organized United Nations Security Council. The world watched in dismay as the two recent allies exchanged harsh words, an omen of what was to come.

While diplomats wrangled at the Security Council, Iran's elderly prime minister, Ahmad Qavam, a seasoned politician, moved cautiously in the interstices of the great powers, seeking a way out of the crisis. Since the early years of the nineteenth century, Iranians had had much experience negotiating with their northern neighbor; many officials in Tehran spoke Russian fluently. Qavam did not want his country to become a pawn in the deepening cold war. In March 1946 he flew to Moscow for meetings with top officials and shortly after his return in April he signed an agreement with Ambassador Ivan Sadchikov, offering the Soviets majority interest in a 25-year northern oil concession with the understanding that they would first withdraw their troops from Azarbaijan.

His agreement with the Soviets has been the subject of much speculation. Did he surrender too much? Did the Soviets need Iranian oil as they claimed or was this a ploy to achieve political domination of the north? Did Qavam trick the Soviets, knowing well that the Majlis would reject the pact once the troops had gone? How could Stalin have been fooled? Or was he? Whatever the answers, and they are far from clear even today, the Soviets did leave in early May 1946. The Majlis vote was delayed until late 1947 when the deputies finally and overwhelmingly rejected the proposed oil concession.

How important was the Iranian role in negotiating an end to the crisis, which some historians consider the beginning of the cold war? The Americans have taken most of the credit for the Soviet retreat, but Iran's action was at least as important as that of the United States. Secretary of State James F. Byrnes did give Qavam room for maneuver by pressing the Soviets in the UN, but the Iranian leader proved how adept he could be when his nation's interests were threatened.

After rejecting the Qavam–Sadchikov agreement, the Majlis turned its attention briefly to the British concession in southwestern Iran, where the Anglo-Iranian Oil Company (AIOC) had been pumping oil since 1909. The deputies passed a vaguely worded motion calling on the government to talk with the concessionaires 'with a view to securing Iran's national interests.' No one knew exactly what that signified, but it became the basis for discussions that stretched out over the next three years.

Well-informed Iranians were aware of new agreements in Venezuela that gave that nation much more for its oil than Iran received. At issue was not just profits and royalties, but national sensitivity to the fact that the AIOC operated as an *imperium in imperio*, to wit, southwestern Iran had become an enclave where the writ of the company went further than that of the government in Tehran. The company shared little information with Iranian officials and blithely ignored increasing signs of opposition. Company negotiators, led by Neville A. Gass, could barely conceal their surprise, therefore, when they received a long list of Iranian demands at their first session in late 1948. Gass promptly postponed further talks until he could consult his colleagues in London.

At Britannic House, AIOC headquarters in London, company officials concluded that Iranian demands were a red herring, and that corrupt Iranian officials only wanted to get their hands on more money, so they dug in their heels, announcing that they expected a quid pro quo for any sweeteners extended to Tehran. Thus, from the beginning, the AIOC and the British government, the majority shareholder, misunderstood the nature of the Iranian demands, assuming that the fundamental issue was financial, when in fact it was political and even psychological. 'The British made us feel like nobodies in our own country,' an Iranian author has written, 'a small, weak people, eternally pushed around by outside interests that only cared about oil money and power.' This was what the British ignored at their peril.[1]

Despite the sensitive nature of the controversy, the Foreign Office provided little direction to the company. This proved disastrous because 'the weakest point in the Anglo-Iranian set up was on the side of the company [led by Gass] which dealt with foreign relations.' The AIOC persisted in resisting all non-financial demands. Talks dragged on into 1949, becoming the focus of nationalist agitation. When a supplementary oil agreement finally emerged in summer 1949, local opinion was so hostile that it stood little chance of Majlis approval.[2]

Nationalists had good reason to protest. The company ignored government suggestions that its accounts should be open for Iran's inspection, that an Iranian should serve on its board of directors, and that Iranians should occupy an increasing percentage of the better positions in the company. Likewise, the AIOC rejected claims that Tehran should share in profits earned outside Iran in ventures developed since 1909 with profits from cheap Iranian oil. In return for relatively little the new agreement would discharge the company of all past obligations to Iran.

Opposition was sparked by Musaddiq and a number of other leaders, who formed the National Front. The corrupt parliamentary elections held in fall 1949 provided the catalyst for the front's formation, with members taking sanctuary at the palace until the young shah agreed to call new elections. Eight National Front deputies won seats in the parliament and although only a small fraction of the 130-member lower house they became an effective opposition for they carried an authority denied other members, who had been put there to represent special interests.

Initially the front focused on corruption within the court–army clique and indirectly on the shah's increasingly bold measures to enhance his power. Since the collapse of the breakaway regimes in Azarbaijan and Kurdistan in December 1946, a development for which the shah received much credit, the second Pahlavi had done all he could to restore powers stripped from the throne when his father abdicated in 1941. He insisted on exercising direct control over the chief of staff of the Iranian army, a possible violation of the 1906 constitution, and wanted to appoint and dismiss key officers. Through control over the army he could influence elections in rural constituencies. He appointed the minister of war and the court minister, presided over weekly cabinet meetings and met frequently with Majlis deputies. A constitutional convention called at his behest in 1949 granted him the power to dissolve parliament and created a senate to which the shah would appoint half the members. His powers had expanded considerably by the early 1950s.

The Americans largely applauded these developments, seeing in them a chance for stability and perhaps even progress. No one in Washington seemed concerned that the shah's enhanced powers might herald a return to the dictatorial ways of his father. Diplomats brashly dismissed any such possibility, concluding that no such development could take place in postwar Iran.

The front only turned its attention to the oil question in summer 1950. A year earlier Prime Minister Muhammad Saed had tried to slip the supplementary agreement through parliament in the closing days of the session. Nationalist deputy Husain Makki led the successful filibuster, asking sensitive questions to which the government did not adequately respond. Thus, the bill, which to nationalists seemed lopsidedly to favor the AIOC, was held over for the meeting of the sixteenth Majlis in May 1950. In the ten-month interlude the National Front was born, and its leaders prepared to encourage popular agitation against the so-called Gass–Golshayan agreement, named after its chief negotiators.

Musaddiq became chairman of the special parliamentary oil committee that would review the supplementary agreement and report to the Majlis. Several National Front deputies joined him on the committee so that they made up one-third of its 18 members. Tensions between Musaddiq and the new prime minister, Ali Razmara, former chief of staff of the Iranian army, rose perceptibly through the waning days of 1950. Razmara, a capable, hardworking, almost puritanical officer, had gained the shah's confidence. He believed he could initiate reform and bring the nation out of its confusion. 'He knew where he wanted to go and expected to make decisions and be obeyed.' Initially Razmara disclaimed responsibility for shepherding the supplementary oil ageement, signed by his predecessors, through the Majlis. But the shah and the oil company pressed him to support it. Hoping he could work out an arrangement with the company for increased royalty payments, he spoke out about the danger to the nation's economy should nationalization come too soon and at the cost of Britain's friendship. In a showdown with Musaddiq and his supporters on the committee, the prime minister boldly declared anyone advocating immediate action a traitor. Four days later, on 7 March 1951, a right-wing assassin gunned him down. The prime minister had been the only leader willing to oppose immediate nationalization, and his opposition cost him his life.[3]

Decisions on oil, postponed for nearly two years, suddenly reached a conclusion in the weeks following Razmara's assassination. On 15 March the Majlis passed overwhelmingly a one-article nationalization bill, followed on 28 April by a nine-point bill authorizing seizure of AIOC properties. [See appendix.] Musaddiq became prime minister the next day. The British and Americans were stunned.

Of the parties to the crisis that erupted in spring 1951 – Iran, Britain and the United States – the Iranians presented the greatest unity of purpose and program. The nation seemed to support nationalization and takeover of AIOC installations centered at Abadan in the southwestern corner of the country. Even in distant, out-of-the-way villages, support for Musaddiq was strong. The press, representing the widest range of editorial opinion, expressed confidence in the new prime minister. The shah, too, after initial surprise, welcomed Musaddiq's accession, believing the time for nationalization had arrived and that Musaddiq would be best able to carry it out. It was hard to find a single friend of the British oil company in Iran.[4]

Iranians had dreamed of the day when mighty Britain would be humbled. For decades it seemed the British government and its oil company had been intervening in Iran's internal affairs, supporting loyal Iranian political leaders, opposing those whom they could not control. It mattered not that many accusations of British machinations seemed improbable, for there was enough evidence to make any conspiracy appear plausible.

During the months following nationalization, Anglophiles among the Iranian elite judged it prudent to assume a low profile.

British officials were divided over how to respond to nationalization. The government held a 54 per cent interest in the AIOC, and operations in Iran represented the largest overseas British investment. This financial interest complicated a settlement, for the AIOC was not just a private company. Since the end of World War II, Britain had faced a seemingly endless series of budget and balance-of-payments crises, stemming from debts incurred during that conflict. The Labour government responded with austerity measures and devaluation, and when these did not staunch the flow of red ink, London went hat in hand to Washington for a loan. All this weighed on the minds of Treasury officials when they contemplated their threatened Iranian investment, which annually returned to Britain over £100 million in taxes, profits and dividends.

The British position came under attack throughout the Middle East at this time, especially in Egypt where nationalists opposed continued British presence in the Suez Canal zone. *Bakhtar-i Imruz*, the newspaper of the National Front, applauded the Egyptian parliament's support for Iran and called for an end to talks with Britain and immediate action to free the canal of foreigners. Whatever the outcome in Iran, Whitehall knew it would influence sensitive relations between London and other regional states.[5]

If officials were divided, the British public was not; it strongly opposed giving in to Iran. There was a sense that Britain had been pushed around since World War II, that it had lost too much of its once-vast empire and that now the government should stand firm. Even Labour backbenchers threatened revolt. One of them summed up his colleagues' response to the crisis in Iran this way: 'Better risk dying on our feet than condemn our children to life on their knees, and if that makes me a jingo, so be it.' The weakened government of Clement Attlee, in power since 1945, could depend on a majority of one in crucial votes of the House of Commons. It faced a string of political crises – no time to chastise jingoists, several of whom sat in the cabinet.[6]

Elected in February 1950, Attlee's second government presented a sorry picture in comparison with its predecessor. A junior minister confided to his diary that 'the senior people are extinct volcanoes, or else were never volcanoes at all.' The prime minister suffered from duodenal ulcers and spent most of the critical month of April 1951 away from his post. During that time, left-wing ministers led by Minister of Labour and National Service Aneuran Bevan resigned in disagreement over Chancellor of the Exchequer Hugh Gaitskell's proposed budget. As if this were not enough, Attlee had been obliged to appoint Herbert Morrison foreign secretary to replace the ailing Ernest Bevin who died in April. Morrison saw the position as a stepping stone to Number 10 Downing Street, and insisted that he have the post despite his inexperience and apparent disinterest in foreign affairs.[7]

While the Middle East boiled, the new foreign secretary spent his first month in office sitting in for Attlee or making plans for the Festival of Britain, an extravaganza of British culture and accomplishments with which he had been closely identified as Lord President of the Council. By almost all accounts he was poorly equipped to handle Middle East problems, and confidence declined even further when he repeatedly referred to the 'U-Frates' river, leaving audiences to wonder who was briefing him. According to the unsympathetic junior minister, Kenneth Younger, 'he is a Little Englander who suspects everyone who is foreign.' He did not do his homework; he quickly became bored. He had difficulty with permanent officials whom he considered snobs. They thought him oversensitive, 'with pre-conceived ideas about them.' Sensing approaching victory after more than six years in opposition, the Conservatives, led by Winston Churchill and Anthony Eden, harried Morrison in the Commons, where the foreign secretary performed poorly in debates on 'Persia.' At an Empire Day rally Eden announced ominously that 'the outcome of these Persian events is bound to have repurcussions throughout the whole Middle East, and indeed beyond.'[8]

Aside from problems within the government, Labour had to deal with the AIOC board chaired by Sir William Fraser, who with his associates adopted an inflexible position *vis-à-vis* the oil question. The Treasury and the Ministry of Fuel and Power usually supported them. As the crisis deepened, the government assumed more control, establishing a Persian Working Party that lower-level officials had suggested months earlier to deal with day-to-day developments. Attlee set up the Defence Committee – a mini-cabinet composed of the prime minister, chancellor of the exchequer, foreign secretary, and ministers of defence and fuel and power – to authorize action if necessary.

The AIOC remained broadly influential because many government officials shared the company view. They saw events in Iran with sensors conditioned by decades of often unhappy experiences with third world peoples. They had developed a 'colonial mentality.' It imposed a heavy burden on the British and one cannot understand all that happened in relations with Iran, nor with Egypt later, without some feeling for British attitudes of superiority toward 'lesser' peoples. A good example appeared in a diplomat's note on Iranian society penned to instruct the Persian Working Committee on the background of the crisis. The 'expert' saw in Iranians

> an unabashed dishonesty, fatalistic outlook, [and] indifference to suffering. . . . The ordinary Persian is vain, unprincipled, eager to promise what he knows he is incapable or has no intention of performing, wedded to procrastination, lacking in perseverance and energy, but amenable to discipline. Above all he enjoys intrigue and readily turns to prevarication and dishonesty whenever there is possibility of personal gain. Although an accomplished liar, he does not expect to be believed. They easily acquire a superficial knowledge of technical subjects, deluding themselves into the belief that it is profound.[9]

How could anyone negotiate with such a people!

Fraser himself had had an unhappy experience with Iran in the 1930s, which must have contributed to his outlook. In the face of declining royalties associated with the depression, Riza Shah in 1932 had cancelled the oil concession. On behalf of the then Anglo-Persian Oil Company, the British government refused to accept his unilateral action. The case came before the Council of the League of Nations, which encouraged negotiation in Tehran between company directors and the Iranian ruler. Fraser took a prominent part in these difficult talks, which resulted in a new agreement in April 1933. That experience must have reinforced the belief that firmness with the Iranians paid dividends and that money was what mattered most to them.

British officials often expressed surprise that Iranians thought themselves capable of operating the complex oil industry, including the immense refinery at Abadan, the largest in the world; hence they had difficulty taking nationalization seriously. Either the Iranians were bluffing to squeeze as much money as possible from the AIOC or, like unruly children, they had determined to turn everything upside-down, without quite knowing – or caring – what would result. In either case the British had responsibility to restrain them until the nationalist 'fad' subsided and normal conditions returned.

The AIOC seemed so entrenched in southwestern Iran, it was little wonder officials responded slowly to Iranian demands. Abadan was a company town where British employees lived in isolation from the natives, their every want supplied by the company. There were company bungalows, shops, churches, restaurants, and, for the many cholera and typhoid victims, a company cemetery. European workers rarely ventured into Iranian Abadan.[10]

Some 'third class' company employees, that is to say Iranians, lived in single-storied barracks where 'discipline and an organized life, including sports and recreation,' came with employment; but the majority lived outside the company precinct, across the narrow, muddy canal in the shabby township. Even here the company exerted its influence, providing not only electricity, drinking water and sewerage, but also advice and direction to local Iranian officials.

The company was a law unto itself, responsible in practice neither to Tehran nor Whitehall. Not only did it exert influence over local Iranian officials, but on occasion it could arrange the transfer of an obstreperous consular official who might have sent too many unflattering reports to the Foreign Office.[11]

Iran and Britain were not the only protagonists. The United States became involved. American support could be decisive, and both sides courted it. Iranian leaders incorrectly assumed that US oil companies waited eagerly to replace the AIOC, while British officials expected the full cooperation of their American ally to enable them to impose a speedy settlement.

The Truman administration had its own ideas. Many officials sympathized with Iranian nationalism, which might fit with the American goal of strengthening the government in Tehran. Few American observers could defend the AIOC's handling of relations with Iran prior to nationalization. Even junior minister Younger confided that the British had largely brought the crisis upon themselves 'by allowing a private company free rein to make enormous profits without considering long term national policy.' The American oil expert, Walter Levy, a close associate of Assistant Secretary of State George McGhee, visiting London for talks in May 1951, criticized the AIOC for its 'lamentable lack of statesmanship,' implying that the British government was also at fault for failing to insist that the right people were in charge. McGhee believed it would be sufficient to give lip service to Iranian nationalization, to salve nationalist pride, without surrendering real control. A State Department report concluded that the AIOC had failed to gauge the strength of anti-British, pro-nationalization forces in Iran and 'increased tension by letting itself be forced to make concessions rather than making them voluntarily.'[12]

Members of Congress, too, criticized Britain's policy toward Iran, with Republicans taking the lead. Three members of the Armed Services Committee, Senators Alexander Wiley (R–Wisc.), Owen Brewster, (R–Maine) and Leverett Saltonstall (R–Mass.) closely questioned administration representatives about any plans to help Britain with troops in Iran. Brewster argued that the United States was 'footing the bill' in Iran by lending London $300000000 to make up for its oil losses. Others claimed that Washington had supported British colonialism and exploitation too long. Representative Jacob Javits (R–NY) called for immediate aid to Iran and Senator Dennis Chavez (D–NM) likened Musaddiq to Benjamin Franklin, seeking aid in France during the American Revolution. The attacks compounded the difficulty of maintaining amicable Anglo-American relations. Much of this was partisan politics, an opportunity to attack the administration, but it revealed American suspicions of British motives in the third world.[13]

Even President Truman criticized the AIOC and the British government, telling the journalist Arthur Krock that 'the British dealt ineptly and disastrously with the Iran oil matter. We told them how to avoid it but they did not follow our counsel.' Later he went further, remarking that 'the British were still back in the nineteenth century in their thinking in respect to Iran. It was they who bore the responsibility for the trouble that now existed.'[14]

But the American official who most vexed the British was undoubtedly Assistant Secretary for the Near East George McGhee. This seemed a strange turn of events to the Anglophile McGhee, a former Rhodes scholar with many friends in the British establishment. Only 39 in 1951 he was already a wealthy man, having made a fortune in American oil; he had married the daughter of oil magnate Everette De Golyer. McGhee offered his services at a dollar a year to Acheson's State Department.

Throughout 1951, whenever the Foreign Office thought it had obtained American agreement on a particular policy toward Iran, McGhee would intervene, suggesting a different approach, more favorable toward Iran. For British diplomats, negotiating with the assistant secretary became only slightly less frustrating than dealing with Musaddiq.

McGhee, who understood the complexities of international oil, had become interested early in 1950 in the developing Iranian situation and had tried to talk reason to the AIOC with little success. His ties to the American oil industry made him suspect to conspiracy-minded Britishers, who thought he might be more interested in gaining US advantage than in resolving the dispute. Following Razmara's assassination a Labour MP charged in the House of Commons that 'things only began to heat up in Tehran when McGhee arrived there on March 17.' Another accused him of 'shooting off his mouth,' leading Iranians to believe American technical assistance would be forthcoming if the AIOC were forced out. 'Perhaps there is more to fear from the US than from Russia,' another declared.[15]

Naturally McGhee bothered the British. Foreign Office experts were diplomatic, to be sure, but troubled by the brash young assistant secretary. They referred to him as 'that infant prodigy' and as 'one of our heavier crosses.' When McGhee complained that Morrison had failed to defend him adequately in the Commons, officials agreed they must go easy for he had Acheson's support and lately, at least, had been working hard for a settlement. Undersecretary Roger Makins, perhaps the most influential official at the Foreign Office, attributed the problem to McGhee's inexperience and overconfidence. 'He also no doubt suffers to some extent from an Irish ancestry and a Texas upbringing,' Makins added. He needed education and encouragement, not abuse.[16]

While the Western allies tried to work out their differences, Prime Minister Musaddiq in far-off Tehran prepared to implement the new nine-point nationalization law. He took pride in this piece of legislation, declaring that the only question remaining concerned compensation for the 'former company.' He boldly requested AIOC assistance in transferring facilities at Abadan and elsewhere to the government.

Refusing to accept nationalization, the company called on Iran to arbitrate as provided under the 1933 concession, but Musaddiq rejected any notion of arbitrating what for him was a purely domestic concern. In the eyes of the prime minister and most nationalists, the 1933 agreement had become discredited because Riza Shah had imposed it on the nation. Musaddiq had repeatedly criticized it as an abandonment of the nation's vital interests because it extended by 30 years the life of the concession without suitably rewarding Iran. He saw danger in delaying the takeover, for he feared that the AIOC (in other words, Britain) would manipulate Iran, as it had done in the past. In the first week of May, when Musaddiq refused to negotiate, the antagonists approached deadlock.

American officials bestirred themselves, urging compromise. In Tehran Ambassador Henry Grady had authority from the State Department to do what he could to bring the two sides together. He had much experience with difficult diplomatic problems – Palestine, 1946; India, 1947; Greece, 1948 – and relished the opportunity. On both Palestine and Greece, however, he had encountered difficulties. Under intense pressure from the Zionist lobby, Truman had dissociated himself from the Grady–Morrison proposals worked out in London. These had called for two autonomous provinces in Palestine, one Jewish, one Arab, and a central government with limited powers. In Greece he had incurred royal displeasure for opposing the king's attempt to install a right-wing government.

Although Grady liked to take charge, one had to wonder how long Washington would leave the crisis in his hands. He probably flattered himself in thinking that his role was crucial. He had been slow to sense the rising importance of the National Front, and then, perhaps, overreacted; recalling his experience in India, he likened Musaddiq to Gandhi. Once Musaddiq became prime minister the ambassador worked tirelessly to influence him 'toward sound thinking.' 'Whatever else

may be said,' Grady cabled, 'he wants to help his people.'
Grady advised Musaddiq that failure to negotiate would have
a bad effect on opinion in the United States.[17]

Grady criticized the British in general and AIOC policy in
particular. This hampered relations with his British colleague,
Francis Shepherd, who came out of the consular service and
lacked the broad diplomatic experience that seemed essential
in Iran. Shepherd had expected an easy post after Bevin assured him on appointment in 1950 that 'he would have no
trouble with the natives.' Events belied that comforting thought.
Now he wanted Grady to be helpful, by which he meant the
ambassador should take his cues from the British embassy, for
'in spite of his long experience he is no less ham-handed than
so many Americans,' Shepherd reported. If the Americans cooperated, he and his superiors never doubted of success.[18]

While Grady and Shepherd sparred, the Persian Working
Party at Whitehall had begun to consider sanctions against
Iran, such as embargoing Persian oil, freezing Iranian sterling
balances and restricting sales of scarce products, such as tires,
sugar and rails. The time for these lay in the future, but the
British pondered how to make such restrictions effective. Other
nations might purchase Iranian oil or supply Iran with technicians, and when the time came, London wanted to guarantee
their cooperation.

Makins traveled to Washington in early May to discuss these
and other issues with McGhee, who told him the United States
could not press small oil companies to stay out of Iran. To
Makins this was unacceptable; the US government must tell
them no. Later, Acheson agreed to do all he could to keep
American companies out but urged the British undersecretary
to recognize the principle of nationalization. Attlee thought
this a good idea, to give Musaddiq a chance 'to save face,' but
his foreign secretary favored caution.[19]

The American oil companies never doubted what policy to
pursue. The five major companies – Gulf, Jersey, Socony, Standard of California, and Texaco – had no intention of interfering in Iran. They knew too well the likely consequences for
their own concessions should Iran's unilateral action succeed.
They saw Iranian nationalization as a threat to them all and
needed no British pressure to stand clear. At a meeting with
McGhee, their representatives admitted the AIOC had created

most of its own problems, but it would be better even to lose Iran behind the iron curtain than to have it succeed on its own terms.[20]

But what of the independent oil companies? Here was cause for Britain's concern, and no one knew how long they could be kept in line. Some companies seemed prepared to take advantage of Britain's predicament, offering to supply oil technicians should the British withdraw. One Los Angeles company promptly offered Musaddiq up to 2500 technicians 'to keep the supply of oil available in Iran flowing to the Western Allies.' Such promises strained Anglo-American relations and fueled the Iranian belief that they could play off the two allies against each other.[21]

What concerned US officials most was the advantage the oil crisis offered to the Soviet Union. Intelligence estimates concluded that the situation was perfect for communist subversion, working through the Iranian Tudeh party. The Soviets could sit back and wait for Iran to drop into their laps. It would take 'every ounce of ingenuity on the part of the West to prevent that from happening.'[22]

McGhee sympathized with the British but would not sacrifice the security of Iran for the sake of the AIOC. Yet the British refused to abandon the company in the interests of the cold war. If the Iranians learned Washington thought the AIOC expendable there would be no possibility of a settlement.[23]

To avoid an impasse Acheson and British Ambassador Oliver Franks worked out a compromise. On 18 May the secretary publicly decried Iran's unilateral action and called for negotiations, advising that US oil companies were unwilling to assist Iran. Ambassador Shepherd followed this with a note to Musaddiq from Morrison, rejecting Iran's right to sever the contract with the AIOC. Without negotiations, he warned, relations would be compromised and serious consequences would result.[24]

Iranians exploded with anger at what they considered Anglo-American collusion. The leading pro-Western newspaper, *Ittila'at,* claimed that 'these two governments have adopted a common attitude unfavorable to Iran in the oil question.' The National Front *Shahid* went further, wondering if the price paid by the British for Acheson's statement might have been a promise not to ship war materials to communist China. Apparent foreign interference strengthened Musaddiq, as Iranians urged him to take over AIOC properties in the southwest without delay.[25]

At this stage of the crisis, the Americans had a better understanding than the British of developments within Iran. They realized how strong was the prime minister's support and discouraged Foreign Office suggestions that they jointly seek the shah's intervention against Musaddiq. Washington had rushed to reaffirm its support for the shah and to strengthen his leadership as 'the only person who can give Iran the leadership necessary to restore stability and prevent the spread of communism,' yet would not encourage him to defy public sentiment and dismiss his prime minister, unless Musaddiq refused to negotiate.[26]

Under pressure from the State Department and its own embassy in Washington to show more flexibility, the Labour government shifted slightly. On 29 May Morrison announced Britain's acceptance of 'some form of nationalization,' although he rejected any unilateral cancellation of the concession.[27]

Would this be enough to bring the two sides together? To encourage the British, Truman sent a letter to Attlee the next day stressing the seriousness of the situation and concern that Iran might be lost to the free world. He urged London to send a negotiating team to Tehran immediately. The prime minister responded favorably, while reminding the president what influence this dispute was likely to have on all other concessions.[28]

Basil Jackson, a company director who had not been involved in the dispute earlier, was to lead the AIOC delegation. Perhaps he would prove a more acceptable negotiator.[29]

There was no agreement on the terms of negotiation. Musaddiq wanted to focus narrowly on compensation, telling the Majlis that nationalization was not open to discussion. The British saw this as an opportunity to convince the Iranians that they lacked the know-how to take over from the AIOC and market oil themselves.[30]

Conditions in Tehran remained tense. On 1 June Radio Tehran announced that 'all of Iran's misery, wretchedness, lawlessness and corruption during the last fifty years have been caused by oil and the extortions of the oil company.' Such charges, widely believed, made compromise difficult. Ambassador Grady exacerbated tensions when he told journalists he thought the AIOC should have sent negotiators sooner and that the company should resume royalty payments cut off in April.[31]

Prospects for success dimmed further with Jackson's arrival in Tehran on 11 June. The Iranian government had been seeking control over all oil receipts collected by the AIOC since nationalization. The government would put aside one-fourth of these as a fund for compensation to the company. Jackson was not optimistic. Exceeding his instructions, he told a news conference that the oil company could never accept such division of profits, that the company would not stay in Iran if it could not fit in with nationalization, and that Iran would not be able to obtain tankers to ship oil. These so-called 'realities' seemed little more than 'thinly veiled threats.' When the delegation presented its proposals, it offered little that was new. It suggested a lease for a new company to be formed by the AIOC to run the oil industry, 'leaving wide open the matter of ownership of the oil.' The Iranian government rejected the offer, which failed to meet the requirements of the oil nationalization law.[32]

Everything collapsed when Musaddiq ordered the immediate takeover of AIOC installations throughout the nation. Ambassador Grady tried to keep the negotiations going, advising Jackson that Iranian intransigence might be a bargaining position and he should remain a while longer, but Jackson was not convinced. He received permission from the British government to break off talks and the delegation returned to London on 22 June. Upon arrival Jackson announced, with more determination than diplomacy, that 'as long as the present government controls Iran, there is no hope in renewing talks.' The two parties had frittered away opportunites for negotiation while positions on both sides began to stiffen.[33]

All eyes turned toward Abadan, where a delegation from the National Iranian Oil Company (NIOC) had been waiting since early June to carry out the nine-point law. Its progress from Tehran had been triumphal – thousands of Iranians had greeted the members at every stop along the railway with shouts of 'Long Live the Shah!' 'Long Live Musaddiq!' At one stop a gaunt old man with a long white beard approached the delegates holding a small tray on which lay an open Quran, a crust of bread and a cracked blue pottery bowl of water. Pointing to the objects on the tray, he said in a quavering voice: 'This is all we have to sustain us under the AIOC.' At this pathetic sight, tears streamed down the delegates' faces. There were many such incidents on the journey south.[34]

At Ahwaz, Minister for National Economy Shams al-Din Amir Ala'i, a prominent anti-court politician, met with the manager of the AIOC in Abadan, Eric Drake, to assure him that the British had nothing to fear. 'We only want what is ours,' he said, 'we have no debts to settle.' As tensions mounted, Amir Ala'i urged Iranian workers to be peaceful and patient while transfer of control was taking place. He knew the task would be enormous, for the AIOC had made no preparations, hoping, perhaps, that the oil committee would go away. Drake admitted as much when he likened members of the Iranian delegation to inexperienced airplane passengers, who demanded to take over the controls in flight, regardless of the consequences.[35]

No one in Iran knew whether or not Britain would resort to force, nor, if it did, what the consequences might be. Once in Abadan, National Front leader Husain Makki could not resist haranguing the crowd. In a speech he referred defiantly to the British cruiser, *Mauritius,* anchored menacingly offshore. 'The British,' he cried, 'cannot frighten us with that matchbox.'[36]

In London the cabinet decided to keep its options open. It had already positioned several more 'matchboxes' in the adjacent waters of the Shatt al-Arab and the Persian Gulf. Earlier it had approved 'Buccaneer,' a plan to seize and hold the oil fields, but it quickly became apparent that the demands of such a scheme would hinder Britain's preparedness elsewhere. The commander of Middle East land forces notified Minister of Defence Emmanuel Shinwell on 1 May that the oil fields objective could only be obtained by weakening forces in the region to such a point that Britain would be unable to oppose any movement by the Egyptians or unrest elsewhere in the Middle East.[37]

Two weeks later a scaled-down plan, 'Midget,' made its appearance. The goal would be to land troops to seize Abadan's airport and to rescue British and foreign nationals from hostile Iranian forces.[38]

Out of frustration Shinwell and Morrison toyed with military intervention. The minister of defence lamented that 'the situation seemed rapidly to be developing where nobody "cared a damn" about this country; this was quite intolerable; we must be prepared to show that our tail could not be twisted interminably.' Morrison continually muttered at cabinet meetings about the need for Britain to stand up for itself. Conservatives agreed. Eden had advocated a show of force in the Suez Canal as a warning to the Iranians, and Churchill was well known for his 'whiff of grapeshot' remark. Appeasement had gone far enough![39]

But force was no alternative. Attlee and Gaitskell opposed it and the military recognized the limits in available manpower. And then there was the United States. Officials in Washington became almost paranoid over the thought that the British might launch an ill-conceived attack on Iran without consulting them. In a National Security Council meeting Acheson declared that use of force would be 'sheer madness' and would open the way to Soviet intervention in Azarbaijan. He told Franks of President Truman's deep concern and reiterated that the United States would support force only in response to a communist coup in Tehran.[40]

After Jackson's failure the British government decided to stand pat, for it received encouraging reports from Tehran that Musaddiq's support had weakened. Perhaps they could return to the *status quo ante*. Ambassador Shepherd now had the inspired assistance of Oxford scholar Robin Zaehner, counselor at the embassy. A Persian language expert who had spent the war years in Tehran as press attaché, Zaehner returned at the suggestion of the dean of British scholars of Iran, Ann Lambton, to do what he could to undermine Musaddiq. He strengthened ties with the Anglophile elite represented most prominently by Sayyid Zia ed-Din Tabataba'i and began drafting hopeful telegrams predicting the weakening of the prime minister. British government intelligence on conditions in Iran thus came from an embassy largely staffed by those opposed to Musaddiq who relied on the Iranian opposition for information.[41]

Buoyed by these reports, Attlee urged the United States to postpone any new approach to the Iranian prime minister. Churchill concurred and sent a letter to Truman, stressing the strategic importance of Iran and the need for the president to take a firm line with Musaddiq. He characterized him as 'an elderly lunatic bent on wrecking his country and handing it over to communism.' The British campaign succeeded, at least temporarily, when the State Department agreed that a rational situation did not presently exist in Iran. Writing Senator Robert Kerr of Oklahoma, Acheson claimed the center of trouble was not money 'but a fanatical idea on the part of the Iranians that they must throw the British out even if it wrecks the country.'[42]

It was a strange situation, indeed, and behind it all lay the sheerest ignorance. Even the British expert, so hastily brought out to Tehran, was more a linguist than anything else. He had been press attaché during the war, no post for making policy. It was advantageous, to be sure, to have someone who could converse in the language, but that was no substitute for good judgment.

Moreover, both Britain and America were too far removed, and their officials were mesmerized by the Korean War – which was going a bit better than in the preceding year, but was by no means over, for the Chinese, after intervening in November 1950, gave no indication of going away. Since 1945, with the victory in Europe and Asia, the two allied powers had been discovering one problem after another, keeping terribly busy trying to solve them. And in the business of discovery and solution the British, of course, were notably the weaker power. They were unduly sensitive to this fact.

What was happening in Tehran was a witch's brew, cooked up by the Iranians for their own noble purposes, without much concern for what it meant to stir things. The Soviet Union, watching the rolling back of its Chinese ally in Korea, was happy to see trouble develop over nationalism in Iran. But, at this point, there was not the slightest indication that the Soviets were remotely involved in what was going on.

3 Peacemaker

Positions hardened during the weeks of early summer. Britain counted on a change of government at Tehran to settle everything. This had happened so frequently in the past, amounting at times to revolving-door rule, that perhaps the wisest course consisted of doing nothing, as the 'experts' in the Tehran embassy advised. Jackson had returned with this very message for Attlee. Nothing he had seen in the Iranian capital, not even a visit to the slums of south Tehran arranged by the wily prime minister, had caused him to change his stance. Attlee had much on his mind that summer, his party's last in power for the next 15 years. There was the ongoing war in Korea, the problem of juggling relations with the Soviet Union, and the continuing weakness in Europe, where General Eisenhower was just putting the 'O' in NATO. At home Labour clung to power with the Opposition hounding it at every opportunity.

Musaddiq, too, must have resigned himself to a drawn-out dispute, with no telling how it would end. He had envisioned a rapid increase in Iran's oil wealth. This, he told Jackson, he would use to improve living standards. His advisers had assured him that Iran's oil production would increase many times over. That development was some way off. Meanwhile the Tudeh party attacked his choice of 'English-leaning ministers,' referring to the fact that Musaddiq, perhaps to reassure the shah, had chosen a surprisingly conservative cabinet. Nevertheless, as the lion and sun pennant of Iran fluttered over the former company director's office in Abadan, it became clear there would be no going back.

Seeing so much at stake in Iran, with its strategic position along the Soviet border, doing nothing was not an option the Americans could long entertain. They could not sit back and await developments, for that could intensify frustration in Tehran, destabilizing the government. All this would play into Soviet hands. The Truman administration found itself in a quandary: a letter from Musaddiq requesting assistance lay unanswered on the president's desk; next to it lay the letter from Attlee recommending procrastination.

On 1 July, Grady sent a personal appeal to Truman and Acheson, warning of chaos if the Abadan refinery should close and urging them to support a policy of reasonableness and conciliation.[1]

To head off either British withdrawal or use of force in Iran, Acheson hastily arranged an informal meeting at Averell Harriman's Georgetown house for 4 July. Present were, in addition to McGhee, the director of policy planning Paul Nitze, Assistant Secretary H. Freeman Matthews, Ambassador Franks, and, of course, Harriman, then special assistant to the president. The secretary suggested sending Harriman to Iran as personal representative of the president to mediate the dispute. Harriman had often served as a trouble-shooter and seemed a good choice. But he had been monitoring the crisis since March and knew how slim were the chances for success. He showed reluctance, acquiescing only at the president's urging.

British approval to dispatch a mission was no foregone conclusion. In response to Britain's appeal, the International Court of Justice had recommended that the Anglo-Iranian Oil Company (AIOC) be reinstated to its properties in Iran, pending settlement of the dispute. Iran rejected this decision, and Morrison wanted the United States to insist that Musaddiq comply with the court's order. The Americans could help most, the foreign secretary wrote, not by sending a special representative but by supporting the International Court. He argued, with truth, that one difficulty in resolving the dispute was Musaddiq's belief that the Anglo-American allies differed on Iran. The American proposal of a mediator would only confirm this notion and make Iran more intransigent.[2]

The foreign secretary could not dissuade the Americans, who agreed only not to refer to Harriman as a mediator. On 9 July, President Truman sent a letter to Musaddiq offering Harriman's services, effectively preempting any British delaying tactics. Meanwhile Acheson recommended that London not refer the dispute to the Security Council, as it had proposed, until Harriman had completed his mission.[3]

Harriman wasted no time putting together an expert group, including the State Department's William Rountree, who had much experience in the Middle East, oil expert Walter Levy, and Vernon Walters, a fine linguist and aide to General Dwight D. Eisenhower at NATO Headquarters. Harriman made a brief stop in the French capital to collect Walters and to confer secretly with Gaitskell, who wanted to make certain the American understood the British position. Gaitskell later assured cabinet colleagues that they could trust Harriman not to act without consulting them.[4]

Harriman had drawn a difficult assignment. His coming produced differing reactions in Tehran. Members of the Iranian government were pleased, hoping his visit presaged a solution favorable to Iran and indicated renewed American concern for their nation. To emphasize the tense situation in the capital, a riot between supporters of the Tudeh party, which opposed the mission, and the National Front left 20 dead and marred the delegation's arrival. Ambassador Shepherd told journalists he thought Harriman's coming a waste of time – a statement he later regretted. Shepherd had his hands full dealing with Grady and now there would be more Americans with more plans. Levy had already loudly announced that he would keep his distance from the British during his stay.[5]

Harriman did not inspire the ambassador's confidence. Despite his friends in the British cabinet, the Foreign Office had written unflatteringly to Shepherd that Harriman's distinguished appointments had been the result of political loyalty and good fortune. 'He is reserved in manner, inarticulate and not very forthcoming in conversation. He also has a strong streak of personal vanity, and is susceptible to attention of all kinds. Experience has shown that playing up to this weakness leads to the best results.'[6]

Ambassador Grady did not welcome the mission either. He had worked for an interim compromise and now Harriman overshadowed his efforts. He did not like special missions, which he claimed undermined the authority of diplomats in the field. More poignantly, he had had an unhappy experience in Greece when Harriman, head of the Economic Cooperation Administration, had visited Athens where Grady was ambassador. Memory of that incident troubled him. A leak in Washington reporting the ambassador's early replacement disturbed him even more. He withdrew with wounded pride to the sidelines, leaving Harriman in the limelight.[7]

In early meetings, Musaddiq rigidly refused to negotiate further with the British government or the oil company, or to discuss any solution that did not conform to the nine-point nationalization law. Harriman met with other leaders – the shah, his adviser Husain Ala, groups of senators and Majlis deputies – to assess the situation and to encourage them to press Musaddiq to reopen negotiations. The American oil expert, Levy, instructed officials on salient features of international oil. In talks with Kazim Hasibi, Musaddiq's oil adviser, and Undersecretary of Finance Allahyar Salih, the Americans discovered that political factors weighed as heavily as economic ones. Harriman accused Hasibi of ignorance about the oil business and of passing on bad advice to the prime minister, which could lead the country to disaster.[8]

Harriman was impressed by Iranian determination to make whatever sacrifices necessary 'to be rid of what they consider . . . British colonial practices.' In reports to Washington he chided the British for failure to keep abreast of the nationalist mood. For years they had sent neither ministers nor company directors to Tehran, and the embassy, he concluded, had not accurately reported the situation.[9]

Little by little Harriman's strategy began to have an effect. He was learning the sentiments of articulate Iranians, who unanimously opposed the return of the AIOC under any guise. Although they recognized the need for foreign technical help, especially regarding the shipment and marketing of oil, they expected a larger supervisory role for themselves than the Jackson proposal allowed. Their responses led him to toy with the idea of an association of oil companies doing business in Iran, in order to take the AIOC out of the spotlight. He felt confident there was enough flexibility for a compromise if he could get the two sides to the bargaining table.[10]

Musaddiq reluctantly agreed to accept a British government delegation and base talks on the original nationalization law of March, rather than the nine-point law of April. Harriman urged the British to seize the opportunity and send out 'one of their most responsible and skillful ministers' if they hoped for success. He wanted his friend Gaitskell to come.[11]

The British were reticent. Harriman had gone beyond his brief, and they were wary of any commitment to negotiations prior to return of the southern fields to AIOC control. To Harriman's consternation, Shepherd was telling Iranian officials to accept the International Court's decision if they wanted talks. Harriman knew that British insistence would scuttle any chance for negotiation; he explained to Acheson how much the Iranians had already retreated. To demand more was to slam the door on compromise.[12]

As the British dickered, Harriman decided to take his arguments directly to Number 10 Downing Street. The cabinet had no time to quash the enterprise for no sooner had ministers decided to oppose the visit than the Americans appeared on their doorstep with Shepherd in tow.[13]

In talks with Attlee, Morrison, and Gaitskell, and separately with Churchill, Harriman reiterated his conviction, without going into detail, that a settlement was possible. Musaddiq had cautioned him not to misrepresent the Iranian position in order to give the British a false impression of what to expect in Tehran, but Harriman saw no need to lay out Iranian terms; that would take place later. He avoided talking about general positions at this stage. His task was to bring the parties together; he hoped negotiation would do the rest.[14]

Attlee and Morrison gave way on 30 July, agreeing to send the Lord Privy Seal, Richard Stokes, who had some business connections with the Middle East and was a man of goodwill. But the choice was not a happy one. Besides the fact that he was not a cabinet member, his character was wrong for these delicate negotiations. He was a bluff, hearty, slap-on-the-back kind of fellow who enjoyed a good joke. 'He was a man for snap decisions and getting things done,' not at all the kind of representative needed in Tehran.[15]

Harriman must have felt relieved that the Labour government would send anyone, for it was under intense pressure from the public and the Opposition not to give in. The cabinet was acutely concerned how the public would react to news of renewed negotiations. In parliament Churchill attacked Labour's weak and inept Middle East policy, and Conservatives insisted that Britain must not abandon Abadan. If the Opposition had known what Levy was suggesting at the Foreign Office, they would have gone into a frenzy. Levy argued that the AIOC would never be able to come back on its own to Abadan and that it might have to form a new company with Shell and others to contract for transport and marketing of oil, leaving exploration and refining to the Iranians. This position closely paralleled Musaddiq's, which was anathema at the Foreign Office.

Ominously, it indicated to the British how far the Americans might go for a settlement.[16]

Stokes arrived in Tehran on 4 August accompanied by representatives of the Foreign Office, the Ministry of Fuel and Power, the Treasury, and the AIOC. Both sides asked Harriman to remain during negotiations. Musaddiq insisted, saying he had accepted talks only on the understanding that the American envoy would stay and 'if this were not the case, he would withdraw his consent.' The day after Stokes arrived, Musaddiq informed the Majlis of Britain's acceptance of nationalization and – rather prematurely, it turned out – thanked Harriman for his help in settling 'the long standing dispute of forty-two years duration with reference to the southern oil concession.'[17]

During the week following its arrival in Tehran, the Stokes delegation busied itself, preparing proposals for the Iranian government. Stokes visited the Abadan refinery to assess the situation and boost the morale of British workers, who told him they would stay only if they received a 50 per cent raise and a British director took charge. In between there were receptions and meetings, enough to keep everyone busy.

Harriman worried that Stokes had become aggressive, that he was pushing the Iranians too hard to accept a partnership with the British and ease tensions in the southern oil fields. He attributed this pushiness to the minister's failure to understand Iranian psychology and to poor advice from Shepherd and the AIOC representatives in his mission. How else to interpret Stokes' warning to Iranians not to commit economic suicide![18]

The British presented proposals on 13 August. They called for transfer to the National Iranian Oil Company (NIOC) of all AIOC assets in Iran on favorable terms, a purchasing organization to market oil, a managing organization which would run the domestic industry on behalf of NIOC with an Iranian at the board level, and a 50–50 division of profits between the purchasing organization and the NIOC. Here were the Jackson proposals camouflaged to keep operations of the oil industry in company hands, 'with no more than a change of name.'[19]

These fell far short of what the Iranians could accept. They wanted real control, not some disguised plan that would allow continued AIOC management. The delegations faced each other across a seemingly unbridgeable gap. The British insisted on stability in the fields and long-term guarantees of oil at competitive prices, hence their proposals for purchasing and management organizations. Investments were so large that there had to be guarantees or the international industry could not function efficiently. The Iranians countered that accepting the proposals would take control out of their hands and behind both new organizations would lurk the hated AIOC. Even the shah, who was no radical on oil, complained when he learned the terms that the British had treated the Iranians as an inferior race for so long that they could not change.[20]

Harriman admitted to Acheson that under the proposals it was possible either to reintroduce British control or provide for a genuinely strong NIOC. Musaddiq would not take the risk. He wanted more than a mere change of words. But he expressed interest in continuing to negotiate. Writing to Harriman on 24 August the prime minister said of his counterproposals, 'we do not claim for a moment that our proposals are adequate enough for the object in mind; but we desire that [they] should become the basis of our new negotiations.'[21]

Stokes had probably done the best he could. After a few more days of desultory talks, the British had had enough. Stokes accused the Iranians of failing to negotiate seriously. He withdrew his proposals and gave Musaddiq an ultimatum: either take the negotiations seriously or the British mission would go home. This was a mistake, but Stokes had become frustrated and was under intense pressure from London not to concede too much. In a meeting with the shah he referred undiplomatically to 'the terrible dishonesty of his people.' He blurted out similar nonsense to Husain Ala over drinks but apologized the next day.[22]

Privately, Harriman blamed the failure largely on Musaddiq, whom he claimed was unrealistic. What the Iranians needed now, he thought, was time to contemplate their situation. Whatever happened, negotiations should be suspended, not broken off. In that way future meetings could take place without loss of face on either side. Stokes agreed and cautioned London before his departure not to take any hasty punitive measures against Iran. He parted on friendly terms with Musaddiq.[23]

The Labour government had been stung by developments in Tehran, which seemed to prove its opponents right all along.

Of uppermost importance to the government now was retriev-
ing what it could of its prestige, while trying to convince the
United States that the Iranians alone had been responsible
for the failure. On the eve of Stokes' departure from Tehran,
Attlee cabled Truman, praising Harriman's efforts and continuing, 'I think you'll agree breakdown in talks entirely due
to Persian side. Only course now is, we hope, for complete
U.S. public support of His Majesty's government's position.'[24]

Attlee had in mind a joint statement on the oil crisis, but
Truman's reply suggested otherwise. Influenced by Harriman,
the president stressed the need for the United States to 'maintain freedom of action . . . to render the most effective . . .
support possible.' Neither the United States nor the United
Kingdom should take action that 'would appear to be in opposition to the legitimate aspirations of the Iranian people.'
Nothing should be done to discourage negotiations. Again the
Americans had rejected the British bit.[25]

Harriman was upset by his failure but recovered quickly,
choosing to emphasize what had been accomplished: the
breaking-down of Iranian intransigence. In London he met
with the cabinet and individual ministers to caution against
precipitous action. He advised them not to take too firm a
stand on old positions that had been rejected. He envisioned
ad hoc interim agreements to keep oil flowing until something
permanent could be worked out. The Americans spoke again
of a consortium to distribute Abadan's oil, making plain they
would have difficulty supporting the AIOC terms laid down in
Tehran. The Persian Working Committee agreed to consider
Harriman's suggestions.[26]

Harriman and Levy urged Sir William Fraser's replacement.
He had, they argued, learned nothing from the past and 'was
completely out of touch with the situation.' This view was widely
shared at the Foreign Office and Sir Donàld Fergusson of the
Ministry of Fuel and Power, a member of the Stokes mission,
agreed, adding that bankers had expressed misgivings about
Fraser's continued leadership. The Treasury, however, had the
deciding vote and would not act hastily.[27]

Back in Washington at the end of August, Harriman reported at a cabinet meeting on the stalemate. The British, he
said, had failed to take Iranian nationalism seriously; the Iranians were ignorant of the oil business. He felt confident pressure

would build against Musaddiq so the shah could dismiss him. This, of course, would take time, and he hoped the British government could resist public pressure to take punitive action against Iran. He had not become disillusioned; he believed patience would bring a settlement.[28]

For two weeks after Harriman left Tehran (24 August) the crisis seemed in suspended animation. The foreign office waited for some new Iranian initiative, while Iran waited for a response to proposals handed to Stokes on 22 August and which British officials had already privately dismissed as impossible. Each side prepared to wait out the other. Musaddiq thought the British would have to come back to the negotiating table because they needed Iranian oil. The British believed that by not negotiating with the prime minister they could weaken him. They would avoid any action that would undermine his opposition in Iran, from whom they expected great achievements.[29]

This ended Harriman's involvement with the Iranian oil dispute. He had to busy himself with his new appointment as Director for Mutual Security. He had acquitted himself well in London and Tehran. Somehow he managed to cope with the daily frustrations and still remain even-tempered and sensible. He resisted British pressure to align with their proposals, and yet he spoke frankly to Musaddiq of the need for flexibility.

He probably understood the prime minister as well as any American did in 1951, which is to say, not very well. His dispatches revealed little sense of the legacy of bitterness in British–Iranian relations. Harriman approached the crisis pragmatically as Americans often did, with slight regard for the past. But Britain and Iran had a long history of unhappy relations, and the Iranians, especially Musaddiq, could not easily put aside their suspicions. To him the British would use any occasion to manipulate his country. Musaddiq had shown considerable flexibility just in agreeing to meet with Stokes. He showed no surprise that London had conceded nothing. If Harriman had understood the depth of distrust, he might at least have encouraged Musaddiq and Stokes to take more time to get acquainted.

With hindsight we can see that the Harriman mission really supported the *status quo*, and in the context of the early 1950s perhaps it would be unrealistic to have expected anything different. The Iranians wanted to be masters in their own house regardless of consequences; this the powers would not accept. Thus, Levy and Fergusson told Iranian officials that they could not hope to break the oil cartel's worldwide monopoly on shipping and that eventually they would have to come to terms. Although the Americans showed greater sensitivity toward Iranian aspirations, they were no more prepared than their allies in London to turn the world of oil upside-down. Forced to choose between what he considered nationalistic idealism and naive intransigence or hard-headed Western pragmatism and order, Harriman, with few misgivings, opted for the latter.

4 Changing the Guard

September 1951 marked a critical point in the Iranian oil dispute, a time when Britain revealed its determination to bring down the government of Muhammad Musaddiq.

With the first signs of autumn the British bestirred themselves, slamming one door and opening another. They decided to reject any further negotiation with Musaddiq and bring the dispute to the Security Council, hoping that there, at last, the Iranian prime minister might receive his comeuppance. They abandoned any plans for military action, leaving the United Nations as the only alternative. The decision to go to the UN really was a measure of desperation, for a general election approached and the government had to be seen to be doing something. London took this step without consulting Washington. This seemed almost an act of defiance, as if to show the world that the British lion could still roar – if only in moderation.

Much of this new resolve emanated from the embassy in Tehran, where Shepherd and his staff predicted the imminent downfall of the prime minister. In meetings with the opposition, including Seyed Zia ed-Din Tabataba'i, Majlis speaker Sadir Fakhir Hekmat and the shah's adviser, Asadollah Alam, diplomats encouraged resistance to Musaddiq and urged them to take action. In early September the prime minister could not muster a quorum in parliament to carry on essential business because many opposition deputies stayed away. Shepherd even sought approval to press the shah for a change of government by hinting of British force if he did not act. Although the Foreign Office hoped Seyed Zia would come to power, London would not yet condone such blatant interference.[1]

Overall, the British government supported the ambassador's hard line. To press Musaddiq more, Shepherd announced his government considered talks broken off, not suspended. With Gaitskell, Morrison, and Shinwell attending to business in the United States, Attlee made this crucial decision on the advice of the Foreign Office's permanent undersecretary, William Strang. He had not even informed Stokes, who fumed when he received the news, no doubt because it indicated how little importance the prime minister attached to his opinion.[2]

Now London could impose economic sanctions. Iran's privilege of converting sterling into dollars was withdrawn and export to Iran of such scarce commodities as tires, sugar and steel was forbidden. The AIOC declared an embargo of Iranian oil, threatening to take legal action against any purchaser of oil which, it claimed, belonged to the company.[3]

These measures, Shepherd assumed, would bolster the Iranian opposition. He was completely unprepared for the criticism that came from elder statesman Hasan Taghizadeh, a widely respected writer and diplomat, and an Anglophile. Taghizadeh decried interference in Iran's domestic politics. What would British reaction be, he asked, if the Iranian ambassador in London suggested a change of government to King George? The Iranian's statesmanlike manner impressed Shepherd, but he would not be deterred, for he saw Iranians generally as people of limited capacity for self-rule. 'Nobody in this country understands anything except the simplest possible statement ten times repeated,' he told the Foreign Office. 'This is a lesson we must learn.'[4]

Still the shah did not act. The counselor at the embassy, George Middleton, referred to him with thinly veiled disgust as that 'weak and ineffectual little man,' who would rather go hunting than deal with politics. But the shah may have had a better understanding of the situation than anyone at the embassy. He told the ambassador that if he dismissed Musaddiq neither Seyed Zia nor Ahmad Qavam would be able to control the situation. He would not take unnecessary risks, and without his leadership the opposition lost heart.[5]

Something had to be done to keep alive the agitation for Musaddiq's dismissal. That something soon turned up. Court Minister Ala had recently passed to the British a set of proposals which were purportedly the work of Musaddiq, although they bore neither date nor signature. London was skeptical, but the Americans urged the British in strongest terms not to reject them out of hand but to consider them carefully. The Americans wanted to confer with the British before any action was taken. Attlee seemed to agree that the notes were worth considering; and Stokes, who had now become a staunch

defender of the Iranian prime minister, went further, arguing that the proposals came close to his own. 'We must desist
from the silly slogan,' he said, 'that we can't negotiate with
Musaddiq.'[6]

At this critical point, Strang received an urgent telegram
from Shepherd, announcing that the shah had sent a message
saying he was prepared to move against Musaddiq. The Majlis
would meet next day, 22 September, and, the ambassador said,
it would strengthen the opposition if Britain immediately rejected the latest proposals. The Foreign Office stampeded and
the government as well, rejecting the unsigned proposals without consulting the United States.[7]

Nothing happened in Tehran, and more than a whiff of
intrigue hangs over this episode. An abbreviated cabinet – in
the absence of Attlee, Morrison, Gaitskell, and Shinwell –
decided to reject the proposals. When Stokes asked to see the
communication from Shepherd to Strang, his request was refused. He learned that the urgent telegram had been based
solely on a conversation between Zaehner and the shah's personal secretary. How could the ambassador and Strang have
convinced themselves that the shah would act despite all evidence to the contrary?[8]

Harriman had observed that Shepherd did not keep his
government well informed. Stokes agreed that a change in
ambassadors might be warranted. 'He is not the right man for
the job. His personality is against him and that counts for
more than anyone can readily add up amongst the Asiatics.'
But Shepherd stayed in Tehran until February 1952, although
he would not again have the opportunity to influence Anglo-
Iranian relations in such a decisive fashion.[9]

The British thus refused negotiations without consulting the
Americans, who had counseled flexibility, patience, understanding. Then London urged Washington not to announce a long-
delayed Export–Import Bank loan to Iran, arguing that it had
become a symbol of US support for Musaddiq and must be
stopped. Morrison ordered the embassy in Washington 'to take
all necessary and emphatic steps to stop US from rewarding
sin against the UK,' adding for good measure, 'I shall be very,
very cross if they do.' Reluctantly, Washington rejected Grady's
advice and incurred Musaddiq's displeasure.[10]

At this unfortunate moment the United States was changing

ambassadors in Tehran. Grady was going home a defeated man, and from this the British could take comfort. A constant critic of British policy in Iran, he had tried to reestablish negotiations after Harriman's departure, appealing to the State Department not to let Iran slip behind the iron curtain. He had urged Washington to show interest by making the loan – all to no avail.[11]

One of the ambassador's last acts was to inform Musaddiq that the loan would not be made – for financial reasons, he added. The prime minister responded knowingly, saying, 'if this loan embarrasses or irritates the Anglo-American alliance, I will be glad to send you a note rejecting [it].' Grady departed with 'a sense of real frustration.' Once retired, the former ambassador gave vent to his disagreement with American and British policies in Iran. He presented to the American public an endearing image of the Iranian prime minister who, he said, is 'a little old man in a frail body but with a will of iron and a passion for what he regards as the best interests of his people' in their struggle against British economic aggression. The British considered Grady 'an inexperienced and amateur diplomatist' and never forgave him.[12]

Loy Henderson replaced Grady. 'Mr. Foreign Service,' as his colleagues fondly called him, was one of Washington's most effective envoys, having served at posts in Europe and the Middle East, and most recently in India. He was no stranger to regional problems, having acted as director of the Office of Near East and African Affairs in the State Department after World War II and as ambassador in neighboring Iraq. Like other cold warriors of his day, Henderson considered the Soviet Union the gravest threat to the so-called barrier states along its southern borders; his goal in Iran was to thwart communist expansion toward the oil-rich Persian Gulf, using whatever means necessary.[13]

While Henderson settled into diplomatic life in Tehran, his superiors continued to urge restraint, knowing that a minority in the British cabinet still desired to use force. To the Americans such a move would be disastrous. The Labour government faced a dilemma. As the general election neared the government had to be seen to be taking action in the Middle East. Yet everything it tried failed, leading to even greater losses in public support.

The Conservatives prodded the Attlee government. In a joint meeting on 27 June, Churchill stressed the importance of Iran. 'It was much more important than Korea,' he said, and he thought 'the moral case for using force to preserve the Company's property at Abadan was a strong one.' Two weeks later he wrote Attlee enquiring about military preparations, saying that Britain could not accept being chased out and promising Opposition support if force became necessary.[14]

In mid-July came the military's turn. The generals pushed for a scaled-down 'Buccaneer,' entailing the seizing and holding of Abadan island. The commander-in-chief in the Middle East urged action at Abadan to preserve British prestige in the region and to punish Iranian truculence and rudeness. The cabinet defence committee wisely chose to keep the plan on hold. July and August passed while the peacemakers, Harriman and Stokes, tried to negotiate a settlement.[15]

The military began to prepare leaflets to drop over Abadan in case of action. Version 'A,' drawn up in June, announced the arrival of troops to protect British lives and added, 'These forces will withdraw from Persia as soon as this task is finished.' In version 'B' officials decided to withhold this commitment, in case the invading force met no opposition and decided to remain. Thousands of each were printed and shipped out to headquarters in Egypt.[16]

With Stokes back in London in early September, Morrison called for reconsideration of the military option. Musaddiq had responded to rejection of his recent proposals with an ultimatum giving British workers at Abadan ten days to leave the country. The cabinet put Midget forces on full alert, while it considered what to do. Attlee read a message from Truman expressing strong objection to any military action. 'This government,' he wrote, 'could not consider giving any support to any such action.' This was the response Attlee hoped for, to silence the jingoist minority in his cabinet. Morrison insisted that Britain should not always be ordered about by the United States and that he still wanted to put in troops, but only Lord Chancellor William Allen Jowitt and Minister of Labour and Industry Alfred Robens supported him. The Truman letter proved decisive. The minister for local government and planning, Hugh Dalton, suggested showing it to Conservative leaders, who would surely not go against the United States.[17]

The British government had to act, for Attlee had scheduled the general election for 25 October and Iran had become a major campaign issue. Ministers spent much time worrying about how failure in Iran would affect them at the polls. Attlee sent a message urging the shah to move against Musaddiq, but that possibility seemed remote.[18]

The cabinet decided to revive an idea that had first appeared the previous May but had been put aside as premature. The government would take its case to the Security Council. Attlee was the mover in this decision and won over those who argued that such a step would be useless.[19]

It had to ensure US support. State Department officials were already considering new proposals for Anglo-Iranian negotiations when news from London reached them. They thought the decision unwise and Ambassador Franks agreed. Would it not be better to delay the UN gambit and accept the American proposals for direct negotiations?

It was too late for talks, Morrison said. Musaddiq's ultimatum was running out and the last thing London wanted was the Iranian telling the world he had received new proposals. That would make it appear that Britain had knuckled under.[20]

At the United Nations in New York City, developments ran counter to British expectations. Security Council President João Carlos Muniz of Brazil refused to ask Iran to delay its expulsion decree, pending outcome of the debate. Prime Minister Musaddiq decided to travel to New York to defend his nation, and Muniz agreed to postpone debate until his arrival. Then the Americans took issue with the original British proposal, which called for Iran to uphold the International Court's request of 5 June. This, they argued, had little chance of passage. They wanted to substitute a resolution calling simply for the United Kingdom and Iran to negotiate. Morrison complained to Acheson of lack of US support, but eventually, after repeated urging from Britain's UN delegate, Gladwyn Jebb, and Middleton, on loan from the Tehran embassy, he recognized the strength of opposition in the council and accepted the American revisions. Even then the prospects were not good, and US delegates suggested an 'out-of-court' settlement with Musaddiq for fear public controversy would only stiffen Iranian resistance and make compromise more difficult. But with the general election approaching, the Labour government, hoping for vindication, insisted on going through with the formal debate.[21]

Anglo-American relations were at an all-time low with regard to Iran. Acheson experienced Morrison's 'arbitrary and unyielding' manner during discussions in Washington. The British had not only rejected negotiations but had also gone to the UN without consulting the United States. Neither would they take American advice to avoid confrontation at New York.

British frustration revealed itself further in a frank exchange between Makins and US Ambassador Walter S. Gifford. The assistant undersecretary of state reminded the ambassador that his country had gone out of its way to adhere to US views and yet no matter how compliant, the United States continually put on the brakes and withheld support. The usually patient Makins complained that 'they were tired of being lectured to by the United States.' He did not like Acheson's recent message suggesting negotiation with Musaddiq in New York City. The British 'had no wish to be made fools of once more.'[22]

Partly the problem stemmed from the fact that the United States had been 'more right' than the British concerning Iran, and some officials found this galling, especially as the Americans were not always discreet in their handling of the situation.[23]

Iran was, of course, only one of many difficult issues challenging the Labour government. It required perspective to appreciate the pressures building in London during the final months of the Attlee government.

The American chargé there, Julius Holmes, sent a lengthy analysis to Washington in late August, explaining Attlee's dilemma. Labour had trouble with its left, the Bevanites, and it was harassed from the right, especially on Middle Eastern policy, by the Conservatives. 'They are tightly stretched, possibly overextended economically, politically, and militarily,' the American diplomat wrote. 'They are conscious of their weakness and extremely sensitive to any hint that we are not four-square with them.' Ministers were worn out after six years in office, and the government, Holmes observed, lacked its former toughness and initiative 'and is sterile in ideas.' All this seemed a recipe for electoral disaster and helped explain why Labour doggedly pursued its policy against Iran at the United Nations.[24]

Iran was becoming a winning issue for the Conservatives. Attlee could hardly have chosen a worse time for an election.

Churchill enjoyed needling him about the triple disasters of Abad*an*, Sud*an* (Egypt) and Bev*an*. The government, preoccupied with Iran, had 'diddled' on presenting Cairo with proposals for a Middle East Command, and in the middle of the campaign the Egyptians announced the abrogation of the Anglo-Egyptian Treaty of 1936 and the Sudan Agreement of 1899. Malcolm Muggeridge of the *Daily Telegraph* observed that 'the government's bungling in Egypt has been well up to the Persian standard.' Events seemed to be turning into a debacle. The British technicians in Iran, having universally rejected individual contracts with the NIOC, withdrew on 3 October, and as they began to arrive back in England, the papers carried their uncomplimentary observations on Iranians and Labour alike. One returnee observed that at departure 'Mr. Ross [AIOC manager] gave such a terrifying word of command in Persian that the policemen and troops were cowed into submission.' Said another, 'you have got to be firm with these people. . . . Stand your ground with the Persians and you have won the day.' Their point was clear – they could have stayed if the government had supported them. 'We are just back in time for the election,' one engineer observed, 'and I know which way we are going to vote.'[25]

Labour candidates resorted to the only reasonable defense, arguing that had the Conservatives been in office they would have used force and risked war. They had the old imperialist outlook, charged Morrison, who presented himself as the unlikely harbinger of peace. 'Only one thing would have justified the use of force in Persia: to save British lives.' Party banners demanded, WILL YOUR BOY DIE IN PERSIA? and WHOSE FINGER ON THE TRIGGER? The Labour counterattack probably neutralized Conservative rhetoric, but the impression lingered that Labour's Middle East policy was a shambles. And then of course there were poignant domestic issues – the high cost of living, deterioration of the economy, continually low supplies of meat and fuel and escalating costs of government.[26]

The election gave a narrow victory to the Conservatives (321 seats versus 295 for Labour), who now inherited the problem of Iran.

Labour had gambled and lost – twice in as many months. Despite Shepherd's prediction from Tehran, Musaddiq seemed stronger than ever. London's rejection of his proposals had disappointed him, and he took the offensive, ordering remaining British workers to leave. London could do little except look with a growing sense of frustration toward the Security Council. And then the election slipped away from them. Attlee could not have been too displeased; his health was poor and his party divided. He had hoped to retire after the February 1950 election but supporters had prevailed upon him to stay.

Labour had been in office over six years, helping its American allies make decisions and create organizations for the postwar world. But by 1951 its once formidable leaders had either departed or run out of energy. Despite a series of foreign policy achievements elsewhere, in the Middle East it left a mixed legacy. Iran and Egypt would demand immediate attention from the Conservatives.

In recent months there had been increasing signs of friction between Washington and London. Morrison had angered Acheson at the NATO council meeting in Ottawa in September. The foreign secretary, who had little experience for the post, let no opportunity pass to criticize US action or inaction. Gaitskell had become worried at the growing anti-Americanism in the cabinet. Perhaps it was fortunate for the Atlantic alliance that Attlee and Morrison had given way to Churchill and Eden. Had they remained, a Suez-like crisis might have erupted earlier, especially if Morrison headed the party, as seemed likely. One could expect Churchill to smooth differences much as he had done repeatedly with FDR during the war. And then, of course, Eden had years of foreign policy making experience, more than any of his contemporaries, excepting the 77-year-old prime minister.

5 Man of the Year

When Prime Minister Musaddiq visited New York in October, he had a splendid opportunity to present his nation's case to the world. He took center stage during the Security Council debate, winning the sympathy of third world diplomats and of many Americans watching on television. He administered a public rebuke to Britain's struggling Labour government just prior to its electoral defeat in late October.

After besting the British he went on to Washington, where Truman and Acheson made him welcome. He spent several weeks meeting with policymakers and came close to a compromise on oil, only to have the new Conservative government back away from the US-brokered agreement. Privately, American officials placed responsibility for failure on London.

Returning to Tehran via Cairo, the prime minister proved again his ability to attract popular support, even among Arabs. Far from weakening him as his opponents had hoped, his six-week progress abroad made him a hero.

British policy toward Iran altered little after the election. The new foreign secretary, Anthony Eden, had some claim to knowledge and understanding of Iran and its culture. He had studied Persian at Oxford, taking a first in oriental languages; he once told George Middleton he read an ode of the great Iranian poet, Hafiz, in the original each night before sleeping.[1]

He had been centrally involved in British foreign policy for 25 years, serving first as parliamentary private secretary to Sir Austen Chamberlain at the Foreign Office, then as Lord Privy Seal responsible for the League of Nation's affairs, and finally foreign secretary from 1935 until he resigned in February 1938 to protest Neville Chamberlain's brazen flouting of his authority. Brought back by Churchill, he headed the Foreign Office until Labour's victory in July 1945. Foreign affairs was everything to him, and he regularly resisted Churchill's efforts to give him experience in home affairs.[2]

Over the years Eden made a better adjustment than Churchill to the rising tide of nationalism in the empire. In one of his earliest speeches he had warned members of the House of

Commons of the danger of pursuing a policy of 'scuttle' in Iraq, which had only recently become a British mandate. Three decades later he would be accused of just such a policy in Egypt.[3]

Franks remained in Washington. He had proven a skilled negotiator and enjoyed friendship with American policymakers, including Acheson, Harriman, General George C. Marshall and McGhee. President Truman liked and respected him, often seeking his opinion.[4]

Shepherd continued in Tehran. It is difficult to assess his importance after his exaggerated prediction in September, but his attitude toward developments within Iran had changed hardly at all – if anything he seems to have become intransigent. A letter he wrote to the Foreign Office in October 1951 provides a remarkable summary of his views. He lamented the fact that Persia, unlike India, had never come under the 'wholesome influence of a Western colonizing power.' The country was 'now paying heavily for her immunity from tutelage.' The salvation of Persia would be a 20-year occupation by a foreign power, but the tragedy was that 'there is no country which either could or would undertake the education of Persia and its preparation for a *renaissance.*' The so-called nationalist movement, the ambassador remarked, was no such thing, rather a will-o'-the-wisp. Persia was still a long way from genuine nationalism. Little wonder the American embassy concluded that Britain's failure in Iran was rooted in 'the apparent inability of the British embassy to properly appraise the local situation.'[5]

While Shepherd had been dashing off his latest assessments of Iranian ineptitude, Prime Minister Musaddiq set off for New York with his son and daughter and a small group of advisers. On 8 October he met with McGhee and Vernon Walters in his hospital room where he was undergoing routine tests. McGhee encouraged him not to burn bridges to negotiation in his appearance at the Security Council. The assistant secretary tried to learn what Musaddiq thought about a renewal of talks and on what terms. The Americans realized they could achieve little prior to the British election, but, looking ahead, McGhee invited Musaddiq to visit Washington after the council debate in the hope progress might then become possible.[6]

The British were suspicious, fearing that US officials might try to commit them to negotiation before there was any indication that Musaddiq seriously intended to seek a settlement. They insisted on going through with their complaint against Iran at the UN. Gladwyn Jebb, who in private revealed a defeatist attitude, did his best publicly to win support for the original resolution, urging Iran to carry out the International Court of Justice recommendations of the previous June. He convinced few members. Musaddiq questioned the council's competency in what was, he said, an internal matter. He angrily denied Jebb's suggestion that the AIOC was trustee for the Iranian people, calling the statement a gratuitous offense to national pride, typical of the smug superiority of both the former company and the British government. After the session, Jebb, who had served in Iran, remarked to Musaddiq in Persian, 'If God wills it we will be friends again.' Without hesitation the prime minister responded: 'We have always been friends with England and the former company dragged your country needlessly into this dispute.'[7]

Musaddiq's arguments touched third world delegates whose nations had experienced colonialism or other forms of imperialism. Even the watered-down American version of the resolution could not collect the seven votes required for passage. On 19 October, the council voted to postpone further debate until the International Court could decide on its own competency in the case. Postponement represented a victory for Musaddiq whose prestige at home soared.

Outmaneuvered in the Security Council, the British accepted the inevitability of United States–Iranian talks at Washington. If they could not stop them, at least they hoped to keep American officials from sacrificing important principles.[8]

On a personal level, Acheson was quite taken with Musaddiq. He later described the old gentleman's arrival at Union Station, where the prime minister hobbled from the train, cane in hand, until he caught sight of the secretary, whereupon he tossed it aside and fairly skipped along. At Blair House, with serious demeanor, he portrayed his country as nothing but camels, sand and barren spaces, prompting Acheson to observe wryly: 'Oh! Rather like Texas.' Musaddiq dissolved in laughter, his ruse exposed.[9]

Between late October and mid-November, McGhee held at least 20 meetings with Musaddiq, trying to work out tentative proposals that would warrant the British sending negotiators to Washington. According to his account, he achieved considerable success, reaching agreement on all questions but price per barrel of oil. Acheson tried to get Musaddiq to understand the need for a two-tiered pricing arrangement, but the prime minister could not accept that the distributing company should receive roughly two times the price given to the producing nation. On this he was adamant, explaining that the Iranian people would not understand. Despite the secretary of state's flattery, he did not give way. Nor would he allow British oil technicians back into Iran. He did agree to turn over the Abadan refinery to a non-British company to own and operate, to assume responsibility for compensating the AIOC, and to give a 15-year oil purchasing contract to foreign buyers.[10]

The Americans kept the new Conservative government informed of every step in Washington, and the British knew that soon the United States would prod them for a decision. By the end of October, London had received the tentative proposals, which inspired little enthusiasm. Only the Foreign Office thought the scheme could work; the Treasury and Fuel and Power considered it unworkable. Fergusson confided to Strang that, despite any gloss, the two ministries would insist that oil operations in Iran remain in British hands. Rejection of the American proposals seemed almost predictable. Everyone agreed that London should not rush into negotiation just because of American optimism. The best course would be to send Musaddiq home and let the United States and Britain discuss terms in leisurely fashion.[11]

Britain's lukewarm reaction was partly the result of ministerial disputes over areas of responsibility. Disagreement over jurisdiction plagued Labour and continued to trouble its successor. The Treasury insisted that it, rather than the Foreign Office, should oversee all government contacts with the AIOC.[12]

Since the end of the war, the Treasury had struggled to make ends meet. The struggle continued under the Conservatives, but Britain lost ground. Dalton, Sir Stafford Cripps and Gaitskell for Labour, then 'Rab' Butler for the Conservatives each tried to stem the flow of red ink. Iranian oil was a major British asset, providing London with cheap oil and hefty profits. No Treasury official could easily relinquish this golden goose.

The Foreign Office viewed the situation differently. Although well aware of the importance of Middle Eastern oil, officials at

Whitehall took a broader perspective. They had to maintain friendly ties with the Americans and if that meant sacrificing something of the British position in Iran it might be a price worth paying.

The powerful Conservative chiefs of the two ministries, Eden and Butler, vied with each other for succession to Churchill, and competition for future preferment might also have contributed to their differences on Iranian oil.[13]

It was clear to Makins that future policy toward Iran could not be charted without a high-level meeting of interested agencies, and a full-scale meeting, with Eden presiding, took place on 1 November, less than a week after the election, to discuss how to respond to the United States. Of all the participants, only the foreign secretary urged serious consideration of the proposals, asking how their rejection would improve the British position in the Middle East. The American approach had been more often correct than their own, and 'he was doubtful whether the right policy was simply to wait for Musaddiq to fall.' The old hands from the three ministries – Leslie Rowan, Churchill's private secretary during the war, Fergusson, Strang, Makins and Shepherd – stressed the impracticability of the proposals and the impossibility of an agreement with Musaddiq. They decided to delay responding to Washington, pleading the need to consult the experts.[14]

During the next few days Eden's thinking underwent a remarkable change. On 4 November he cabled Franks repeating many of the same arguments as his predecessor. He denied Iran was likely to fall to communism as easily as Americans feared. Musaddiq would probably not have survived without US encouragement, he argued. Britain did not consider a bad agreement better than no agreement at all. He asked the United States to join Britain in taking a stiffer attitude toward Iran. He confirmed that he would pursue these arguments with Acheson when they met in Paris a few days hence.[15]

Two factors account for Eden's rapid volte-face. He was not well informed on the details of the dispute, and meetings at the Foreign Office exposed him to the collective wisdom of the old hands, who had been dealing with the crisis for months. Only a forceful, confident individual would have rejected their advice and set a new course; Bevin might have done so, but not Eden, who sought consensus. The second factor may have been even more persuasive. Prime Minister Churchill adamantly opposed the American proposals, minuting but one word, 'unacceptable!' He personally approved the reply to be given to Acheson at Paris. Churchill would have none of this American meddling, and so neither would Eden.[16]

This incident emphasizes the disagreement over Middle East affairs that increased during Churchill's final years in office. He could not tolerate any sign of weakness toward Arabs and Persians, and he subjected Eden to repeated criticism for what he characterized as a policy of 'scuttle.' An influential group in the Conservative party agreed, and the foreign secretary came under intense pressure not to give way either in Iran or Egypt. Eden decided to abandon the conciliatory approach he had suggested on 1 November.[17]

The scene shifted to Paris, where Acheson would not be easily dissuaded. He demanded to know which proposal the British found objectionable, and Eden had to request a team of experts from London, pleading disingenuously that he knew nothing about the Iranian situation. Over they came, Rowan, Fergusson and Martin Flett, representatives of the Treasury and Fuel and Power, all hardliners on Iran. They argued, among other points, for just compensation guarantees for the AIOC, which prompted Acheson to say that such demands were not realistic. Acheson quickly realized there would be no breakthrough and so, sadly, informed McGhee not to detain Musaddiq in Washington. The secretary confided unhappily to his assistants that the new Conservative government had taken a resolute stand toward Iran. Churchill had telephoned Eden in Paris, telling him not to yield even an inch. They would accept no settlement that would threaten their overseas investments even if it meant Iran went communist. Musaddiq could not be allowed to profit from his takeover of AIOC properties, nor humiliate them or discriminate against them. The new government had the same advisers as Labour, so they got the same arguments and analysis. Any change in British policy would come slowly.[18]

Acheson had a brusque final meeting with Eden. He recommended the foreign secretary obtain advisers other than those 'who had led British policy into the present trouble.' To avoid disintegration in Iran, the United States might have to extend financial assistance even though this would embitter Anglo-

American relations. He contended that negotiations would press the Iranian prime minister and show his weakness if he failed to reach a settlement. Eden agreed with none of this.[19]

And so ended the American autumn offensive. McGhee and his assistant Paul Nitze were depressed. In order not to put the British in a bad light, they told Musaddiq the whole problem had centered on his failure to agree on price, but he knew exactly what they were doing. He took the British response calmly, observing that they still believed they could force Iran to capitulate through economic pressure.[20]

As Musaddiq prepared to leave the United States, he penned a long letter to President Truman in which among other points he raised the possibility of an internal crisis in Iran. He hoped the US government would assist him with loans, pending settlement. Musaddiq knew how concerned the Americans were to maintain stability in his nation to thwart a communist takeover, and he must have been toying with their fears, for although such assistance would represent a symbolic victory for the prime minister, foreign loans were not yet essential to Iran's well-being.[21]

This game could be dangerous. There is little evidence the prime minister understood the possible negative consequences. Should Musaddiq's prediction come true, claimed the Joint Chiefs, the Soviet Union would have a springboard for domination of the entire Middle East, and McGhee told the House Foreign Affairs Committee that the Tudeh party in power would likely ask immediately for Soviet assistance. Henderson, always an ardent anticommunist, was even more concerned than officials in Washington. He sent urgent reports to the State Department throughout Musaddiq's stay, warning of communist support for the anti-British line as part of the Tudeh party's plan to destroy its rivals and seize power. He predicted Iranians would turn toward communism before bowing to Western imperialism, and he conjured up a horrifying scene: a nation of serfs, the Western-educated intelligentsia eliminated, and a strong army launching adventures in all directions, making the region indefensible. To forestall such a calamity, he recommended continued support, given Musaddiq's 'demonstrated political ability.' Should the internal situation worsen, or the prime minister lose control, Henderson and policymakers in Washington might quickly switch American support to another.[22]

Curiously the Soviets were slow to take interest in all this, prompting a former Tudeh party member to accuse them of doing nothing. Soviet writers treated Musaddiq's premiership with caution, evidently doubtful of the significance of his movement. Mirroring Moscow's indecision, the Tudeh party divided over how to respond to the prime minister. Party intellectuals opposed him, whereas workers and military officers wanted to extend support.[23]

Within the National Front there was suspicion of the Tudeh party and the Soviet Union. One of the most vocal critics was Musaddiq's adviser, Khalil Maliki, a former Tudeh member and co-founder of the Zamat Kishan-i Millat-i Iran [The Toiling Masses of Iran], who advocated a 'third force' in international affairs, an ideology positioned between the twin evils of capitalism and communism. He spoke for a socialism arising from the people and their national traditions and cited Iran, Egypt and India as contemporary examples. Whereas citizens of third world nations recognized the dangers of imperialism, Maliki argued, they worried less about the equally dangerous embrace of communism, which could destroy nationalist movements as it had done in Eastern Europe after World War II. 'It has become clear after Czechoslovakia that if socialists work with communists eventually communists will take control by force.' Maliki and other front leaders saw the Tudeh as serving the interest of the Soviet Union, not Iran. Tudeh reluctance to support Musaddiq and his policy on oil confirmed their suspicion.[24]

Neither the Soviets nor the Americans trusted the so-called third force. For the Russians, at least while Stalin lived, its advocates seemed tools of the imperialists; US officials considered them naifs who would prepare the way for communist takeover. Few in the West considered Musaddiq a communist, but many worried where his policies would lead. Western powers, seizing on Maliki's example, feared Musaddiq might end his days like the non-communist president of Czechoslovakia, Eduard Benes, who had been overthrown by his communist coalition partners in 1948.

During the Truman years, it is clear, the Americans reluctantly accepted Musaddiq as the alternative to communist domination of Iran, hence their frequent assertions to the British that they would take unilateral action if necessary to support

Musaddiq to keep Iran from falling under Soviet control. For their part, the British believed their ally suffered from the 'loss of China' syndrome, and they tried to convince Washington that supporting Musaddiq would guarantee instability and increase the likelihood of communism.

From time to time the Americans worried about the economic situation in Iran. They feared collapse would result in Musaddiq's replacement by the Tudeh. And yet the Iranian economy performed better than anyone could have predicted. Shortages of raw materials associated with the Korean War drove up the price of cotton, of which Iran had a large surplus. In 1951 Iran became self-sufficient in agricultural products except sugar and tea and bartered for the former with the Soviet Union and the nations of Eastern Europe. After September 1951, the Iranian government paid the wages of former employees of the AIOC and with less delay than under the company.[25]

It would take time for the British oil embargo seriously to affect the Iranian economy. An American officer in the US Mission to the Iranian Gendarmerie (GENMISH) reported to the Pentagon on the 'phenomenal tenacity for independence and for survival' of Iran. 'Events are weathered here which would be disastrous in any other country.' He did not foresee the nation 'going down the drain' in the near future.[26]

Although the US government was unwilling to make loans to Musaddiq, it maintained an active Point Four program in Iran, and during these years it became the only dependable source of US assistance. Point Four, under the direction of former New Dealer William Warne, developed a fine reputation for technical assistance in the countryside, sinking wells for pure water, spraying malarial mosquitoes and helping improve livestock. In spite of the prime minister's suspicion of foreign experts, Warne experienced little difficulty working with Musaddiq; he often had more problems with bureaucrats in Washington.

One of the recurring difficulties of technical exchange was the tendency for Western specialists to become impatient with Iranian colleagues, to disparage their abilities, and to adopt a superior attitude. Lack of respect had hampered Overseas Consultants Incorporated (OCI) and led to cancellation of its contract. Such difficulties frequently interfered with the work of US military missions as well. Iranian officials came to expect complaints from foreign advisers; only occasionally were they surprised. Musaddiq's minister of agriculture told the US agricultural attaché that the usual advice he heard from foreigners was that everything was wrong in Iran and that Iranian specialists were incompetent. Iranians responded by being stubborn and dilatory. They were sensitive to foreign criticism and yet most Westerners failed to understand this. Musaddiq often spoke in the Majlis against foreign experts who seemed to forget whom they were working for in Iran.[27]

But communist threats, US assistance and foreign advisers: all were forgotten in the triumphant arrival of Musaddiq in Cairo, where he had decided to make a brief stop on his way home. The prime minister's decision to visit Egypt was symbolic, its import not lost on the British government whose experts had long discerned an interrelationship between the crises in these two nations. Musaddiq received a jubilant popular reception, as adoring crowds chanted, 'Long live the leader in the fight against imperialism!' He in turn praised Cairo's stand against British imperialism. The leading Egyptian newspaper, *Al Ahram*, editorialized that he 'represents the vital and alert spirit of the East and its will to smash the iron fetters of politics and economics. It is this which binds us together.' These two ancient nations, land of the pharaoh and of the shahanshah, at either end of a great arc transcribing the Middle East, centers of powerful dynasties and age-old cultures when Britain was an island of rude and warlike savages, threatened to join forces 'to close down the oil fields and fill in the Suez Canal, if necessary,' to expunge all traces of imperialism.[28]

Yet despite crowds of well-wishers packing Cairo streets, closer observation would have confirmed that ties between Iran and Egypt were tenuous and did not extend beyond occasional incidences of symbolic support. Arabs and Persians had never been fond of each other and although both enjoyed twisting the British lion's tail, mutual support did not go beyond rhetoric that made everyone feel good but added little strength. Iranians were suspicious of foreigners, even co-religionists, and the leaders of Egypt considered themselves more progressive, more civilized than those who inhabited the distant plateau of Iran. In short the British worried unnecessarily over Egyptian–

Iranian collusion for neither side would derive much long-term benefit from Musaddiq's hurried visit.

By the time his plane touched down at Tehran's Mehrabad Airport on 24 November, Musaddiq had been abroad six weeks, and he soon discovered that matters were in disarray. Initially angry that the British had offered Musaddiq an international forum by hauling Iran before the Security Council, the opposition quickly changed its mind, using the prime minister's absence to organize. The British encouraged them. The oriental counselor at the embassy, Lance Pyman, canvassed senators and other officials, telling them the United States and Britain were now working as a team, indicating now was the time to act against Musaddiq.[29]

The British sought royal intervention to embolden Musaddiq's opponents, but this seemed increasingly unlikely after Musaddiq returned from the United States stronger than ever. The shah appeared more afraid of Musaddiq in opposition than as prime minister. He realized he could do little when even the leading cleric in Iran, Ayatollah Muhammad Husain Burujirdi, urged Iranians to stand together in the face of British threats. The shah enquired of Henderson, 'Can appeals to balanced budgets and increased national incomes have much effect when deep national passions have been aroused?' The shah would continue his waiting game.[30]

The opposition decided to act without the shah, and as soon as the prime minister appeared in the Majlis, Jamal Imami, a prominent opponent, proposed postponement of the scheduled parliamentary elections. Musaddiq refused. He intended to pursue his legislative program as long as the Majlis supported him and to delay elections would play into Britain's hands. London wanted his government to fall and be replaced by a pliant successor; this was not a propitious moment for them and so the call had gone out to delay the elections. Having cast his critics in the role of British lackeys, and thereby disarming them, he received a vote of confidence in both houses.[31]

Failing to bring down the prime minister in November, opponents renewed their attack the following month, when events again seemed to play into their hands. Violence had broken out on 6 December among Tudeh supporters, anticommunists, and the police. Twenty-five demonstrators died. Clashes continued among spectators in the visitors' gallery in parliament. The opposition used these incidents to renew its attack on the government. Not surprised by their tactics, Musaddiq shrewdly arranged for his opponents to make their complaints over national radio, where several used coarse language and insults when referring to the prime minister. Jamal Imami asked Musaddiq what he would report to the nation: 'Do you want to report that you killed innocent children on December 6th?' 'Pity this poor country and its poor people who have entrusted you with their destinies.' In conclusion he observed: 'Sometimes God sends a sickness to punish a people. Musaddiq is one of those sicknesses that God has sent to Iran.'[32]

Musaddiq spoke only after opposition deputies had been heard. He made a calm, well-reasoned speech, citing the importance of an opposition for effective government. He reiterated familiar nationalist appeals against Britain and succeeded in blunting all opposition charges, reestablishing his support across the nation. He promised to resign whenever he lost the confidence of the Majlis.[33]

It was a forensic *tour de force*. Even politicians who mistrusted Musaddiq's leadership showed enthusiasm for the skill he exhibited in parliament. Minister of Court Ala's son and daughter, university students, told Henderson how much the prime minister's oratory thrilled them. Even their father praised Musaddiq for his great success in ridding Iran of the AIOC.[34]

One note in Musaddiq's speech should have caught Washington's attention. The prime minister claimed Britain had come to dominate the United States with regard to policy toward Iran. If the Iranian government believed this, it could limit any future intermediary role for the Americans.[35]

Musaddiq's assertion came as Acheson prepared for a conference with the British in Washington, and he could be certain the Iranian government would scrutinize these proceedings.

Americans meanwhile could peruse copies of *Time* magazine, which proclaimed Muhammad Musaddiq 'Man of the Year.' The editors seemed neither to admire the Iranian prime minister nor understand him. They cited few of his accomplishments, telling readers of his tantrums, his grotesque antics, his oiling of the wheels of chaos. But they admitted he did pose a moral challenge, which the United States had to meet.[36]

Unlike the editors of *Time,* Asian correspondents found much to praise in Musaddiq's character. Indian journalists in particular, whose nation had experienced its share of crises with Britain, could sympathize with the Iranian prime minister. They considered him neither a neurotic nor a fanatic but rather a revered champion of the masses, an intellectual and a patriot whose people had 'at last found a leader who could not be bought.'[37]

Time's response was typical of many Anglo-American journals and newspapers. At first the press had been mildly sympathetic toward Musaddiq, portraying his struggle with the AIOC as strictly a case of British imperialism versus third world nationalism. As events in Iran spilled into crisis, interpretation changed. More foreign correspondents arrived and few had experience in the region. Many had difficulty adjusting to local conditions, and their reports seemed to reflect their discomforts and frustrations. Even an old 'Persia' hand like Basil Bunting of the *The Times,* who had served in Iran during World War II, complained that 'Mossy Dick' could not make up his mind whether to let him stay or expel him and so he remained in limbo 'without any legal papers.'[38]

Of course, Musaddiq's habits seemed peculiar to Westerners and provided wonderful opportunity for satire from journalists and cartoonists alike. Carried away in his speechmaking, the prime minister would often shed copious tears or swoon at the rostrum in the Majlis. He could laugh uproariously at his own jokes. Frail, chronically ill and tiring easily, he preferred to meet dignitaries in his house, usually in his bedroom, lying in striped pajamas on his wrought-iron bed. He continued this practice during his visit to Washington, where McGhee and Walters huddled at his bedside.

When he rejected one proposal after another, journalists focused more on Iranian intransigence and lack of reality and less on the issue of colonialism. Again Bunting wrote of being lied to by officials and of trying constantly 'to guess the truth.' Moreover, journalists were briefed by embassy personnel, many of whom had little sympathy for the National Front. When at a press conference the prime minister explained that British technicians were spies, that Iran's problems resulted from foreign 'lust for wealth,' that Iran (like the mythical land of Oz) had once been full of happy people bursting with a 'traditional love for liberty and national integrity,' journalists privately guffawed. When he insisted that what he told them were 'undeniable facts,' their doubts only deepened.[39]

In such encounters Iranian spokesmen often weakened their own positions. They were suspicious of Western journalists and this made communication across cultures difficult. They did not have the experience of a free press, believing from the shah down that representatives of the media had at least semi-official connections with various factions at home. Although Musaddiq and his ministers gave interviews to the press, these often appeared so full of propaganda that they did little to convince the journalists who attended.

For their part, journalists often misinterpreted what Musaddiq was saying. They failed to look behind his words. Predisposed toward consensus and conciliation, order and efficiency, they found more to criticize than to praise in Musaddiq's Iran. This proved unfortunate, for like *Time* magazine in January 1952, they alarmed Americans unnecessarily about the fate of Iran under the present government.

Many, like Bunting himself, Leopold Hermann of Reuters and the American Michael Clark of the *New York Times*, were expelled in retaliation for their increasingly hostile articles in the Western press. There were only a few exceptions to the generally negative line of reportage coming out of Tehran. Clifton Daniel, who had visited Iran briefly during the Azarbaijan crisis of 1946, returned for a short while in 1953 and wrote some sensible stories about what he saw. Perhaps the most even-handed of all the Western journalists at this time was Clark's replacement, Albion Ross, who wrote several excellent interpretive pieces on Musaddiq for his paper. He seemed somehow to have looked into the soul of Iran in a way few Westerners ever did. But overall the negative media image of Musaddiq continued to grow.[40]

Despite his apparent successes in New York, Washington and Cairo, one might wonder what Musaddiq had achieved. He had embarrassed Britain at the UN, but this may have made London more resistant to compromise, more determined not to negotiate with him. In spite of his cordial reception in the American capital, he came away empty-handed. He did not succeed in dividing the Anglo-American allies as he no doubt hoped to do, and he left with only vague promises of future assistance. In Egypt he charmed the masses, but not the politicians. The shah had opposed his Egyptian visit, and with some justification the opposition charged that his going antagonized the British and made compromise more difficult.[41]

At home he skillfully fended off the most determined opposition attack since taking office, but as long as the oil issue remained unsettled, Musaddiq presented it with the means for his undoing. He mistakenly believed time was on his side. Sooner or later his popular support would weaken in the face of economic hardship and enemy propaganda, and then Musaddiq would meet his greatest challenge. He was certainly right about collusion between domestic and foreign opponents, but he did not take from them their most effective weapon, the unresolved oil dispute.

6 Failed Plot

The first six months of 1952 – the only full year Musaddiq spent in office – brought a rush of events, but no solution to the crisis. At home the prime minister achieved a long-sought-after goal, holding free elections for the seventeenth Majlis. Concurrently, he negotiated with a delegation from the International Bank to resolve the oil dispute. Abroad, British and US officials met repeatedly to work out policy for Iran, and by mid-year the Americans had accepted a British plan to replace the Iranian leader.

The year opened with Anglo-American talks in Washington. The Americans had prepared well for their first high-level discussions with Churchill and Eden since Potsdam, drafting and redrafting position papers on a wide range of issues. Concerning Europe, the United States was anxious to reintegrate West Germany into the Western European community and to establish the European Defense Force, incorporating German military units. For all Churchill's apparent acceptance, wrote Acheson, 'at heart he did not approve of it.'[1]

Outside Europe the two areas of concern were East Asia and the Middle East. Here the two allies pursued revealing strategies. The Americans pleaded for British support and understanding in Asia, especially concerning China where it might be necessary to extend the air war beyond Korea and to blockade Chinese ports, should an armistice fail to end the conflict. In the Middle East attention focused on Egypt and Iran. Acheson considered the proposed Middle East Command (MEC), which he hoped Egypt would join, a panacea. More important for the secretary of state was Iran, the key to Middle East security.[2]

'Iran is a dam which keeps Soviet power from flooding the Middle East Corridor,' reported one intelligence study. It stood on the Soviet periphery, in the first line of defense against communist expansion. Should the Soviets breach that barrier – a flimsy one in early 1952 – its troops would quickly reach the Persian Gulf, around which lay the world's greatest oil reserves. Western oil companies had huge investments there, and production supplied Western Europe and Japan with the cheap oil needed for rapid economic growth. Discovery of oil in North Africa lay in the future, and most Middle Eastern oil then came from Iran, Iraq, Kuwait and Saudi Arabia. If the Soviets could shut off or reduce the flow of oil to the developed world by seizing the fields or disrupting tanker traffic, Europe would be at its mercy, and Western rearmament would suffer a major setback. The Americans concluded it would be foolish to sit tight in the face of increasing instability in Iran. Britain should seek a settlement based on proposals that would work to everyone's advantage.[3]

Churchill offered to follow the US lead in East Asia if the United States would follow Britain in the Middle East; the Americans found this unacceptable. They could nót conceive of the United States in a subordinate position. Henderson wrote to reinforce the belief in Washington that the British had pursued a destructive policy in Iran. If the Iranians had reacted unreasonably, the ambassador said, it was not without provocation. Perhaps the time had come for the British to allow the United States 'a free hand in an endeavor to save Iran.'[4]

The talks on Iran and Egypt thus got nowhere. Acheson pressed Eden so hard over what he considered the dangerous British policy toward Iran that he offended the foreign secretary, to whom he later apologized.[5]

At this juncture the International Bank for Reconstruction and Development (IBRD) entered the oil dispute. An American vice-president of the bank, Robert Garner, who was himself suspicious of foreigners, had contacted Musaddiq to discuss the possibility of an interim agreement under which the bank would operate Iran's oil industry. The prime minister had shown enough interest to warrant sending a bank mission to Tehran after approval from the State Department and the Foreign Office. Talks in December and January, however, offered little prospect of agreement, and when the British came to Washington, Acheson expressed doubt that the bank would succeed where so many others had failed.[6]

There was perhaps more to the secretary's dismissive comment than first appeared. The bank had an unfortunate reputation in Iran, where successive governments had requested development loans and officials – among them Garner – put them off under one pretext or another. Making loans to developing nations, which it considered credit risks, really worried the bank in those early years. The details of these failed negotiations were widely known and had become the butt of jokes in the Iranian press. Musaddiq had shown some courage in welcoming the bank's representatives.[7]

The bank suggested operating the oil industry for Iran as an independent and neutral agent, dividing the profits between Iran, the purchasing group and an escrow fund that could be used later to pay compensation. At first this arrangement seemed acceptable. Soon, however, Kazim Hasibi questioned the arrangement, arguing that it would harm Iran's interests by raising doubts about its claims to the oil reserves. He suggested the bank act as an Iranian agent, and upon reflection, Musaddiq agreed. Other problems remained as well. There was the unresolved problem of price, which had proven so intractable in Washington in November. Perhaps most difficult, Musaddiq would forbid employment of British technicians, for, as he explained to Henderson, 'if we let in only two or three Britishers, Britain will in a short time be ruling Iran. Don't you know if you let in one Britisher he will soon be manager and director and will fill it with Britishers.' It would be difficult to dispel the suspicions of a lifetime.[8]

Cool at first toward the bank's proposals, the British began to see the advantage. Although they had little hope of a settlement, at least negotiations in Tehran would keep the State Department from pushing them too hard for new proposals. Whenever the Americans suggested devising a back-up plan should the bank fail, or discussing economic assistance to stabilize Musaddiq's regime, the British put them off with the observation that they should await the outcome of the bank's negotiations. Whatever the result, London was determined that any failure should be seen as the responsibility of Iran, not Britain.[9]

Throughout the winter and spring of 1952, IBRD delegations came and went between Washington, London and Tehran, without much progress. Not only were the British suspicious of American plans, but the Treasury and the Ministry of Fuel and Power considered their own Foreign Office a weak link because the diplomats believed they had no choice but to accept the State Department's lead on Iran. Eden, they complained, had not kept in touch with the AIOC nor informed Fraser of the latest developments. When Treasury members of the Persian Working Committee were not invited to the minister of state's dinner for the bank mission, their suspicion seemed confirmed. At that gathering, Middleton of the Tehran Embassy hinted that his government might now consider compensation for physical assets only, rather than for oil still in the ground. On learning this, the Treasury complained loudly to Eden and made clear to the IBRD that such was not the government position.[10]

Fraser maintained a proprietary interest in all that happened, staunchly defending his company's record. He told Acheson's representative, Nitze, that the AIOC 'had trained the Persians, educated them, taken care of their housing and social services in a way which the Persians themselves were totally incapable of doing. He felt that most of the Persians with whom they had dealt recognized this and would welcome the return of AIOC.' Fraser's continuing lack of realism brought renewed recommendation in Whitehall that he be replaced but, as before, nothing happened.[11]

In mid-March negotiations in Tehran were broken off over the unresolved problems of price, management and British technicians. On this last point, Musaddiq assured US officials who might think him paranoid that just as the United States suspected Russian intentions, so Iran with even more justification suspected those of the British. An American diplomat in Tehran, summing up the growing frustration there, wrote, 'personally the whole thing seems to me to be like a Grade B movie being played over and over.' But he quickly added that they could not give up trying, for the alternative – a communist Iran – was too horrible to contemplate.[12]

Thus ended another attempt to defuse the crisis. This was, of course, no plan to resolve differences, merely a two-year stopgap to allow Iranian oil to flow again while the principals negotiated. It is tempting to conclude that Musaddiq ought to have endorsed the bank plan, for in the short run it would have relieved pressure on his government and provided money for necessary projects. And yet how would Iranian nationalism have fared under such an arrangement? The people could not remain in such an excited state indefinitely, and once they turned their attention to mundane matters, Musaddiq would have difficulty stirring them again. The present course, he could easily conclude, provided the best opportunity to push through to success.

And then, of course, the bank plan would lessen pressure on Britain and the United States. Musaddiq believed – mistakenly – that the West could not do without Iranian oil. Why then surrender his strongest weapon by allowing it to flow again? He thought time was on his side. To settle for an interim arrangement could sacrifice all the previous months of national effort, without resolving anything. Given his understanding of events, the failure of the negotiations was no catastrophe.

The British hastily prepared for the renewed American offensive. They had to deflect the Americans, who considered the cold war paramount; for the British, maintaining their economic strength was fundamental. They would try to engage US officials on plans for a successor government in Tehran, as if Musaddiq's demise was a foregone conclusion. They would chip away at Washington's determination to deal with Musaddiq. In early 1952 the Truman administration was having difficulty justifying continued US economic and military assistance to the Iranian government. The British were delighted, arguing as they had all along that US aid only strengthened Musaddiq and made him more intractable (and more difficult to replace).[13]

The State Department insisted on maintaining support for Point Four and the two US military missions in Tehran. Under the Mutual Security Act of 1951, nations receiving economic and military assistance had to agree to use it in defense of the free world. Arguing that such a statement would violate Iran's neutrality, Musaddiq refused. Through compromise the pledge was waived and the United States assigned $23.4 million to Iranian training and development projects. Continuing military assistance was more problematical, for requirements here could not be easily circumvented. Shipments of materiel were temporarily halted in January while Henderson dickered with Musaddiq over a statement to allow the missions to continue and the military supplies to flow. The Joint Chiefs recognized the critical importance of continuing the missions and yet could not defy the law. By April they despaired of accommodation and made plans to divide Iran's Mutual Security money between Greece and Turkey. At the last moment Musaddiq offered a letter, giving assurance that 'Iran supports and defends the principles of the United Nations.' Officials grasped at this statement, judging it sufficient to fulfill the spirit of the law and to justify resuming military aid. The Americans bent the rules in what seemed a good cause. Acheson went further, somehow interpreting Musaddiq's letter as a retreat by the prime minister.[14]

All the talk of aid presumably showed continued support, yet Musaddiq would have preferred budgetary assistance. He had requested this in his November letter to President Truman, and the Americans said they would consider it. The president responded in March, saying that Iran could have all the money it needed if it settled the oil dispute. Musaddiq rightly interpreted this as a not-so-subtle refusal.

The January announcement of renewed assistance came at the worst possible time for Musaddiq's opponents; elections had just begun and the news could only boost the prime minister's support at the polls. Musaddiq chose this time to confront the British for 'open interference' in Iran's internal affairs, forcing them to close their consulates in provincial centers. The public applauded his decision.[15]

At this juncture Musaddiq determined to conduct free elections, a goal he had pursued for 50 years. To ensure this he even rotated provincial governors to lessen their influence at the polls. The elections began in January and National Front candidates won easily in Tehran while their allies, followers of Ayatollah Kashani, carried Tabriz, Iran's second largest city. In smaller provincial centers, however, the landlords and army used their influence to elect right-wing, anti-Musaddiq deputies. The prime minister had been naive to think that free elections would allow voters to express the popular will. What happened was that landowners herded peasants to the polling places to vote for approved candidates.[16]

By April it became clear that the seventeenth Majlis might contain a majority against the government. Still Musaddiq would not condone interference to ensure favorable results. Instead, he decided to suspend the elections after a majority of seats had been filled (80 out of 134). This unprecedented step solved the immediate problem, but left him without a solid majority in the Majlis. He could count on 30 firm votes; others supported him conditionally until an alternative presented itself. The truncated elections provided opponents with a grand opportunity to attack the prime minister as a would-be dictator, a charge that many in the West readily believed. Musaddiq had played his hand badly. The question became one of who would replace him.

It was sad indeed that Musaddiq, a real patriot, certainly also an idealist, with much political good sense, might be downed because of a political miscalculation. He could not quite believe that with a good, lively case against the British, and much careful maneuvering on his own part, his fellow countrymen would not see that after all he was working for the country. He could not think they would allow his opponents to remove him in order to bring in some appointee of the young shah, hoping to prop up the dynasty and return to business as usual.

But Musaddiq had stumbled, and the opposition settled on Ahmad Qavam, who had a long career in politics. Since early in the century he had occupied the highest offices, serving several times as prime minister. He came from the Qajar family that had ruled Iran before the Pahlavis. Musaddiq, too, belonged to this extended family. Despite his age – he was into his seventies – Qavam eagerly sought office. In London he had visited cabinet members to press his case. More than any other leader he had experience at manipulating Iranian factions, and supporters predicted he would find the means to govern.

Qavam admittedly did not have the shah's support. The shah did not share Musaddiq's commitment to a constitutional monarchy and yet could not embrace Qavam. During World War II, and more recently in 1946–47, the young monarch had encountered many difficulties with the wily, ambitious Qavam, who as prime minister had seemed bent on limiting royal prerogatives. The shah vacillated, frustrating the opposition and the British, who wondered if a diminution of royal power might not be such a bad idea. The shah had his own candidate to replace Musaddiq, Allahyar Salih, member of the National Front and, as leader of the Iran Party, a close ally of Musaddiq. He was certainly ambitious and his appointment might divide the National Front as Qavam's would not. As minister of the interior, Salih had impressed the shah by his firmness toward Ayatollah Kashani. Perhaps the shah was shrewder than anyone imagined.[17]

The Americans and British were skeptical. Washington considered Salih anti-Western and no more likely than Musaddiq to solve the oil crisis; London worried because Salih's brother was the long-time Oriental secretary at the US embassy. Henderson and Middleton scheduled long, separate meetings with Qavam to signal their preference to the shah.[18]

In early July the shah seemed ready to move. According to constitutional procedure the prime minister had to resign following the general election. Musaddiq's resignation would offer opportunity to call on the Majlis to nominate a prime minister, and the shah might even recommend Qavam.

When Musaddiq resigned, a muddle ensued, and soon he was back in office. The shah urged the speaker to obtain a vote of inclination for Qavam, but when he addressed committees of the Majlis and the senate at the palace, he spoke in such ambiguous terms they assumed he favored Musaddiq, and the Majlis duly extended its support. The senate – strongly opposed to Musaddiq – would not vote. Musaddiq refused to assume office without senatorial support, so the shah pressed them. Reluctantly, they obeyed and then adjourned, in disappointment and frustration.[19]

But it was only the beginning of the crisis. Returned to office, Musaddiq requested that parliament grant him six months' unlimited power to introduce new laws without delay. Then, on 16 July, he proposed to take over the ministry of war in his new government. This latest news stunned the shah, who considered appointing the war minister a royal prerogative. Although the 1906 constitution had intended to put control of the military in the hands of the government, not the ruler, the shah had exercised this power since the first years of his reign and would not yield. In 1942 Qavam's cabinet had fallen over this very issue.[20]

Who should control the military became a question crucial to the survival of Musaddiq's government, hence his decision to retire if he could not obtain control over the post. The armed forces had become a major prop for the Pahlavi dynasty. Riza Shah had lavished energy and resources on developing a modern army, and his successor continued the policy. As commander-in-chief, the shah had appointed all high-ranking officers, basing decisions on loyalty to the throne rather than on ability or honesty. A close friend of the monarch, General Murtiza Yazdanpanah, had occupied the ministry of war and repeatedly ignored Prime Minister Musaddiq's requests for transfer of officers.[21]

Corruption and incompetence had plagued the officer corps for years, resulting in constant complaints from American military advisers. There could be little improvement as long as the shah remained personally in control.

US policymakers were aware of the problem and the resulting weakness of Iran's army, but faced a dilemma – to press the shah too hard for reform might lead him to pursue a neutralist policy and thereby open the door to the Soviets. During the Musaddiq years their worries compounded because they viewed the shah as the principal stabilizing force in Iran, and he in turn relied on the military to sustain him. Thus they ended by trying to restore the political importance and prestige of the Iranian military establishment to counteract Musaddiq's policies.[22]

Meanwhile discontented junior officers, often denied promotion regardless of ability, listened to appeals not only from nationalists but from Tudeh propagandists as well, both of whom promised to sweep corruption and inefficiency from the officer corps. It was a time of restiveness among younger officers throughout the region, especially in Egypt and Syria, and the Pahlavis could hardly forget that their own dynasty had arisen out of these same ranks.

The army frequently interfered in elections; it had done so again in the recent voting, and the prime minister insisted that the military be responsible to his government. Further, he argued that Iran needed only a small force to maintain internal stability. Ironically, the Americans would have agreed.[23]

Explaining to the nation his inability to govern without control over the military, Musaddiq suggested that the shah find someone in whom he had confidence. He withdrew to his house and refused to meet with any visitors.

As this crisis-within-a-crisis unfolded, the Americans finally adopted the view that Musaddiq was impossible. After more than a year in office, resolution of the oil dispute seemed further away than ever, and US officials increasingly blamed Iran more than Britain for the impasse. Now Musaddiq had moved to weaken the throne. With backing from the State Department, Henderson told the shah that rumor of US support for the prime minister was unfounded and that he personally thought Musaddiq was leading Iran toward disaster. The shah had to face up to his responsibility to change the government if Musaddiq would not or could not settle the oil dispute. Assistant Secretary Henry Byroade informed the House Committee on International Relations that 'there cannot possibly be a settlement of the oil issue in Iran while Musaddiq is Prime Minister.' Acheson met with Eden in London where they discussed the crisis. The secretary of state felt confident that Musaddiq would fall, but when Eden assured him the prime minister would have to be pushed, Acheson did not protest.[24]

The Foreign Office breathed more easily, knowing that at last the Americans shared their perspective on Musaddiq, but no one in London could guess how long their views would coincide.

Still, the British had prepared no better than the Iranian opposition for a change of government in Tehran. They realized a new prime minister would require immediate financial assistance and early resolution of the oil crisis, yet they had no plan ready when opportunity came. They could not provide emergency assistance; the Americans, Eden remarked, would have to contribute that.[25]

Nor had the British worked out a new oil proposal. The Foreign Office had sponsored a move to replace Fraser, but the Treasury and the Ministry of Fuel and Power resisted, leading Deputy Undersecretary Makins to complain of 'a solid wall of Bourbonism and Micawberism.' Eden saw Fraser as being in 'cloud cuckoo land.' The AIOC leadership assumed that their company would return to Iran once Musaddiq fell. They wanted to deal directly with Qavam, who would need money and therefore be unlikely to raise difficulties.[26]

At first everything appeared quiet in Tehran following Musaddiq's resignation. Groups of deputies met to determine strategy. Although National Front leaders announced support for Musaddiq, Qavam's supporters held a rump session of the Majlis and recommended their candidate to the shah, who promptly called him to form a government. Qavam spoke out strongly for law and order, threatening woe to 'those who obstruct by sabotage my well-intentioned measures or try to disturb public order . . . I am warning you all,' he said, 'the period of transgression is over. The day has come to obey the government's orders.'[27]

And how long might Qavam last? He had only half-hearted

support from the shah, who was terrified that the movement to replace Musaddiq might backfire and bring down the throne. Qavam wanted stringent measures, a declaration of martial law and dismissal of parliament, but the shah demurred. Now his ill-tempered speech had enraged his opponents.

National Front deputies arranged an audience with the shah on the morning of 18 July, while the new prime minister was battling for survival a few blocks away. Led by Ali Shayegan, the delegation of five deputies argued that the shah's advisers must have misinformed him, for the Majlis had lacked a quorum and its vote of inclination for Qavam was therefore illegal. The shah disclaimed responsibility for Musaddiq's resignation, calling on the Majlis to vote if it wanted him.[28]

Qavam reacted angrily to news of the opposition deputies' audience, and turned to Henderson for emergency aid, which could determine success or failure. Henderson was sympathetic, telling Washington speed was essential. An early decision 'might play an important role in maintaining internal security.' Officials hastily put together a $10 million package. On 21 July, Acheson informed Truman of the critical situation.[29]

Henderson did all he could to bolster Qavam. He kept secret the request for emergency assistance, for the United States had repeatedly denied such funds to Musaddiq. He met with the prime minister, with the shah's Swiss confidant, Ernest Perron, and with Minister of Court Husain Ala, trying to strengthen their resolve. He and Middleton would have welcomed a royal audience, but the court feared it would be misconstrued. He did speak with the shah by telephone, advising him 'not to be too scrupulous, saying that the constitution was not meant to paralyse the executive in moments of extreme danger.'[30]

Crowds in the streets of Tehran and other cities across the country influenced the shah more than counsel of the two ambassadors. The people of Iran were sending a message he could not ignore. Musaddiq's supporters took to the streets soon after the resignation – students, workers in the bazaar and industrial workers all rushed to join the demonstrations. A key figure in rousing the masses, Ayatollah Kashani, denounced Qavam as 'the enemy of religion, freedom, and national independence.' Kashani suspected a foreign plot and threatened to put on a shroud and take to the streets himself, if necessary, to overthrow Qavam. He refused to negotiate with the prime minister's emissaries, and Qavam's order to arrest him on 20 July could not be carried out because of the throng surrounding his house.[31]

The National Front called for massive demonstrations on 21 July, which according to Henderson resulted in civil war. The Tudeh joined with Musaddiq's supporters to battle army tanks, and 29 rioters died. The shah feared for the loyalty of the army and worried that anger directed at Qavam might come to focus on the throne.

Qavam felt powerless to put down demonstrations without the shah's support and alternated between action and indecision. Perhaps age weakened his will. At 5:00 p.m., 21 July, against Henderson's advice, he resigned and went into hiding. The embittered old man sent a desperate message to parliament, comparing himself improbably to Imam Husain, grandson of the Prophet, who had been called to power by supporters in Kufa in Iraq and then left to perish at the hands of his enemies.[32]

Then came another turn of the wheel. The shah rushed to recall Musaddiq to end the violence. He returned in triumph, made sweeter by news of the International Court's decision that it had no jurisdiction in the oil dispute. In order to reassure the young shah, Musaddiq inscribed a Quran for him, affirming his loyalty to the constitution and swearing he would have nothing to do with anyone proposing to alter Iran's form of government. He broadcast this pledge to the nation. Yet his new cabinet reflected a move toward the left. As minister of war he retired many officers, transferred others, and appointed a trusted general as chief of staff. The Majlis granted him full powers for six months to speed the process of law-making, and when the unpopular senate resisted, Musaddiq disbanded it.[33]

Success did not come without a price. After July 1952 fissures appeared within the nationalist movement, and Musaddiq's enemies exploited them. Ayatollah Kashani expected to exercise more authority after he helped remove Qavam, but Musaddiq kept power in his own hands, although he supported Kashani's election as speaker of the Majlis. Clerics, including Kashani, criticized increasing Tudeh activity and Musaddiq's refusal to crack down. The gap widened.

After Qavam's overthrow and the shah's humiliating retreat, Britain and America moved again in opposite directions. The

Americans worried that Musaddiq might turn against the United States and throw out the military missions and Point Four. Concluding that only Musaddiq and the National Front stood between the Tudeh and its domination of Iran, the United States decided to do all it could to rescue the situation by co-operating with the government. It was difficult work. On 28 July, Henderson reported on his first post-Qavam meeting with Musaddiq. 'I could not but be discouraged at the thought that a person so lacking in stability and so clearly dominated by emotions and prejudices should represent the only bulwark left between Iran and communism,' he related. 'I had the feeling at times that I was talking to someone who was not quite sane.' The prime minister had been sane enough to question US diplomacy, claiming the Americans were willing to lend money to Qavam when they refused it to him and that the United States had encouraged Qavam to take power. The ambassador lied, stoutly denying both charges.[34]

In spite of his feelings, Henderson urged Washington to support Musaddiq, recommending up to $50 million in loans and grants with as few strings as possible to stabilize the Iranian government. Perhaps he was responding to the sober analysis of a US Army officer who suggested that the United States had a rare opportunity to support the choice of the people, who was also an anticommunist.[35]

After the recent fiasco in Tehran, officials concluded that the United States would have to support Iran more to save it from the Soviets and that Britain should accept American leadership as right and necessary. Charles Bohlen, Counselor at the State Department, accused the British of being more interested in a satisfactory oil accord than in keeping Iran from becoming communist. The National Security Council (NSC) advised consultation but cautioned that London should not be allowed to veto any US action essential to getting oil flowing again.[36]

Whether by impish design or pure coincidence, Musaddiq hurled one further chastisement at the Americans when he appointed the outspoken nationalist, Allahyar Salih, ambassador to the United States. Musaddiq actually questioned Salih's loyalty and shipped him to Washington for safekeeping. In his first meeting with President Truman, Salih criticized the United States for following Britain's lead in Iran, whereupon Truman responded with some 'give "em hell Harry" language.[37]

The British reacted to these events with bitterness toward the shah, whose fear, they claimed, had overcome his reason. The Foreign Office now realized that Musaddiq's removal would have to come from military action, a *coup d'état*; given the shah's weakness, constitutional measures would not work. Within a week of Musaddiq's return the Rashidian brothers, who worked with British agents, were recommending General Fazlollah Zahidi as leader of a coup. One British diplomat asked Middleton for advice because he did not want 'to set him off on a coup d'état and then have to call it off should we decide, which heaven forbid, to support Musaddiq.' Middleton met with Zahidi who implied he would lead a coup. The chargé cautioned London that any such project would have to take place without the shah's knowledge, for he might ruin it at the last minute.[38]

What, then, had happened was that the man in striped pajamas, with whom the patience of Washington and London had snapped, was back in power, and the question was what the two nations, sometimes known as the powers, would do about it. By avoiding Musaddiq, trying not to deal with him, the British, with American sufferance, had brought about their own discomfort, and with it the discomfort of their American ally. The British were virtually reduced to scheming against Musaddiq through a plot with Zahidi, while the Americans reluctantly mended fences with him.

7 Britain Departs

The late summer and autumn of 1952, as matters turned out, was a seedtime in relations between Britain, Iran and the United States, although it is fair to say that none of the principals, the Iranian premier or leaders in London and Washington, understood just what was happening.

Such is the manner in which great events occur. The usual belief is that change comes from gradual accumulation of *démarches*, each almost like a trumpet call, and as the exchange becomes more shrill the evidence of crisis accumulates and then, finally, in a clap of thunder, a shriek of trumpets, all is new, nothing remains of the old. But in actuality the changes of this world are not like the movements of a symphony. They are gradual accumulations of smallnesses, sometimes – as in the autumn of 1952 – of personal smallnesses, from which history moves to a conclusion that afterward seemed predictable, evident, and yet really was not.

One event in the summer of 1952 that made a real difference was the disappearance from the Foreign Office of the foreign secretary, the prickly and stiff and sometimes old-fashioned Anthony Eden. Behind all his fuss and feathers the latter was not really as formidable as he seemed. He was, instead, a sort of pussycat. Behind the appearance of decisiveness was weakness born of being the heir apparent, of waiting for Churchill to get out of office. So long as Eden was around, one could take comfort in believing that not much of a serious sort would happen between Britain (and its ally, the United States) and Iran. Eden simply was not decisive enough to do that. But then in the summer of 1952, Eden went away for a short time. He married the niece of his prime minister, Clarissa Churchill, on 14 August, and the newly-weds went off to Portugal.

It fell to Prime Minister Churchill, who even in his old age was a far more decisive figure, to contain the American rush to pacify Musaddiq. History exercised a powerful influence over his decisions on the Middle East. The old imperialist had displayed keen interest in the region since the early years of the century – even before, for he had served with victorious British forces under Kitchener at the battle of Omdurman in

1898, which put the Sudan firmly back in the empire. As First Lord of the Admiralty during World War I he had negotiated government purchase of a majority share in the Iranian oil concession, to guarantee fuel supplies for the Royal Navy, which was converting from coal at the time. He had helped organize the disastrous Gallipoli campaign of 1915–16, which brought his ouster from the Admiralty. As colonial secretary in the immediate postwar years, he organized British control in the new mandates of Iraq and Palestine. Long sympathetic to Zionism he had done what he could to foster a Jewish homeland in the latter. With decades of experience in the region he was not about to give in easily to the demands of Middle Eastern nationalists, especially not to those of the Iranian prime minister, whom he despised.

Churchill's intervention began when Musaddiq, returning to power, to the complete surprise of Washington and London suggested arbitration of the oil dispute, without providing any details. Perhaps he felt greater confidence after recent events. Certainly he trusted the International Court of Justice more after its recent nine to five decision favoring Iran. Then, just as quickly, and inexplicably, he withdrew his offer. Acheson would not let the opportunity pass and immediately proposed a simple US–UK approach, combining economic assistance and arbitration. After many twists this suggestion became the joint Truman–Churchill proposal of 27 August 1952.[1]

Churchill presided over Iranian affairs in the absence of the foreign secretary. In London the cabinet aired concerns regarding Acheson's proposal, in particular wanting any joint approach to set conditions, for otherwise the Americans might end up rewarding Musaddiq at AIOC expense. At least a joint offer would keep the United States from independently offering Tehran financial assistance. While they deliberated, Musaddiq issued a demand for compensation for losses related to the oil embargo. This did not improve the mood at Whitehall. Nine days passed before Acheson finally received an answer to his urgent communication. Foreign policy was in something of a hiatus, with Eden away in Portugal. The sense of urgency that infused officials in Washington was not shared it seemed by their British colleagues across the Atlantic.[2]

The initial exchange with Acheson went out in Eden's name. The response was unsatisfactory in every way, and the secretary of state told Ambassador Franks that the only resemblance between the *aide-mémoire* and the reply was that 'they were both written on paper with a typewriter.' American officials considered the British terms so narrow as to invite Iranian rejection, to hinge too much on the cooperation of the AIOC. Franks convinced the department to rephrase its terse reply in which it threatened a unilateral approach to Iran, but he agreed with several of the American points, and he advised his government to rethink its position carefully.[3]

What inspired the next action in London was news that W. Alton Jones, head of the Cities Service Oil Company, the major American oil distributor, planned to accept Musaddiq's invitation to visit Iran to advise on the oil industry there. The State Department tried to dissuade Jones but to no avail. Secretary of the Interior Oscar Chapman, interested in a larger role for himself on Iran, arranged a meeting with President Truman before Jones's departure. The Foreign Office deplored the whole affair, fearing it would indicate a break in company embargoes against Iranian oil, encouraging Musaddiq to be less accommodating with the AIOC.

Churchill wrote the president, hoping he would discourage Jones, but Truman said the visit might result in much good. He reassured the prime minister that American oil companies wanted no advantage from Britain's discomfiture, but urged Churchill not to reject Musaddiq's proposal of arbitration at the World Court. Truman added, in a phrase that makes it almost certain the president was dictating the letter, 'If Persia goes down the Communist drain, it will be little satisfaction to any of us that legal positions were defended to the last.'[4]

Sensing Truman's willingness to take a more active part in the Iran problem, and no doubt relishing the leader-to-leader diplomacy reminiscent of World War II ties with President Roosevelt, the prime minister now suggested a joint US–UK note; a combined approach might convince the errant Musaddiq. 'The alternative,' he warned, 'is the United States taking on the burden of being indefinitely blackmailed by Persia to the detriment of its greatest friend. It will be worse for you even than for us if . . . Persia thinks she can play one off against the other.'[5]

But the Americans had second thoughts after Acheson's

proposal three weeks earlier, and Truman now asked for separate messages to avoid any indication of 'ganging up' on Iran. When Churchill wrote again, resurrecting memories of wartime solidarity, of two good men doing what was right 'against a third who is doing wrong,' the president relented.[6]

The Americans had made an important concession. Previously the two allies had maintained separate approaches toward Iran, Britain setting narrow conditions, allowing little room for maneuver, the United States more pragmatic, willing to change details, even principles if necessary, to reach agreement. Now London had succeeded in linking itself with Washington in the joint representation. Even if the British had to give a little to get Truman's assent, they knew the combined approach would strengthen their position. It mattered little whether Musaddiq accepted or not – they did not expect him to do so – at least they had the Americans temporarily on board. They would do what they could to keep them from getting away again, to prevent them from pursuing heaven knows what other scheme concocted by junior officials at the Pentagon or in Foggy Bottom.

Churchill's act might have been appropriate, for Musaddiq was anxiously awaiting a reply to his earlier proposal, failing which he threatened to consider severing relations with Britain. Still, Churchill's intervention came at a price. When Eden, honeymooning in Lisbon, learned that the prime minister had avoided channels at the Foreign Office by writing directly to the president, he complained that Winston had stolen his own 'personal thunder.' Their differences, of course, became more frequent the longer the prime minister busied himself with foreign affairs and postponed his promised retirement. Here was the spectacle of the middle-aged Eden, at long last married to a woman younger than himself, a wife he cherished, happy in Lisbon, awaiting his translation to the prime ministry, a little fearful however in pushing his opinionated senior colleague with whom he had worked over many years. Eden felt slighted, but he could do little except let off steam in fits of pique. Musaddiq may even have sensed this confusion, and if so he would have profited from it.[7]

Henderson and Middleton presented the joint note unofficially on 27 August, proposing arbitration by the International

Court on compensation and negotiation between Iran and the AIOC to allow Iranian oil to move again into world markets, all sugared over with a US advance of $10 million.

Musaddiq's reaction was hostile. He regretted United States association with Britain and sarcastically referred to the $10 million as charity. When he indicated he would publish the note, the two diplomats decided not to deliver it formally before seeking advice from their governments. Henderson was reluctant to take action that might damage US–Iranian relations, now that Britain's position was so tenuous.[8]

Since July he had done what he could to strengthen the American position in Iran. He met with Ayatollah Kashani to explain why Britain and the United States had to work together as pillars of the current world system. Kashani did not agree, demanding that the United States be as outspoken against colonialism as it was against communism, threatening to denounce it if it was not. Henderson talked with Husain Makki about his upcoming trip to Washington and tried to defuse the deputy's opposition to the American military missions. He advised the State Department that Iran needed massive economic aid on the scale of Greece and Turkey in 1947. Iran, he argued, was an American problem and the British would just have to accept this. He disliked the notion of a joint approach from the start because Britain had become a source of weakness for the West in the region with its unwise decisions to stand firm on outmoded treaty rights and privileges. It was difficult to keep the American and British representatives together; to achieve this, Middleton spent hours with his colleague discussing the crisis. The chargé assured London that Henderson, not he, had been responsible for the delayed delivery of the note.[9]

Truman praised the diplomats for acting wisely, and indicated he would change the note as Musaddiq wished, if Britain agreed. But Churchill did not agree, referring contemptuously to 'the drivellings of this old man in bed.' The note, he said, should be formally delivered, and 'let the world judge.' And so it was.[10]

Musaddiq did not reject the note officially until 24 September, but it was clear long before what the result would be. He realized the inherent danger for Iran in the Truman–Churchill proposals. To accept them would have turned a dispute with a private company into a public affair in which Iran would confront not one power, but two. Furthermore, the compensation article did not explicitly recognize the nationalization law and under the 1933 concession agreement, which would run until 1993, the AIOC might claim losses from future earnings. Iran required some limits on how much the British could claim, otherwise Iran might have to assume a huge debt. Musaddiq must have been encouraged by Jones's recent visit, hinting of cracks in the British blockade, without which Iran would be free to sell its own oil.[11]

In this litany of proposal and counterproposal, Musaddiq quickly added another passing idea, suggesting compensation to the AIOC be limited to physical property in Iran (thereby excluding any claims for loss of future earnings); that Britain make an advance to Iran of £49 million, which he claimed it owed under the unratified supplementary oil agreement of 1950; and that Iran remain free to seek compensation for losses from the British embargo.[12]

What followed was a three-way struggle in which Musaddiq sought to divide the United States and Britain, the former tried to work out new proposals, and Britain tried to get the Americans to stand by the joint note. On 8 October, Musaddiq wrote thanking the American government for its efforts and accusing the British of procrastination. Next day Acheson told Franks of a tentative plan to create a new international distribution company to take off $25 million of Iranian oil. More important was his proposal for cutting the compensation knot. It seemed clear that the British and the Iranians could not agree on particulars of arbitration, so, suggested Acheson, why not have Iran provide a single, lump-sum payment in settlement of all claims. This could be calculated in oil and because of its simplicity might attract Musaddiq's support.[13]

His suggestion never reached Tehran, for Churchill and Eden opposed it. They rushed a note to Tehran reiterating their position and raising anew those issues of compensation that had alarmed Musaddiq from the outset. Roger Makins and the head of the new Ministry of Transport, Fuel and Power, Lord Leathers, agreed that the latest American proposal was unwise, but Makins worried that the Americans would not stay put unless given some alternative to keep them happy. So intent were the British on maintaining the appearance of US–UK accord that they agreed to send parallel messages to Musaddiq rejecting his reply to the Truman–Churchill note. This was less than the strong, joint note they originally demanded but far better than the wholly separate ones favored by Acheson.[14]

Events were hurrying toward memorable trouble, and even such an expert on Persia as British scholar Ann Lambton could offer nothing but recrimination and grim predictions. Musaddiq was impossible, she concluded, and the Americans were responsible for the lack of British success in Iran. She advised the government not to give in, even though the United States might make a deal with Persia eliminating Britain.[15]

The longer the crisis lasted, the more the British blamed the United States – often with good reason. Continuous leaks in the American press made Anglo-American differences apparent to all. What could the Americans be thinking, they wondered, when they invited Musaddiq's 'right-hand man,' Makki, to visit the United States as a guest of the government. Furthermore, the administration's attack on the oil cartel would destroy the companies' control over international markets, 'the best safeguard against a repetition of Persia's action.' These concerns came from a diverse group of oil executives and government officials, who did not often find themselves in agreement with the antediluvian head of the AIOC.[16]

In retaliation for Britain's rejection of his counterproposals, Musaddiq now announced the severing of diplomatic relations. And so, after 18 months of intense diplomatic activity and over a century of ties, British diplomats packed their bags.

Even the departure of the diplomats was not without drama. They had to go out to Baghdad in a caravan of automobiles led by Chargé Middleton, who recalled that after several days on the road, 'we came toward Baghdad at sunset driving West, and they had mounted guards with lances and banners all along the route into the city . . . and as my Rolls came by they all dipped their lances – marvellous drama.' It was all reminiscent of Kitchener and Khartoum, of Allenby and Zaghlul Pasha in 1924, of running the tanks up to Abdin Palace in 1942, or so Middleton seemed to be dreaming. At least the memories, though surely not the reality, were there on the outskirts of the Iraqi capital. By the middle of the twentieth century, memories were all that remained of Britain's imperial glory.[17]

While the British careened in their caravan to Baghdad, to

receive the dipping of the lances, Ambassador Henderson shouldered the Anglo-American burden. His reports to Washington would provide the Foreign Office with information on internal Iranian developments, and London made an arrangement for its diplomats to read his dispatches twice a week at the State Department. The American envoy had to proceed cautiously in his relations with Musaddiq, for if he had to leave like his British colleague, the Western position would be lost. Henderson, in the foreign service for 30 years, no stranger to ceremony (albeit to American ceremony, one might add), would have no dreams or memories of past glories to accompany him. He would simply have to pack up, get in some airplane, and fly back to Washington – hardly a romantic enterprise.[18]

Reactions in the American capital to yet another setback revealed the variety of interests surrounding Iranian developments. The American oil companies all along had opposed compromise unless Musaddiq paid a penalty sufficient to keep leaders of other concessionary states from following Iran. Company officials reported King Abd al-Aziz Ibn Saud becoming more difficult. 'Today the victim is Britain in Iran,' revealed one intelligence report, 'tomorrow it may be an American company in another Middle East country.'[19]

In summer 1951, major US and foreign oil companies had joined in a voluntary agreement under the auspices of the Petroleum Administration for Defense headed by Oscar Chapman to deal with production shortfalls and disruption of the market due to loss of Iranian production. At first the antitrust division of the Department of Justice had opposed the agreement, but the president exempted the companies from antitrust laws under section 708 of the Defense Production Act of 1950. In some sense the Korean War had come to the aid of policy toward distant Iran. The voluntary agreement provided that US companies would decrease imports of Middle Eastern oil, relying more on domestic production. This would release Middle Eastern supplies for Western Europe and East Asia. Production of crude oil could be increased quickly in Saudi Arabia and Kuwait, although refinery capacity was limited. With Abadan out of production, it became necessary to distribute refined products carefully to avoid shortages. The greatest problem was high octane aviation fuel, but even it resolved itself as new refineries came into production in the Eastern hemisphere.

As a result of government and industry cooperation, the AIOC continued supplying its customers. Despite the loss of profits from Iran, the company's dividends for 1952 were maintained at the 1951 level.[20]

Within the American government the Department of Defense admittedly took a more accommodationist view. The Joint Chiefs argued that the continued orientation of Iran toward the United States transcended both the British position in the Middle East and Britain's collaboration with the United States in the region. Secretary of Defense Robert Lovett told George McGhee he thought the plan worked out with Musaddiq in Washington and then proposed to the British was better than they could have expected given their weak position. He tried to convince his friend the secretary of state to seize the initiative on Iran. Lovett interpreted the severing of Anglo-Iranian relations as proof the United States could not rely on the British. The United States would have to take prompt economic and political action to revive Iran's oil industry and bolster the Iranian government. To wait would play into the hands of the communists and might necessitate US military intervention. The prospect concerned him, for the Joints Chiefs reported that the United States could not respond to an emergency in Iran without grave risks – withdrawing troops from somewhere else (presumably Korea) or expanding the armed forces. An early settlement seemed to offer the best solution for the military's dilemma. Lovett knew such a change would cause difficulties for Anglo-American relations, but he believed there had to be action, with or without the British.[21]

Even within the State Department support for unilateral action was increasing. The new Assistant Secretary of State for Near East Affairs, Henry Byroade, agreed with Lovett. Yet Acheson rejected unilateral action; he would not risk the British pulling away from the United States. 'We have to go just like pigeons,' he wrote, 'when one turns the others do it too. We have to fly wing to wing.' Iran just was not worth losing 'our closest ally.'[22]

The secretary did suggest a new approach; this time he offered something different. American proposals had envisioned a one-to-one agreement between Iran and the AIOC. Now Acheson suggested a consortium including American companies. The companies would take off Iranian oil and sell most of it to the AIOC. After October 1952, US proposals routinely incorporated this consortium idea.

Such a suggestion encountered plenty of problems on the American side, and at first they seemed almost insurmountable. The US companies, which had been indicted by the government in an oil cartel suit, showed little interest in the scheme. Certainly they would refuse to participate unless the suit were quashed. The Justice Department did not accept the 'interests of national security' argument put forward by supporters of the consortium idea and wanted time to think about the proposition.[23]

Then, too, the British wanted no part of yet another American plan. But Ambassador Gifford in London advised the Foreign Office that if Britain rejected the Acheson proposal, Washington might go ahead anyway and break the united front. After all, this was the autumn of 1952, an electoral year, with President Truman retiring in January 1953, and Dulles threatening to use failure in Iran as an election issue. Whoever his successor, and the odds were on Eisenhower, this meant a change of some sort. Perhaps, he must have reasoned, it was better to do something rather than nothing. The cabinet decided to stall. When Paul Nitze and Walter Levy came to London in mid-October, officials listened politely and at every opportunity affirmed their attachment to the Truman–Churchill proposals of August. The strategy seemed to pay off, and at the end of the month Makins concluded with relief that 'Nitze has gone home in a happy frame of mind and the UK position is now held for a week or two!'[24]

One must say, in conclusion, that the cheerful words of Makins were hardly on the mark. The Foreign Office had become far too philosophical, too observational. It was like the American State Department during the 1920s and 1930s, when its officers believed their duty was to observe the actions and frequently the foolishness of their European opposites, to take all this into consideration, think idly of what they (the Americans) might do or have done in a similar situation, pronounce a curse upon all of them, and then do nothing, observing, not very wistfully, that what had come up would go down, and that if kind words sent off an inquisitor that was all that needed to be done. In the case of Makins it was foolhardy to believe that just because Nitze went off in his plane to the United

States, Britain's diplomacy on Iran had succeeded. After all, Middleton's untimely parade to Baghdad in his Rolls had left the Foreign Office in the not very gentle hands of the Americans. Within the American government there was confusion over Iranian policy in the Department of Defense, and some wistfulness, some thought that an agreement was possible, even within the State Department. Acheson had many problems on his hands, unlike the dreamy Makins and the self-satisfied Middleton. To most officials in Washington it was apparent in the autumn of 1952 that the Truman administration was going to give way to a Republican administration under the questionable leadership of a World War II general. Acheson – contrary to Makin's musings – may well have thought that autumn that he, the secretary of state, had only a few months to tidy up affairs in Iran. He did not like to fool with countries outside of Western Europe, the more so when East Asia was still aflame, but he had to make a final try.

The situation had taken a bad turn. Everything had fallen into the hands of Musaddiq, whose intense feelings for his own country made certain he would stand firm.

8 Time Runs Out

It is an extraordinary thing that after all the negotiating that seemed to go on interminably, and the resistance in London that seemed likewise, it took the end of the Truman administration to bring ginger, so to speak, to the negotiations between Washington and Tehran. One can of course almost imagine what happened. When it became clear that the Democratic administration was going to be replaced by a Republican administration in the November election, President Truman may well have said to Secretary Acheson, 'Let's do our best to tie up as much loose business as we can, before those Republicans take over.' Or, along the same lines, perhaps Acheson thought, 'I can do better than General Ike, with all his talk of Republican virtue, and certainly better than Foster Dulles who has had no real diplomatic authority since he was his grandfather's secretary at the Second Hague Conference in 1907.' Whoever broached the question of resolving the Iranian Crisis before Eisenhower's inauguration on 20 January, this indeed was the purpose of the Democratic administration in the time remaining to it. By all evidence, it is clear that Truman and Acheson got promptly to work on this matter.[1]

The Americans were reluctant to get caught in the middle of the British–Iranian antagonism. They knew full well that they had enough on their agenda. They believed that apart from their own country, Western Europe was the most important place in the world, at least for them. Second at that time, rather to their consternation (for they would have preferred no second), was East Asia – the locus of the Korean War that by November 1952 had turned into a stalemate, the Americans having redeemed South Korea, the North Koreans now propped up by the Chinese and simply refusing to make peace. With its worldwide concerns, the Truman administration preferred to have Britain handle the Middle East. In the absence of much enlightenment in London, Truman and Acheson now, in their last weeks of power, sought to bring some to the matter themselves.

Despite their disdain for the incoming Republicans, Truman and Acheson may nonetheless have sensed that innocence could bring greater confusion than the Republicans might have anticipated, that in a sense the new administration might prove almost dangerous in its desire to be a new broom, and sweep out the – mostly Democratic – cobwebs. Eisenhower was accustomed to military solutions, even though most of his army service over the past decade had been diplomatic in nature. Dulles, so long without power, would naturally expect more to come from the exercise of power than he should have. And the Republicans generally, with a right-wing group in the Senate and House that constituted an embarrassment even to Eisenhower and Dulles, were inclined toward rash statements in their discussions, foreign and domestic. There was danger in the air with the change of administrations.

During the Truman administration's lame-duck period between November 1952 and January 1953, there was much activity in Washington as outgoing officials tried with a final burst of energy to resolve the Iranian oil dispute. Like the Carter administration three decades later – which was also involved in negotiations with Iran – the efforts of Truman and Acheson fell just short of success.

One obstacle in this final diplomatic offensive was Britain's reluctance to sacrifice its Middle Eastern interests to make the American plan succeed. The British had tired of Acheson's lectures. As before, London stalled, letting time slip away, hoping the new administration would be more understanding.

Soon after the Republican victory Eden traveled to New York to attend the UN session and to meet with President-elect Dwight D. Eisenhower. Eden and his aides spent more than two weeks in New York City, meeting with world leaders at their headquarters in the Waldorf Astoria Hotel overlooking the nearby East River. These were not easy days for the foreign secretary. He did not approve of Eisenhower's choice for secretary of state, John Foster Dulles, which made for a certain awkwardness. And he repeatedly ran afoul of Dean Acheson, not only on policy toward Iran but also on Korea and Trieste, where the American secretary of state seemed prepared to offend Yugoslavia in order to give the Italians the territory they wanted.[2]

Strangely Eden got along better with the president-elect than with the outgoing secretary of state with whom he had worked so closely during the previous year. According to one source

Acheson appeared in Eden's suite one evening slightly tipsy and over another martini commented undiplomatically on Minister of State Selwyn Lloyd, holding him responsible for Britain's failure to support the American position on Korea.[3]

Eisenhower knew a good deal about the Iranian problem. He had had long talks about Iran and Musaddiq with Vernon Walters, who translated for Harriman in July–August 1951 and for McGhee in October–November of the same year. Furthermore, two days before his meeting with Eden in New York City, Acheson had briefed Ike on Iranian policy, explaining that the United States intended to seek a settlement by taking a series of apparently unilateral steps, which he speculated would stimulate British cooperation. Ike showed interest in a settlement, suggesting to Eden an easing of British terms for arbitration. But to his query as to whether a solution was likely before he took office, Eden responded negatively.[4]

Meeting with Eden later, Secretary Acheson said he wanted the United States and Britain to enter into serious, non-stop discussion to find an agreeable plan; barring this the United States might have to act on its own. The State Department planned to send Nitze to London again for further talks, and he hoped a new approach could be ready for Ambassador Henderson to take back with him to Tehran in late December.[5]

The Foreign Office had to keep the Americans in play, trying to uphold the joint proposals of August while ascertaining the likely policy of the new US administration toward Iran. Postponing talks as long as possible would delay the risk of an American ultimatum.

Internal divisions at Whitehall resurfaced. The Foreign Office thought that if all else failed a bad agreement might be better than a break with the United States. (This, of course, is what the Americans were counting on.) The Treasury, and Fuel and Power, did not agree. The Treasury warned of the effect that a bad agreement would have on Iraq and Kuwait, leading Eden to comment icily that the Treasury was responsible for most of the present difficulty because it had squeezed AIOC profits after the war and done nothing to improve the company's mediocre board.[6]

Eden and Permanent Undersecretary Pierson Dixon's talks with Nitze, and later in Paris with Acheson, proved inconclusive. Acheson raised again the possibility of a lump-sum compensation if necessary to get an agreement, but the British would not abandon arbitration. They prevailed upon Acheson not to grant the long-delayed Export–Import Bank loan to Iran, leaving Henderson to return to Tehran empty-handed.[7]

Acheson continued to pursue the idea of a consortium. Knowing that any agreement would depend on the cooperation of US oil companies, he persuaded President Truman to instruct him to open negotiations. On 3 December he held an important preliminary meeting with the reluctant oil executives in Washington, where they explained to him just how difficult a settlement would be. The ARAMCO representative argued that Saudi Arabia would be angry if his company cut output to assist the movement of Iranian oil into the world market. Finding a place for it would not be easy. The leaders again expressed their concern that Iran should in no way be rewarded for its action, which would set a bad example. Acheson assured them that no other producing country was likely to emulate Iran for the Iranians would come out of all this with less production and profit than under the previous agreement with the AIOC.[8]

Meetings with the oil executives continued off and on into January. With the oil cartel suit still pending, the companies saw little reason to cooperate; after all it was that kind of cooperation that had gotten them into trouble with the government in the first place. Nor did they want to upset the principle of the 50–50 agreement in the Middle East.

It took a presidential decision to make the oilmen more cooperative. Truman removed one barrier at a National Security Council meeting on 9 January 1953 when, acting on General Omar Bradley's advice that national security was at stake, he designated the cartel suit a civil rather than a criminal case. Thereafter, if the companies were found guilty, punishment would be greatly reduced. The Justice Department was not pleased. The incoming Eisenhower administration, which had been kept closely informed, developed this budding relationship with the major oil companies and eventually dropped the case entirely.[9]

With the oil companies moving, albeit reluctantly, toward cooperation, the Americans prepared to approach London again. While Prime Minister Churchill bade farewell to President

Truman in Washington, taking time incidentally to caution John Foster Dulles that the new administration should let events in places such as Egypt, Korea and 'Persia' simmer for several months, Assistant Secretary Byroade traveled to London for what he hoped would be the final working out of a proposal on Iran.[10]

It took only a few days for the two sides to agree on a three-point set of proposals: arbitration by the International Court using the same principles as those for nationalization of coal in Britain; commercial negotiations between Iran and an international firm composed of the AIOC, US and French oil companies to arrange the sale of Iranian oil; and advance payment by the US government against future oil deliveries for the US stockpile ($50 million when the agreement was signed, $50 million more in five installments).[11]

Optimism ran high in London and Washington. Henderson had urged speed, saying that Musaddiq this time seemed genuinely interested in agreement. Eden sanctioned sending Sir Pierson Dixon to Tehran to initial the accord. To save time the foreign secretary even signed a letter to be delivered to the Iranian leader at the appropriate time:

Dear Prime Minister:

My good friend Sir Pierson Dixon will hand you this letter and tell your Excellency how very glad I am that the differences which have so unfortunately divided us are now well on the way to being honourably settled.

I look forward with confidence to the new era which the conclusion of the agreement will open in the relations between our two countries.

Yours sincerely,
Anthony Eden[12]

One wonders whether this letter would ever have been written had Churchill not been vacationing in distant Jamaica. The prime minister was too far away to transform his strong views on the Middle East into effective pressure on the Foreign Office. For once the foreign secretary could follow his own inclination, not only on Iran but on Egypt as well, where negotiations for a new Anglo-Egyptian treaty were underway.

When the prime minister returned on 29 January, he was furious over what he referred to as Eden's 'Munich on the Nile' and called for a stiffer policy toward Cairo.[13]

In Tehran, Henderson tried his best to make the 20 January deadline of the outgoing administration. He presented the proposals to Musaddiq on 15 January, spending seven hours with him trying to answer numerous objections. Two days later Musaddiq rejected this latest plan and submitted his own. Time had run out for the Truman administration.[14]

Henderson, intensely frustrated, described for Washington the difficulties of negotiating with the Iranian prime minister, who could, observed the ambassador, be petty, overcautious and suspicious when faced with a document. Musaddiq was not duplicitous but insisted on negotiating alone, and was incapable of continued, complicated negotiation in one direction for a length of time. 'He becomes confused, changes his mind, forgets, heeds advisers who pander to his suspicions, thinks up new ideas, or never frankly explains what is in the back of his mind.' This last observation may have been especially pertinent, for there are indications that Iranian leaders – like their British counterparts – expected a better settlement from the Eisenhower administration. Despite evidence of goodwill, many Iranians considered the Truman administration to be dominated by Britain. Musaddiq had admitted this in a letter to Eisenhower on 9 January. The prime minister knew that W. Alton Jones of Cities Service, a close friend and frequent bridge partner of Eisenhower, sympathized with Iran since his visit there in August–September 1952. In fact Jones had promised to send five US oil technicians to operate a small lubricating plant to satisfy Iran's domestic needs, and he convinced Ike to approach the British on this matter. Why not wait and learn what the Republicans might propose?[15]

Coming late to the crisis, the Truman administration had done its best. McGhee, Harriman, Acheson, Lovett, Truman himself, each had tried, only for their efforts to end in frustration. Truman railed against 'the blockheaded British' who said they knew how to handle Iran and did not.[16]

But neither he nor Acheson was prepared to act unilaterally. And unilateral action would have been necessary to get Iran's oil industry moving again. Like their British counterparts, the Americans saw too many problems in Iran which defied quick solution. They had in mind the orderly operation of the international oil industry on which the economic well-being of the United States, and more particularly Western Europe, depended.

What if the Iranians had been allowed to sell their oil to anyone at any price, would that have undermined the orderly marketing arrangements with other concession states? Probably, at least in the short run. The risks seemed too great. Furthermore, if Iran had to sell cheaply to attract customers, this might have meant lower prices – and lower profits – for everyone. There would be less certainty of supply as well and this possibility concerned government officials and oil executives alike.

There was also the question of compensation. If Iran had been allowed to pay only for assets of the AIOC in Iran, not for oil profits still in the ground, would this not make nationalization attractive to neighboring Iraq, Kuwait, or Saudi Arabia? And then there were the intangibles to consider: pride and prestige. If Musaddiq came out the victor, and hero to Iranians and other third world peoples, how would Western powers maintain their regional interests? Had not the British surrendered one point after another, agreeing that the AIOC would not return on its own to Iran, and that the NIOC could select whomever it wished to run the industry, including the Abadan refinery, and take the oil? All of this seemed to place more confidence in Iranian competence than Britons a few months earlier would have thought advisable.

Action by the United States to take off Iranian oil, in defiance of British policy and of the leaders of international oil, would have required a courage – perhaps rashness – lacking in officials who had spent the postwar years patiently and painstakingly building up the defenses of the free world. They could deprecate the inflexibility of their British allies, they could advise and warn them, but in the end they could not, would not, act against the interests of London.

It was a nice question how much of all this Musaddiq understood. Scholars have given the prime minister little credit, considering him naive, confused and obstinate. Perhaps he was all these things. Ambassador Henderson certainly came to this conclusion, and he had as much contact with Musaddiq as any American. Yet there is a problem here, for experts focus narrowly on particulars – compensation, arbitration, price per barrel, the usual paraphernalia of Western commercialism. They overlook the larger picture, or dismiss it. One of the most revealing insights to this controversy came out of a conversation in summer 1951, when Musaddiq was pressed by the oil expert Walter Levy to be more reasonable in seeking a settlement. He responded with an analogy, comparing Iran's relations with Britain to those of the American colonists at the time of the Boston Tea Party. 'What would American independence leaders have responded if some Persian mediators had come aboard the ships anchored in Boston and asked the colonists not to throw the tea overboard?' No one in the embassy or in Washington paid attention to this quaint comparison, and yet it contained the essence of Musaddiq's world view. Americans expected Iranians to show a degree of reasonableness that was unrealistic given the difficult historical relationship between the AIOC and the British government and Iran.[17]

Nothing in recent Anglo-Iranian relations gave Musaddiq reason to trust the British. They repeatedly sought to maintain *de facto* control over Iran's oil industry under the guise of accepting change. As if there were no difference in the position of a prime minister and a director of the board, they continually equated the AIOC and the government of Iran, arguing that if Fraser had been obstinate, so, too, had Musaddiq.[18]

Solving the oil dispute, which was much more than a dispute over oil, required a dramatic step, a leap of faith. Britain and the United States responded in a business-as-usual manner. None of the negotiators who came out to Iran in 1951 or 1952 had enough independence to bargain like an Iranian bazaar merchant. None, that is, until the consortium negotiations of 1954. Earlier proposals had to be approved back home and this took time; they fell prey to changing moods. A generous gesture might have captured Iranian imagination. Middleton was closer to the truth than he realized when he light-heartedly suggested that London send him a poet rather than an accountant.

What might have been acceptable in 1951 was rejected in 1953. This might seem strange if one believed that tightening the oil embargo would make the Iranians more amenable. Passage of time had the opposite effect. Musaddiq's credibility was tied to resolution of the crisis. He would not endorse a few cosmetic changes such as Jackson and Stokes had proposed. When the Anglo-Americans finally offered real changes in January 1953, the climate for compromise had badly deteriorated.

When British and American observers concluded that Musaddiq could not reach any agreement because it would cost his political life, they were missing the point. He would accept nothing that did not accord with his own high resolve to further Iranian independence. This approach may have been impractical, but we should not think the prime minister would have accepted what was offered were it not for fear of repercussions at home.

The issue of British technicians was a case in poiñt. In June 1951, Musaddiq welcomed them to work on individual contracts with the NIOC, but by the end of the summer when they rebuffed his offer he rejected any British participation in Iran's oil industry.

One cannot help but compare the Iranian crisis in 1953 to that in Mexico 15 years earlier. Indeed, throughout this later period American officials referred back to that dispute as an example of the effectiveness of enlightened policymaking. The Roosevelt administration had refused to press Mexico City to meet immediately the exaggerated compensation claims of US oil companies whose concessions President Lazaro Cardenas nationalized. After years of desultory negotiations the companies settled for 10 per cent of their original demands, less than they deserved, but the settlement created a priceless reservoir of goodwill during World War II. After nationalization the Mexican oil industry limped along, losing its formerly large share of the world market as foreign capital turned to Venezuela and then the Middle East. But the Mexicans accepted the sacrifice; it seemed to them a price worth paying, although it left foreign oil executives shaking their heads in dismay.

Some such arrangement might have been possible in Iran. At least one sympathetic writer, comparing Mexico and Iran in 1951, understood what lay at the heart of the dispute:

Mexico could be producing two or three times the amount of oil it does produce. Mexicans know that, but are they sorry they nationalized oil? Not in the slightest! Do they want the American companies back? Emphatically no! They would much rather own their oil industry and run it badly than have it well run by foreigners. They do not care if they have less oil, poorer in quality, higher in cost and badly distributed – so long as it is their oil.[19]

The Iranians had Mexico's experience very much in mind when they sent a delegation to Mexico City seeking technical assistance and legal advice. To their requests the Mexican government turned a deaf ear, pleading insufficient resources. The Mexican revolution was over, and as they struggled with social and economic problems, Mexico's new leaders wanted no added difficulties with Washington. The only friendly response came from former president Cardenas, who cabled Musaddiq his admiration, comparing Iran's action to Mexico's in 1938, and congratulating the prime minister on this successful blow against imperialism. Alas, Cardenas had no influence over his country's foreign policy.[20]

Iran's neighbors similarly did little to assist Tehran. Iraq, Kuwait and Saudi Arabia took advantage of Iran's distress as Western oil companies pumped more petroleum in these three states to make up for lost Iranian production. In Iraq and Kuwait, where British oil interests predominated, production rose respectively from 6.5 (1950) to 18.45 million tons (1952) and from 17 to 37.1 million tons. In nearby Saudi Arabia, where American companies held sway, the increase was slightly less although still considerable, rising from 25.9 to 41 million tons. In Baghdad there was no official sympathy for Musaddiq's National Front. The royalist, pro-British regime of General Nuri al-Said put down pro-Iranian demonstrations with dispatch. Iran had seldom enjoyed close ties with its Arab neighbors; there were none now.[21]

The Indians showed more understanding. The *Times of India* saw parallels with Gandhi's 'quit India' movement of 1942, during which he told the British rulers of the subcontinent: 'Leave this country to chaos, if you like. Leave it to God. But you get out!' Unfortunately for Musaddiq, support from the subcontinent did not extend much beyond a favorable press.[22]

While Washington and London negotiated the final proposals of the Truman administration, events in Iran took a dramatic turn, holding out to the British the prospect that their policy of standing firm against Musaddiq might soon be rewarded. Not that Britain's blockade had forced Musaddiq to surrender, for Western analysis indicated that the Iranian government was in no imminent danger of economic collapse. Indeed, prospects for 1953 appeared good. Although the regime's fiscal position would remain precarious, it would probably be able to assure basic requirements of food and fuel, limit unemployment and control inflation. The government had even sold several tanker loads of oil to Italian and Japanese buyers and courts in both countries upheld the legality of the transactions. To observers in Tehran this indicated a weakening of the British blockade.[23]

What made the British optimistic were increasing signs of stress within the National Front. Merely rumored in early fall 1952, they had become openly apparent by January as, one after another, Husain Makki, Dr. Muzaffar Bagha'i and Ayatollah Kashani publicly rebuked Musaddiq.

Makki, member of a prominent merchant family from Yazd, had entered the Majlis in 1947 as a supporter of Qavam but soon abandoned him and organized anti-government demonstrations in the Tehran bazaar. His popular book, *A Twenty-year History of Iran* (1945), criticized the Pahlavis and aligned him with the liberal nationalists. He had supported nationalization early, filibustering the supplementary oil agreement in the waning days of the Majlis session in August 1949. He had served on the delegation from the NIOC to take over the Abadan refinery in June 1951, haranguing crowds in Khuzistan with his jingoistic speeches. In elections for the seventeenth Majlis, he received more votes than any candidate in Tehran. (Musaddiq, as prime minister, did not run.) Unfortunately, he had an inflated sense of his abilities and was easily offended. Musaddiq gave offense when he failed to include him in his delegation to the United States the previous year. In December he resigned as a member of the Supreme Council of the NIOC to protest the council's selection of Dr. Riza Fallah as director of the Abadan refinery.[24]

Bagha'i, a European-educated lawyer and publisher of the influential nationalist newspaper, *Shahid*, broke with Musaddiq in November 1952, ostensibly over the prime minister's soft policy toward communism. His defection was more serious than Makki's because of his greater forcefulness, intelligence and organizational support in the bazaar. When he broke, he split the Toilers' party; the social democratic element went with Khalil Maliki to form the Third Force, loyal to Musaddiq. Bagha'i aspired to succeed Musaddiq and was more comfortable in the traditional world of conservative religious leaders.[25]

Of all the defectors the most important was Ayatollah Kashani, a politically pragmatic cleric who avoided the extremes of some of his associates. He had taken up arms against the British in World War I, had opposed Riza Shah in the 1920s and had been sent into exile by the British in 1941 for his ties to the Grand Mufti of Jerusalem, who had challenged British policy in Palestine. His anti-British, anti-imperialist statements led Westerners to dismiss him as nothing but a rabble-rouser. He could bring out crowds of lower-middle-class supporters as proven on 21 July 1952 when he helped unseat Qavam. He represented the conservative, traditional wing of the nationalist movement, as Musaddiq did the liberal and progressive. He influenced many clerics who sat in parliament. Kashani had pledged not to interfere with Musaddiq's appointments, but soon after the prime minister's return to power the ayatollah announced that he would have to leave Tehran, perhaps Iran, if such poor appointments continued. Musaddiq left such appointments to his advisers, reserving himself for what he considered important problems. He responded sharply, saying 'If you want reforms to take place, you must abstain from interfering in matters for a while.' Publicly Kashani urged support for Musaddiq, but their differences increased. Public defection came in early January, a few days after the prime minister received an overwhelming vote of confidence (64 to 1), for on 9 January, apparently without much consultation, Musaddiq asked the Majlis to extend his special powers, due to expire 9 February, for an additional 12 months.[26]

Makki resigned his seat immediately, criticizing Musaddiq as another Hitler. Bagha'i took a leading role in opposing the extension. Kashani wrote an open letter condemning the move as a violation of the constitution (although he had remained silent when similar action was taken in August 1952). In a test of the prime minister's support, the Majlis voted 59 to 1 to extend the emergency powers.[27]

What prompted the prime minister to seek this extension? To a meeting of National Front deputies he explained that reform bills took too long going through parliamentary stages.

More importantly he argued that an extension of his plenary powers would send a message to Britain that his government had strong support, that despite minor differences the nation stood united in the struggle to free itself of foreign control. This would improve the chances of an oil settlement. He disclaimed any intention of reducing the power of the Majlis, which would retain the right to reject laws decreed by the prime minister every three months.[28]

In this contretemps Musaddiq revealed the extent of his popularity among all classes. He appeared a national leader. After the defections the National Front was more cohesive.[29]

Yet there was a subtraction from his power. Even supporters admitted his partial repsonsibility for the defections. 'Whenever right is at stake,' he declared, in the manner of an Old Testament prophet, 'I will oppose any power.' According to a deputy minister in his government, Shahpour Bakhtiar, Musaddiq was certainly honest, but he could be intransigent and brusque. 'Issuing a law, he expected it to be applied today or tomorrow – he would not make exceptions.' These characteristics could estrange him from supporters. At age 73 he was unlikely to modify his behavior.[30]

Members of the two wings of the National Front had come together because of opposition to the court–army clique and to foreign meddling in Iran's affairs. They found Musaddiq an attractive leader. By the end of 1952, the conservatives had second thoughts. They had always been uncomfortable associating with secular intellectuals, and now they feared the growing strength of the Tudeh party. They sought assurance in the stabilizing forces of crown and army. They wanted an oil settlement to calm the nation but believed Musaddiq incapable of negotiating one.

All this was transpiring while Henderson negotiated with Musaddiq in his bedroom over the latest US–UK proposals. There is no evidence the prime minister rejected the plan because he feared for his safety if he approved it. This idea was popular in the West but had little foundation. The opposite argument could just as reasonably have been offered, that Musaddiq should have accepted the plan because it would have quieted such opponents as Bagha'i. If, that is, expediency moved Musaddiq, rather than principle as he claimed.[31]

As to the future, it became increasingly clear that officials of the incoming Eisenhower administration would have less sympathy for his policies than had their predecessors. Earlier, American assessments of Musaddiq and his government had referred only incidentally to a lack of conscience, dictatorial tendencies, or a trend toward fascism. After January 1953 these considerations became the focus of Washington's assessment, without any corresponding change in Tehran. Henderson, whose analysis carried weight in Washington, referred to the regime as representing 'one of the most dangerous kinds of dictatorship.'[32]

The Eisenhower administration would base its eventual decision to move against Musaddiq partly on the allegation that extension of his plenary powers indicated a move toward dictatorial rule. Scholars have argued that the request for plenary powers was constitutional and did no violence to parliamentary rule. The Majlis had granted emergency powers in the past and could revoke such grants at will. No part of the constitution was suspended in January 1953, and Musaddiq reaffirmed the power of the Majlis to remove him at any time by a vote of no confidence. The press remained free to criticize, and many papers, among them *Shahid, Atish* and *Bisu-yi Ayandah*, availed themselves of the opportunity. Up until the *coup d'état* of 19 August 1953, such headlines as 'Musaddiq Must Go,' 'Musaddiq's *Coup D'état*,' and 'Musaddiq Is Doomed,' appeared regularly in the opposition press. If anything, Musaddiq treated opponents too leniently and thus contributed to his downfall.[33]

According to Richard Cottam, American officials, acting out of fear of chaos and instability in the region, adopted a cultural stereotype of Musaddiq, finding in him not 'the proponent of liberal democratic institutions and the symbol of his people's quest for national independence and dignity,' but 'a demagogic agitator who was leading his immature public' in a dangerously pro-Soviet direction. The new perspective, simple and judgmental, came to dominate the thinking of most American officials – none more important than Ambassador Henderson – in a way largely unknown during the Truman administration. Frustration produced a change in US policy. The old nationalist's ploy, therefore, to use fear of communism to secure assistance would soon contribute to his undoing.[34]

9 Coup

By all accounts the transition from the Truman to the Eisenhower administration was a rough one. Acheson recalled that at their first meeting following the November election the president and the president-elect eyed each other nervously as if the other had designs on his pocket watch. Following 20 years of Democratic control of the White House, the breakdown of bipartisan foreign policy over Korea and the unremitting attacks by Republican conservatives and McCarthyites on the Roosevelt and Truman record in world affairs, this suspicion is not difficult to understand. And yet the president-elect had been well-briefed on the Middle East and particularly on the Iranian situation. Eisenhower and Dulles at first moved cautiously, doubtless reluctant to take any action before 20 January that could be construed as interference. Dulles told oilman W. Alton Jones that he and Eisenhower did not want to risk being blamed by the Truman administration should the last-minute negotiations in Tehran fail.[1]

But in the early weeks of the new administration a subtle shift took place in the relative prominence of Britain and the United States *vis-à-vis* the crisis in Iran, with Washington beginning to dominate. This was partly the result of the breaking of diplomatic relations in October, which left the British dependent on reports from friendly nations – Pakistan, Switzerland, France, and especially the United States – to keep abreast of internal developments. In this respect Henderson's accounts were indispensable. There was another factor, too. The new administration intended to pursue a more aggressive foreign policy, not only with respect to the Korean War but also in trouble spots such as Egypt and Iran.

Eden welcomed the more 'robust' approach of the Eisenhower administration because, on Iran at least, it appeared 'rather tougher than the previous administration.' He failed to see, as did his boss Churchill, that the Republican administration had no special fondness for Britain, nor for any foreign government, and was going to go its own way, everywhere. He simply did not understand that a party out of power for 20 years, during which time it was blamed for every unhappiness that occurred in the United States or as a result of failure in foreign policy, was bound to try, with more than usual effort, to make its mark.[2]

At first the Americans continued their penchant for compromise and the British had to watch closely to safeguard their interests. Eisenhower had promised his friend Jones he could send five American oil technicians to Tehran. When the British learned of this, they convinced the president to withdraw permission. But generally the Republicans indicated that they would not go on indefinitely trying to work out an agreement with Musaddiq, and this was the message the Foreign Office found so hopeful.[3]

Dulles and Eisenhower urged the British to make one last approach, assuring London that if the Iranian prime minister rejected it, Henderson would not try again. Based on the advice of its new ambassador in Washington, Roger Makins, who pointed out that Musaddiq would likely reject the proposals in any case and that London's flexibility would put the onus for obstruction on Iran, Britain agreed to try, even agreeing to limit compensation from Iran to a 20-year period.[4]

At the end of March, as Makins predicted, Musaddiq rejected the latest package, essentially what Truman had offered in January. The prime minister would submit to arbitration only if Britain stated the compensation it sought in advance and if Iran found the sum reasonable; that is, it did not include 'lost profits.'[5]

This would be the last Anglo-American proposal. The British dreamed on. They wondered whether settlement was even in their interest now that crude was so plentiful. Perhaps the best policy would be to let Iran sell a few million dollars of oil on the sly and scrape by with American aid indefinitely. Musaddiq too turned away from the oil question, telling Henderson he wanted to forget oil, for the British would never accept a settlement suitable for Iran.[6]

Dulles appeared more sympathetic than Eisenhower to the British position. When he visited London in February, officials cautioned him that throwing money after Musaddiq would not resolve the communist threat in Iran. Shortly after that meeting, he agreed with his brother Allen, now director of the CIA, that Musaddiq could not afford to reach agreement with the British lest it cost him his political life. For his part Eisenhower still entertained thoughts of finding a solution. He told Eden during a visit to Washington in early March that the United States might have to have a freer hand with relation to Iran. The United States would have to do something, the president said; it could not just sit by, as the British preferred. Eisenhower told Eden he would like to give Musaddiq $10 million. That, assuredly, would be doing something.[7]

But the administration's essential pessimism appeared in the National Security Council (NSC) meeting on 4 March, just a few hours before Eisenhower's session with the foreign secretary. At that meeting Iran took up half the discussion, revealing a remarkably pessimistic Dulles. When Secretary of the Treasury George M. Humphrey asked if he was convinced the Soviets 'would ultimately secure Iran,' the secretary of state replied affirmatively. This prompted Dulles to complain loudly against the British, French and other allies who constantly slowed American actions abroad. Distressed by the prospect for the West in the Middle East, especially in Iran, Eisenhower blurted out, 'If I had $500 000 000 of money to spend in secret, I would get $100 000 000 of it to Iran right now.' Harold Stassen quickly assured the president that his Mutual Security Administration had 'as much as the situation required,' and the president's specialist in cold war strategy, C.D. Jackson, volunteered to produce the mobs if the president wanted them.[8]

Eden was momentarily able to reassure Eisenhower by reminding him how reasonable the British had been in contrast to the Iranians. Had they not welcomed the attempts of the World Bank to resolve the crisis, modified their own demands for compensation and joined the United States in a combined approach to Musaddiq?[9]

Eden's success was all the more remarkable because British leadership seemed rather in a muddle. Eden continued to suffer from gall bladder complications, and in April almost died on the operating table. He was on sick leave from April to October. Lord Salisbury agreed to serve as acting Foreign Secretary, but Churchill meddled constantly, especially in Middle East problems. In mid-March he sent an unhelpful letter to Eisenhower, hinting that Britain would not assist the United States in East Asia unless Washington helped more in the Middle East. The prime minister suffered a mild stroke in June, which slowed him down. He recovered, but the Foreign

Office found it exasperating to conduct policy through his residence, Chartwell, where, when urgent decisions had to be made, he seemed 'always in the bath or asleep or too busy having dinner.' Chancellor of the Exchequer R.A.B. Butler, whose name was mentioned increasingly as a successor, later summed up this period: 'Churchill was practically lying down the whole of 1953. . . . The country was undermanned at the top.'[10]

It was a stroke of good fortune for the British, therefore, when the Iranian government antagonized Eisenhower by moving to curtail the shah's powers. The Americans had come to see the shah as a source of stability in Iran, the key individual for maintaining order. This belief had developed slowly after World War II, but crystallized before the end of the Truman years. Not that US officials were unaware of the shah's limitations – his frequent bouts of depression, his preference for a bloated military force, his failure to pursue reform – but for them the monarchy represented a force for order in a troubled land.

Since coming to the throne in 1941 on abdication of his father – an act forced by Britain and the Soviet Union – Muhammad Riza Pahlavi had worked methodically to restore the prerogatives of the crown. By 1951 he had become the single most important leader in Iran, wielding decisive influence over parliament and the selection of prime ministers and other ranking civil and military officials. The shah made certain no leader with independent power should become prime minister. Some Iranians, recalling the rise of his autocratic father in the 1920s, took alarm, but could do little.

Then the oil crisis thrust Musaddiq and his associates into the spotlight as representatives of the nationalist crusade against the oil company. The National Front rode the wave of popular opposition to the AIOC, to Britain and to earlier Iranian governments that had signed away the nation's oil resources so cheaply. The shah realized he could not control the movement, and after Razmara's assassination in 1951 could not even direct it. Whatever his abilities, rousing the masses was not one of them. How he must have envied Musaddiq his rapt throngs.

But the rise of the National Front was not without benefits for the monarchy. The shah had no love for the oil company nor for the British – he trusted neither. If nationalization succeeded, Musaddiq would have increased the national wealth and rid the land of British influence, fitting revenge for Riza Shah's disgraceful removal a decade earlier. Inevitably, Musaddiq would lose popular support to a more manageable leader. Then the shah could again pursue dominance of the nation's politics.[11]

The shah willingly signed the oil nationalization laws and publicly supported Musaddiq. In those early days of the reign the shah had a sense of what the people wanted. He bided his time, waiting for a swing away from the prime minister.

From the outset Musaddiq planned to turn the shah into a constitutional monarch on the British model, transforming him from a George III into a George V. He acted to limit royal prerogatives, little ones at first such as canceling Monday cabinet meetings at the palace in the shah's presence, or refusing to make calls on members of the royal family. He became bolder, taking the post of minister of defense, forcing members of the shah's family and leading courtiers into exile, denying foreign envoys and members of the opposition access to the shah without permission, and assuming control over crown lands. The shah resisted in July 1952, with results approaching a debacle. Then, in small symbolic ways, Iranians began to show disrespect for the monarch. Theater-goers did not stand in his honor at the beginning of performances; demonstrations took place during his birthday celebrations in October.

Musaddiq became more determined to transform the monarch into a figurehead but apparently had no plans to establish a republic. Some supporters, however, most notably Foreign Minister Husain Fatimi, made no secret of their preference for such a solution.[12]

As he curtailed the shah in one area after another, the Americans took alarm, worrying what might happen if Musaddiq should die or be overthrown and the shah left powerless, unable to stabilize the country. This would play into the hands of the communists. These fears increasingly concerned officials of the Eisenhower administration.[13]

In late February trouble began when Musaddiq accused the shah of continuing to interfere in politics. He had learned that General Zahidi was plotting to succeed him. Zahidi sent word through the US naval attaché, Captain Eric Pollard, to

Ambassador Henderson that he was prepared to assume power as soon as the shah appointed him. Henderson advised Husain Ala what the shah should do if Musaddiq resigned. Under no circumstance should the shah accede to Musaddiq's demands. To ensure Zahidi's success the ambassador urged inclusion of some National Front members in any cabinet he might form.[14]

In the last week of February, Musaddiq demanded, and the shah refused, control over the revenues of Imam Riza's shrine at Mashhad and other less important shrines and crown lands throughout the nation. The shah suddenly requested permission to vacation abroad, which was promptly given. His approaching departure was a badly kept secret. Ayatollah Kashani's followers and royalist groups such as the right-wing Sumka party used the prime minister's farewell visit to the palace as occasion for pro-shah, anti-Musaddiq demonstrations. Musaddiq's house came under attack from a crowd led by a gang leader of south Tehran nicknamed Shaban-the-Brainless. The prime minister fled in his pajamas over the garden wall to seek refuge in the Majlis; his narrow escape elicited taunts from opponents. It took several days for loyal units to restore order.[15]

Kashani had been deeply involved in the disturbances, but his bid to reduce Musaddiq's power failed when the prime minister emerged stronger than before. The shah used these demonstrations of apparent support to justify giving in to popular demands that he stay in Tehran. He cancelled his plan to go abroad.[16]

Relations between Musaddiq and the shah deteriorated steadily, and the prime minister, who considered the incident outside the palace an attempt on his life, did not visit the shah again. Only 18 Majlis deputies attended the shah's traditional salaam ceremony at the New Year (21 March).[17]

Order restored, Musaddiq set about further limiting the monarch. He had the shah dismiss Minister of Court Husain Ala, who had been meeting with Zahidi, and appoint in his place Abul Qasim Amini, who was more loyal to the prime minister. A royal decree transferred the shah's private estates to the government. Musaddiq set up an eight-man parliamentary committee to study the relationship between the shah and the military and to make recommendations concerning removal of the monarch as commander-in-chief of the armed forces.

No one knew what military units remained loyal to the government and what to the crown, and Musaddiq, who had advocated reduced expenditures and a smaller armed force, feared an army-led coup. In this tense atmosphere a widely circulated anti-royalist tract appeared, presenting the radical views of Major Seyed Mahmud Sakha'i, commander of the Majlis guard, who no doubt expressed the sentiments of many other junior officers. He called for a non-political military and hinted none too subtly of disturbing similarities between the present ruler and the last despised shah of the eighteenth-century Safavid dynasty, Sultan Husain. He cautioned that if the earlier shah had not been so weak and not wasted so much money he would never have been overthrown with the support of his own people.[18]

Balancing such sentiments, a group of royalist officers, many of whom Musaddiq had retired, formed the 'Committee to Save the Fatherland,' and gradually included key air force and tank commanders in a conspiracy against Musaddiq.[19]

Fighting between pro-shah and pro-Musaddiq crowds took place. General Afshartous, chief of police and a loyal, courageous Musaddiq supporter, was kidnapped and murdered by members of the opposition. This act should have warned the prime minister to take greater precautions, but he continued much as before.

After the events of February, Musaddiq criticized Henderson for advising the shah not to leave the country. The prime minister could rightly have handed him his passport for such interference, and Henderson realized he might have 'put his head on the chopping block.' Eisenhower briefly considered replacing him, but the State Department advised against this. When Musaddiq did not press the issue the ambassador remained.[20]

By this time Henderson was clearly out of sympathy with Musaddiq, having abandoned all hope that the Iranian crisis could be settled while he headed the government in Tehran. At first he viewed Musaddiq as a force for stability, but as the National Front fragmented, Tudeh activity increased and the prime minister's differences with the throne deepened, he began to see him as a threat to good order. The ambassador judged governments on the basis of where they stood in the great struggle between the United States and the USSR; it seemed to him that Musaddiq had moved in the direction of the Tudeh party and the Soviet Union. Like the new secretary of state, Henderson was a dedicated cold warrior who believed that local and regional problems must be subordinated to the greater global struggle against communism.

Henderson continued to send reports to Washington, exaggerating Tudeh party influence on Musaddiq and his government, heightening fears in the already jittery State Department, encouraging policymakers to consider alternatives. Henderson reported that Musaddiq intended to depose the shah because he could not break the army's support for him. He ridiculed the prime minister's claim that the British were paying for crowds to masquerade as communists 'in order to frighten the United States into believing that under my premiership the country is going communist.' He did all he could to panic Washington, pointing to signs of approaching bankruptcy, Musaddiq's growing reliance on communists and fellow travelers, and 'the fact that the Iron Curtain was about to envelop Iran.' He urged Dulles not to visit Iran on his forthcoming trip to the area as this might be interpreted as support for Musaddiq. Undersecretary W. Bedell Smith quoted Henderson to Eisenhower saying, 'only those sympathetic to the Soviet Union and to international communism have reason to be pleased at what is taking place in Iran.' All this, of course, fitted with anticommunist attitudes then prevalent in Washington.[21]

Henderson did his job well, and after his talks with Dulles in Karachi, the secretary became even more convinced that Musaddiq must go. He told the head of Point Four in Iran, William Warne, that not a nickel would be allotted for projects because, according to Warne, 'they were going to starve Musaddiq out of office.' Dulles reported to the National Security Council that Iran 'woefully lacks any prospect of effective political leadership' and that 'the United States must concentrate on changing the situation there.'[22]

Despite Henderson's dire warnings, there was little evidence that Musaddiq had moved closer to the Tudeh to offset his losses among the conservative nationalists. He kept them at arm's length, refusing to lift the ban on the party and to enter into a united front after the events of 28 February. There would be no Tudeh ministers in the cabinet as there were in

1946 under Qavam. Although the party had gained strength under Musaddiq due to their superior organization and popular anti-imperialism, their principal support remained focused among young intellectuals, university students and some industrial workers. The rural masses, conservative by tradition and circumstance, lay beyond their reach. Mutual suspicion continued between the nationalists and the communists. Musaddiq refused to issue weapons to civilians, and the police regularly intervened to break up Tudeh demonstrations. The prime minister believed that the communists would be less of a threat if they were not driven underground – as they had been under Riza Shah and again during the years, 1946–51 – but were allowed to participate in elections and set up front organizations, newspapers, and so forth.[23]

The Tudeh opposed Musaddiq right until the end. They considered him an American lackey, who brought the capitalist Harriman to Iran in summer 1951, went meekly to Washington to seek a solution, and refused to expel American economic and miltary missions. No doubt the Tudeh would have seized power if the opportunity had been offered, but in 1953 the party was in no position to take control. Members were divided; the hardliners in the leadership did not trust Musaddiq. They had only a narrow base of support in the cities and cadre in the military held few posts in the crucial sectors such as motorized divisions or the air force, units that would be essential to a successful coup.[24]

The Tudeh threat would have magnified had the party received support for action from Moscow, but after Stalin's death in March the joint Soviet leadership was uncertain and contented itself with watching developments in neighboring Iran, not becoming 'directly active' against Musaddiq. Nor, of course, did it support him nor attempt to modify the Tudeh hardline. 'It could have paid its war debts to Iran, which were long overdue and in the absence of oil revenues, badly needed.' Instead, it settled them later with the shah.[25]

By early June, when Henderson was preparing to return home for consultation, Musaddiq had become almost irrelevant to US policymakers. When the ambassador delivered a message of support to the shah from Churchill, the two discussed the shape of a future government under Zahidi, Henderson telling the shah that both the United States and the United Kingdom could support the general as long as he had royal backing.[26]

In Washington the decision was taken to proceed with 'Operation Ajax,' a CIA-assisted coup first proposed by British intelligence. According to one expert, the British played on the American paranoia concerning communism, in order to persuade Washington to become involved in the *coup d'état*. Henderson supported this decision, admitting to Makins that 'nothing at all can be expected or hoped for from Musaddiq.'[27]

Eisenhower's experience as a young officer in the Philippines prior to World War II might have had some bearing on his decision to approve the operation. When he served in Manila under General Douglas MacArthur, he engaged in protracted discussions with Filipino military and political leaders, trying to agree on the shape of a Philippine army. Every time Eisenhower thought he had an agreement, it came unraveled, and he realized that the Philippine officers had not agreed after all. He recognized this failing as a grave impediment to progress, an indication that nothing whatsoever would be done. In 1941 Manilla became an easy prey for Japan. A decade later Musaddiq's behavior must have reminded him of those earlier frustrations, only now the threat came from the Soviet Union.[28]

In Tehran nationalist opinion had turned against the United States after the events of February, with calls for the prime minister to eradicate US influence and to seek withdrawal of American advisers from the Iranian army. The Americans, it was charged, had consistently upheld the British, and Allahyar Salih's Iran party called on the government to sever relations with Washington. Musaddiq told Henderson that the United States could halt the rise of anti-Americanism by helping Iran more substantially, and when the ambassador bade him farewell on 31 May, the prime minister gave him a secret letter for President Eisenhower, asking for a loan to save Iran from serious consequences. The letter avowed that 'Tomorrow might well be too late.' This was a disastrous ploy, for it confirmed all that Henderson had reported. Musaddiq's 'secret' letter and the president's refusal soon appeared in the American press, further undermining the prime minister.[29]

During the final weeks of Musaddiq's government the prime minister still believed he could maintain control and in his confidence took few practical steps to avert his own downfall. Reassured by the outcome of events in the previous July and February, he relied on the support of the people, trusting his ability to rally them when danger threatened. He underestimated the determination of his opponents, refusing to arm supporters for fear of bloodshed.[30]

By July Musaddiq's patience with opposition deputies in parliament wore thin. They absented themselves regularly so the Majlis could not vote on recommendations of the prime minister's 'Committee of Eight,' transferring control over the miltary from the shah to the prime minister. When they did appear they launched attacks on Musaddiq and members of his government. Frustrated, the prime minister encouraged National Front deputies to resign, leaving the Majlis without a quorum. Then the government organized a referendum on whether the seventeenth Majlis should be dismissed and new elections carried out. Held between 3 and 10 August, balloting was arranged so that those opposed to the measure would have to cast their votes at a place separate from affirmative voters. The government won a resounding victory of 99.93 per cent and Musaddiq asked the shah to call new elections.[31]

This time Musaddiq had gone too far. His methods alienated many Iranians. Their disaffection came at the worst possible time, when secret plans for a *coup d'état* were about to be put into action.

The quixotic American CIA agent, Kermit (Kim) Roosevelt, now took charge of coup preparations in Tehran. He was an interesting character indeed. Born in 1916, grandson of Theodore Roosevelt, he inherited the family penchant for derring-do. As for so many other members of that generation, his introduction to the Middle East came in World War II when he went to work in Egypt for the Office of Strategic Services. Stationed in Cairo he traveled extensively in the region, making his first trip to Iran in 1944. During that short stay he became fascinated with the country, its lofty, snow-covered peaks and migrating tribes, and made contact with American expatriates and Iranians who would help him in his exploits years later. After the war he returned to civilian life but was recalled to service in 1950 with the outbreak of war in Korea. He became an agent for the CIA, specializing in the Middle East, which had become a ferment of local nationalisms.

He visited all the major capitals. In Cairo he established good relations with a rising young army lieutenant colonel, Gamal Abdul Nasser. During meetings of Anglo-American intelligence officials in Washington in February 1953, the British, who knew his exploits, urged he be put in charge of Operation Ajax and his superiors agreed.

Roosevelt traveled to Iran several times in winter and spring 1953, and after the go-ahead from Washington, he returned to contact opposition leaders and bring the shah, without whose support the plan would fail, into the scheme. The shah was cautious, insisting, contrary to Anglo-American advice, that Zahidi must come to power through parliamentary procedure. Only after a secret meeting with Roosevelt and confirmation of US–UK support did he agree to assist Zahidi's coup.[32]

At this crucial time Musaddiq took almost no action to control the opposition press, which blasted away at his government. *Atish* prodded the shah to save his throne before it was too late. 'Will you stand by and let one old man ... play with your throne and crown?' it challenged. The paper's owner, Mihdi Mir-Ashrafi, a deputy elected through army influence in Azarbaijan, busied himself attending secret meetings with Zahidi and other conspirators.[33]

State Department experts on Iran set out to destroy any lingering American support for Musaddiq. Appearing before the House Foreign Affairs Committee in executive session on 17 July, Arthur Richards, head of the Office of Greek, Turkish and Iranian Affairs, who had spent several years in Tehran as political counselor at the embassy, simplified the situation there for committee members. 'The Persians are dreamers,' he observed. 'They live in a world of fantasy. They are probably the most impractical people in the world ... if you have to bring them down to the hard facts, especially in a mechanical age, they are lost. Practical matters just do not mean anything to them.' The British had failed because they had not understood Persian psychology. A short while later he assured the committee that 'the more practical people' in Iran would like to throw out Musaddiq but he was too powerful. No one questioned Richards' conclusions. Whenever Iranians appeared difficult, they were dismissed as children living in a fantasy world; when their goals coincided with American or British views, they appeared as practical, sensible people.[34]

While lower-level officers calmly assured Congress of the soundness of US policy toward Iran, their superiors pondered nervously what might happen to US–Iranian relations should the coup against Musaddiq fail. Allen Dulles assured his brother that plans were progressing well, but there was always the chance the shah might pull out at the last minute. He requested that the State Department issue another bulletin decrying conditions in Iran and emphasizing Musaddiq's increasing reliance on the communists.[35]

Washington officials suspected the worst when Musaddiq sent a delegation to Stalin's funeral, or when he allowed Soviet military personnel into the southern province of Fars to fight locusts. Most sinister of all to those who sensed a conspiracy, he approved the appointment of Anatol Lavrientiev as ambassador at Tehran. The latter was considered Moscow's specialist on *coups d'état*, having put Czechoslovakia 'firmly behind the Iron Curtain' in 1948. There seemed no time to waste.[36]

According to plan on 13 August the shah, vacationing at the Caspian shore, issued decrees dismissing Musaddiq and appointing Zahidi his successor. When Colonel Nematollah Nasiri, commander of the Imperial Guard, delivered the *firman* to Musaddiq at his house two days later, he and a group of the guard were arrested.

The coup, it seemed, had failed. On 16 August the dispirited shah set off with Queen Soraya in his private plane for Baghdad. There, desperately seeking advice from the United States, he held a secret meeting with US Ambassador Burton Berry. Before Berry could respond officially, the royal couple flew on to Rome to escape the heat, and it was then that the United States advised the shah to assert his constitutional position and the illegality of Musaddiq's action in holding the referendum. Privately neither the State Department nor the Foreign Office was sanguine about his return. Bedell Smith told Eisenhower they would 'probably have to snuggle up to Musaddiq' now, and the British commented that 'one day he [the shah] might play a useful part as figurehead in a truncated non-communist Persia.'[37]

But Roosevelt and his conspirators in Tehran did not give up so easily. They decided on a second coup attempt. This became possible when the prime minister failed to act against the conspirators over the next few days. When a correspondent asked Foreign Minister Fatimi about government measures, the minister replied almost casually that 'the government is considering what to do after the incidents of two nights ago and the results of these studies have not yet reached the stage of decisions.' The government had been lulled into such a sense of security that on the day of the second coup Army Chief of Staff General Taqi Riahi planned a pleasure trip into the mountains.[38]

Opposition newspapers were describing Musaddiq as 'a hypocrite and a demagogue,' warning that 'the people of Iran must be aware that the terrible power of communism is behind Musaddiq,' arguing that 'in the absence of the Majlis, the shah is in a position to appoint and dismiss prime ministers.' But then such sentiments had been heard before. They hardly seemed more than pleasantries.[39]

CIA officers hid Zahidi in a safe house and prepared for his evacuation in the US military attaché's plane if necessary. US funds, perhaps those offered by Stassen in March, were distributed to mobs. On 17 August, a violent anti-shah crowd of 100 000 tore down statues of the Pahlavis and cheered the end of the monarchy. Recent evidence indicates that hired thugs, posing as members of the Tudeh party to frighten the general population with visions of communist-inspired disorder, formed the nucleus of this demonstration. Later, real Tudeh activists and others joined in.[40]

Henderson, who had remained abroad for two and a half months because he could not deal with Musaddiq 'openly and frankly' once he knew of the plot against him, returned hurriedly to Tehran. He met with Musaddiq on the evening of 18 August and told him he would have to advise evacuation of Americans if the government did not take steps to restore order. Although Musaddiq suspected US involvement in the coup attempt, he ordered the police to move against the roving gangs, which included some communists. The police did their job, cracking heads and causing Tudeh leaders to order members of the party off the streets.[41]

Matters continued in an apparently confused state. During a four-day interlude, the prime minister failed to act decisively. His foreign minister went on the attack as editor of *Bakhtar-i Imruz*, the unofficial government newspaper. Fatimi lashed out at the shah, accusing him of organizing the events of 28 Feb-

ruary, of being worse than the recently deposed Farouk of
Egypt, 'a deceitfully pretty young man,' a snake 'who bites
mortally when the opportunity presents itself.' He referred to
the monarch as the 'Baghdad fugitive' and to the court as a
center of prostitution. 'O traitor shah, you shameless person,
you have completed the criminal history of the Pahlavi reign!
The people want revenge and they want to drag you from
behind your desk to the gallows.' (Fatimi burned all his bridges.
He was the only National Front leader executed after the shah's
return.)[42]

Tudeh papers called again for a united front to defeat imperialism in Iran, but many of Musaddiq's advisers opposed
such a step, and when the royalist mob appeared on the
morning of 19 August the communists stayed home. The Tudeh
Central Committee met throughout the day but could not
decide whether to assist Musaddiq. First Secretary Nur Al-Din
Kianuri telephoned the prime minister twice but procrastin-
ated and soon it was too late.[43]

Taking advantage of public disenchantment with the violence of 17 August, the conspirators organized a pro-shah,
pro-Zahidi mob in south Tehran, which gathered strength as
it proceeded north toward the city center. A soft, incompetent
officer, General Riahi failed to disperse the first protesters,
assuring ministers that 'we will hold them.'[44]

The end came quickly. Confrontation of military forces
around Musaddiq's house left several hundred dead and the
prime minister in flight. He surrendered next day to Zahidi.
In a speech at 1:25 p.m. over Radio Tehran, the general ush-
ered in the post-Musaddiq era by promising to raise workers'
wages and distribute free medicine to the poor.[45]

The question arises: how important was CIA assistance in
the overthrow of Musaddiq? Responses have ranged widely,
and yet it does seem that its role was crucial. To be sure,
Musaddiq had lost much support. The referendum tarnished
his image as a democrat. The overthrow was indeed a complex
affair. Still, the Roosevelt team provided the catalyst for the
coup, without which the shah would have been reluctant to
act. Any ranking of factors must grant a prominent place to
US covert activity. Without it Musaddiq could have maintained
himself indefinitely.[46]

It is not easy to assess the Musaddiq years. To supporters,

the old man in striped pajamas quickly became a larger-than-life figure, symbol to Iranians of a wise, patriotic, benevolent leader whose promise to transform Iran was defeated by a conspiracy of corrupt Iranians and their foreign masters anxious to dominate Iran's affairs. To opponents, domestic and foreign, he became a symbol of the naive leader who in treading the path between the power blocs would unintentionally deliver his nation to communism; or alternately the would-be dictator seduced by power into abandoning democratic pretense. His supporters came closer to the truth. In a March 1952 letter to Musaddiq, the highly respected Dr. Qasim Ghani wrote, 'We need an individual who is wise, resolute and cautious of people's trust – these characteristics are combined in your personality.'[47]

Musaddiq was no saint, as even his advisers recognized. He could be stubborn and narrow-minded. Yet he was the most popular leader in modern times – at least prior to the revolution of 1978. The oil issue so occupied him and his ministers that little was accomplished in social, economic and political reform. Perhaps if he had been freer to attend to other matters his incapacity would have become apparent, leading to removal or resignation. Then again he might have resolved some of Iran's longstanding problems.

There is convincing evidence that Musaddiq never planned to create one-man rule such as developed in the 1960s and 1970s under the shah. He relied on the army, did not create a secret police like the shah's SAVAK nor a paramilitary organization similar to the *pasdaran* of the Islamic Republic. He did not violate the constitution as did the shah repeatedly in later years; he never put himself beyond control of parliament and to the end allowed the press to speak its mind. These are not methods of would-be dictators.

If Musaddiq was a prisoner of the past – opposed to dictatorial rule, supportive of constitutional government, hating foreign influence – the Americans were no less prisoners of the cold war mindset that would not tolerate neutralism in the struggle against godless communism. Since the constitutional revolution of 1906, Musaddiq had sustained a vision of an Iran he hoped to fashion. He found it impossible to trim his vision to the realities of the postwar world. This proved his greatest failing.

10 Second Chance

American leaders breathed a sigh of relief with the overthrow of the contentious Musaddiq and his replacement by the more tractable Zahidi. But feelings of satisfaction were short-lived as officials pondered the difficulties that remained. They would spend the next four months trying to return Iran to normalcy. Musaddiq still enjoyed widespread support and Zahidi wanted immediate assistance to bolster his own popularity. Musaddiq's fall did not end Iranian disagreements with the British; if anything it exacerbated them. Policymakers puzzled over how to resolve the oil dispute and reestablish diplomatic relations between Britain and Iran, without weakening the Zahidi government.

Exactly five days after his pell-mell flight to Iraq and thence to Rome, the shah returned in triumph. Queen Soraya remained in a swanky Roman hotel, resting it was said – but, of course, awaiting her husband's trip back home to see how it would go. She need not have worried in the slightest; to shouts of 'long live the shah!' that echoed down the boulevards, that almost ricocheted from the minarets, and to the clapping of tens of thousands of hands, the monarch's motorcade of limousines slowly wound its way through friendly crowds lining the streets from Mehrabad airport to the palace.

A casual observer might have concluded that a genuinely popular uprising had occurred, that a beloved monarch had returned to an adoring nation. The truth naturally was more complex. Many of the Iranian middle class, bazaar merchants, members of the ulama, military officers, and more humble folk too, welcomed what they hoped would be the end of stringencies associated with the final months of Musaddiq's government. The previous 28 months had brought recurring crises so that even those who supported the prime minister had wondered how much longer the struggle could go on. For many Musaddiq's removal was bittersweet – relieved at the prospect of better economic times, an end to political crisis, they were saddened to see the courageous old man in chains, put there through a conspiracy of his enemies. Although the shah's return proved reassuring after the uncertainties of recent weeks, Iranians none the less approached the situation cautiously. They worried what the Zahidi government would do, especially with regard to the oil question, withal they shouted and clapped their hands.

The British and Americans received the news of Musaddiq's overthrow with relief. Months of careful planning had met with reward. As Secretary Dulles told his colleagues, 'We now have a miraculous second chance.'[1]

The two Western allies had to use the opportunity wisely for paradoxically they found themselves in a more sensitive situation than under Musaddiq. If the restored regime of the shah and the general should fail, Iranians would blame Britain and the United States, which had manifested their antagonism toward Musaddiq and support for the shah.

Zahidi's success was by no means assured. The allies appreciated the weakness of his government. British officials declared privately that there was no certainty the general could make his position secure. Up to March 1954, families of American embassy personnel were forbidden to travel to Tehran, to limit numbers there in case of evacuation. Brigadier General Robert A. McClure, head of the US military mission, reported that everything depended on the Iranian army, which alone could keep the government in power. Yet its morale was low, its standard of living pitiful and its loyalties throughout all ranks none too certain. Despite concern about the Soviet reaction, the Joint Chiefs of Staff even considered the feasibility of deploying a US infantry division to Tehran, should the Iranian government ask for it. The next several months would prove crucial. The crisis in Iran was far from over.[2]

The Americans wanted to settle the oil dispute quickly in order to stabilize the new regime, but in the meantime some assistance seemed essential. In separate meetings with Ambassador Henderson, the shah and Zahidi urged the United States to extend grant assistance without delay. The nation had been rescued on the brink of the communist abyss, now the people expected action, said Zahidi; his government had to keep its promises. To do this he needed US aid.[3]

Zahidi impressed Henderson as a leader of vigor and determination and once the prime minister had given assurance that he, too, wanted a rapid settlement of the oil question, Henderson recommended immediate aid. On 5 September,

President Eisenhower, who earlier had rejected Musaddiq's pleas, announced a $45 million emergency grant.

Everything momentarily settled, then the flighty British, as they had so many times, raised up the host of questions and concerns that seemed always on their minds. They never felt the Americans were doing enough, and always came to the same thumping conclusion that you could not trust those wily Persians. American largesse did not find favor in London, where the British had different ideas on policy. The Foreign Office worried that Zahidi's government might prove nationalistic and anti-British; after all, it was they who had interned the pro-German Zahidi early in World War II. Would he hold it against them now? They knew how widespread were Iranian suspicions of British interference. Even the shah had doubts, re-marking to Henderson shortly after his return that he discerned treachery behind failure of the coup of 15 August: could it have been British agents? Henderson reminded him that Iran could not expect US assistance if it planned to make Britain 'the whipping boy.' The shah changed the subject.[4]

The British believed the shah had an 'almost pathological distrust' of them. They confided to the Americans their concern that grants might be unwise, for such aid would relieve pressure on the new government, thereby making settlement of the oil problem less urgent. Reluctantly, London gave way under US pressure but only if Washington made clear the short-term nature of assistance. Churchill would have extended British support to forestall the Americans from reaping 'all the benefits of many years of British work in Persia,' but Chancellor of the Exchequer Butler, facing recurring budget problems, refused to consider loans not tied directly to an oil settlement.[5]

Once the immediate financial problem had settled itself, the allies had to face the thornier issue of how to proceed on oil. Zahidi told Henderson that a misstep here might be fatal to his government. Any solution, he warned, must be fair and reasonable to Iran.[6]

At this juncture the Americans took a large view. Dulles wrote to the Marquis of Salisbury, who was standing in for Eden, urging an early meeting of officials to discuss proposals for a settlement to close 'the most dangerous gap in the line from Europe to South Asia.' The Americans had in mind 'a new look without abandoning basic principles.' The new look was a military policy within the United States symbolized by the gauche phrase of 'more bang for the buck,' but here Dulles centered on the idea of a consortium of oil companies to replace the AIOC in Iran. McGhee had suggested this approach during Musaddiq's visit to Washington in 1951, and Secretary Humphrey pursued it with the British on his own initiative in May. The Americans returned to it because they believed the Iranians would not accept any scheme that Musaddiq had rejected, such as the principle of arbitrating compensation claims. If Anglo-American oil companies bought out the AIOC's interest in Iranian oil, the issue of compensation would be moot. With this solution in mind, the State Department began talking with US oil companies.[7]

Now arose the need to appoint an oil expert, someone who could coordinate the delicate negotiations that lay ahead. By 8 September Dulles and Humphrey had settled on Herbert Hoover, Jr. as special adviser for petroleum affairs. He seemed the perfect choice. He was not only an acknowledged expert but knew the terrain, having spent much of the war in Iran advising the government on a proposed concession to the American-owned Stanvac company. Moreover, he had impeccable Republican credentials. He accepted on condition that the oil companies would cooperate and that the Eisenhower administration would not press the cartel suit. Dulles reassured him on both points. The National Security Council had already agreed that Attorney General Herbert Brownell should consider settling the cartel case out of court. Hoover set to work familiarizing himself with details, conferring with US oil company executives to gather their views.[8]

The special adviser suspected State Department officials of having encouraged the Iranians to nationalize oil. In a conversation with Vice President Richard Nixon prior to his departure for Iran, Hoover charged that support for nationalization had become a department policy even though everyone knew that communists spearheaded such movements. Had Iran succeeded, he continued, Saudi Arabia and Venezuela would have been next, tying up this strategic material and denying it to the West. Surprisingly, given Dulles's selection of Hoover for the special assignment, he did not limit his suspicions to

Acheson and Byroade, but included Henderson and even the secretary of state.[9]

If the Americans had too many players, the British had too few. They still found themselves embarrassingly 'undermanned at the top.' Churchill was recovering slowly from his stroke, and Eden did not return to the Foreign Office until 6 October. Differences continued among the several ministries. The Foreign Office began to consider the consortium idea, whereas the Treasury and Fuel and Power demurred. The AIOC was considering return to positions abandoned in the 20 February proposals. In fact, Sir William Fraser was unconvinced that the AIOC could not go back to Iran in its own right.[10]

The Foreign Office urged an oil agreement within six months to sustain Zahidi and to maintain friendly Anglo-American relations, but not everyone in London agreed that speed was essential. When it circulated a draft accepting the Iranian nine-point law of 1951, not insisting on effective management or inclusion of British firms in an agreement, Fraser protested so vigorously that substantial changes had to be made. All this took time, and it was the end of September before London submitted a draft, proposing settlement along the lines of 20 February, including arbitration for compensation. London also argued for direct talks between Iranian and British delegates, which would require resumption of diplomatic relations *before* negotiations.[11]

The government followed its proposals to Washington with a delegation headed by Victor Butler of the Ministry of Fuel and Power. In discussions with State Department officers, including Hoover, a possible interim agreement was drawn up calling for the World Bank to operate AIOC properties in Iran until a permanent settlement could be arranged, but nothing came of this suggestion. It seemed fresh ideas were rare, in spite of Dulles's reference to a new look. It was indeed pretty much the old look. At least Butler had an opportunity to assess Hoover, and he reported his very favorable impression, which may have been the most important result of the meetings.[12]

What to do next? Henderson had declared the impossibility of basing negotiations on the 20 February proposals. The Iranian government was confused. Neither the shah nor Zahidi knew what proposals would be acceptable, but they wanted negotiations to begin so as to find out what Britain wanted. The British were stalling until Iran's wishes became clearer. Urged on by Henderson, the State Department cut the knot, announcing that Hoover would undertake a mission to Iran to assess the situation. Privately they confided he would try to educate Zahidi and his advisers.[13]

The Foreign Office acquiesced in his going, and Eden, now back at work, urged Hoover to explore the possibility of reestablishing diplomatic relations so that direct Anglo-Iranian talks could take place. During the next two months, this became a top priority for Britain.[14]

Hoover declined a suggestion he stop in London on his way to Tehran, for the Iranians would misconstrue such a visit as an Anglo-American plot. He agreed to meet secretly with representatives of the AIOC in Amsterdam. Herbert Gass and Basil Jackson, both with considerable experience in Iran, were impressed with Hoover's understanding of the oil situation. The American expert preferred a consortium, a solution the AIOC had not yet accepted. But when he flew off to Tehran on 17 October, the two officials believed he would represent British interests there fairly.[15]

The situation in Iran did nothing to foster optimism. The shah's triumphant return, with all it seemed to anticipate, had been naught but a return – one of the many comings and goings, it appeared, that had given the impression of change in the capital but, then, had amounted to nothing at all. The most serious problem concerned increasing hostility and mistrust between the shah and Zahidi. The shah had become much more assertive after his triumphal return to Tehran, confiding to the retiring US naval attaché, Captain Eric W. Pollard, he felt now he was the shah of Iran, not just the son of his father. He seemed to believe that his restoration had been due 'entirely to his popularity with his people and to resent suggestions that any participating groups assisted in the process.' Later he would write: 'I defy anybody to prove that the overturn of Mossadegh was not basically the work of the common people whose hearts held a spark of the divine.' He suspected any alternate source of power, such as Zahidi represented. He was determined to regain absolute authority over the army, despite American observations that this would be unpopular. When the prime minister issued instructions to the Iranian chief of staff, the shah protested. Zahidi rushed to assure him he had no intention of usurping royal prerogative. But it was all shadows. According to Henderson, the prime minister spent most of his time trying to make the shah feel better. Nothing could make the shah feel better. He was absolutely incapable of gaining enough confidence to cease requiring confidence; in the game of making him feel better, appetite improved with the eating. Henderson had to remind the shah and prime minister of larger issues, but he remarked, to no one in particular and only half in jest, that he had to 'introduce the two every other day at 9 o'clock in the morning.'[16]

While the introductions, figuratively speaking, were taking place between Zahidi and the shah, the serious business of government almost stood still. What to do with Zahidi's predecessor? With National Front leaders? With an eye on public opinion, the shah and Zahidi paid unprecedented calls at the home of Ayatollah Kashani shortly after the restoration. They kissed his hand in respect and thanked him for his assistance. Kashani for his part promised to support the government as long as it ruled according to the constitution and Islamic principles. These visits did them little good. Neither could inherit Musaddiq's mantle as a nationalist leader, for they were too closely identified with the United States and Britain. The best they could hope for was acceptance as the upholders of stability.[17]

Despite disenchantment with his regime, Musaddiq remained popular. Iranians continued to view him as a symbol of freedom from foreign political influence and economic exploitation. Those of the secular middle class considered him a patriot and the National Front as 'a noble if unsuccessful experiment.' All attempts to nullify these impressions, to link the nationalists and the communists, failed. As an American observer aptly put it, Musaddiq became 'a sort of demi-god who is too good to live among ordinary Iranians.' The government would have to move cautiously in bringing the aged nationalist to justice, and in the meantime the nation remained under martial law.[18]

The shah took charge of arrangements for Musaddiq's trial, insisting – against the advice of Zahidi, the United States and Britain – on an open trial where the defendant would be able to say whatever he liked. The shah wanted to make a show of democracy and thereby win over some of the former prime minister's supporters. On 4 October, the government issued a 24-page indictment. This was followed ominously by the closing of the Tehran bazaar, a traditional form of popular protest.[19]

During a two-week stay in Tehran, Hoover tried to go about his business as if everything had returned to normal. He worked closely with Henderson to get a sense of what Iranian leaders expected but found them very confused. Eventually, Foreign Minister Abdullah Intizam drew up a memorandum for the British. It opened with a stinging attack on the AIOC's past activities in Iran, concluding it was impossible for the company to return. He suggested a consortium to buy and market Iranian oil, no more than half of which was to be controlled by British companies. Members of the consortium, not Iran, would pay compensation to the AIOC.[20]

The talks that followed between Hoover and Eden in London did not go well. It came as no surprise to the British that the unsigned memorandum Hoover brought from Tehran mirrored the American's thoughts. Hoover urged the foreign secretary not to reject it because of a pro forma attack on the oil company. To do so would offend the Iranian government. Most points, he advised, were open to negotiation, but under no circumstances could the AIOC go back to Iran. Of that he was certain. The foreign secretary refused to accept the Iranian statement as a basis for discussion and pressed again for direct negotiations, meaning an early resumption of diplomatic ties.[21]

Convinced the British had no intention of seeking a speedy settlement and were waiting for the Iranians to come around, Hoover packed his bags and departed for Washington, leaving behind a deeply offended Eden. His action underscored the fact that the United States and Britain were far apart on Iran. The Americans wanted a speedy solution, preferably before resumption of relations, and preferred a consortium with the British share held to a minimum.[22]

Then the weeks and months passed, with no settlement. Washington officials became impatient. One suggested that perhaps British commercial interests in the Middle East were better served by the *status quo*, with the AIOC receiving oil from elsewhere in the region and the United States continuing to subsidize the Iranian government. Even Henderson became exasperated. Writing in mid-November, he rejected the idea that the AIOC could have controlling interest in any consortium. The British, he argued, were counting too much on American goodwill. If they continued making impossible demands, they would help drive Zahidi from office.[23]

This time the American feeling that something needed to move, that (to use one of their phrases of a few years later) push should come to shove, that one could not spend one's life waiting for an adversary to come around – in short, all the American instincts that diplomacy meant activity, not passivity – came to an impasse at this juncture. The truth was that the Americans had seen British inaction for so long they had ceased making any explanations for it, believing this was the way the Britons, with their marked lack of national power, now behaved, almost like children who thought that somehow they should get what they wanted because in the past they always had. This time, however, they needed subtlety in dealing with their British cousins. They failed to understand that Eden was not in a strong position regarding his Middle East policy. He had to put up with Churchill's interference, which continued after the foreign secretary's return. Fraser was determined to go back to Iran, and had support from the Treasury and Fuel and Power. Even in the City, where many men of power criticized Fraser, business leaders resented the idea of 'another surrender' to the Americans by allowing them a stake in Iranian oil. More serious for the foreign secretary, who paid close attention to sentiment in the House of Commons, was a report from the Conservative whip that members opposed American participation in any oil agreement. The less such involvement the better, he said, and 'if there was no US participation there would be delight.' No wonder Eden appeared reluctant to embrace the United States on Iran.[24]

And the allies had many more serious disagreements than those related to the Middle East. In East Asia they had contrasting views on China, Korea, Japan and Indochina, in Europe on Austria, East–West trade and the European Defense Community. Shortly after Stalin's death in 1953, the Soviets made overtures for an East–West summit, and the Big Three needed to discuss this proposal and iron out what differences they could.

At Churchill's invitation everyone assembled at Bermuda in early December: Churchill and Eden; Eisenhower and Dulles;

and Joseph Laniel and Georges Bidault for France. Preparations were inadequate and the conference achieved little. The French premier took to his bed almost immediately with pneumonia. Eisenhower became frustrated with the wrangling and vowed never to attend another such meeting unless everything had been agreed beforehand.[25]

With regard to the Middle East the conferees resolved little. The Americans had come prepared to raise with the British the delicate issue of their respective roles in the region, where Washington believed Britain refused to recognize its declining power. The United States would continue to support London when it could but would not give a blank check or a right of veto over US action. Moreover, during the three-day conference there was little opportunity to discuss the Middle East with such contentious issues as policy toward the Soviet Union, the EDC and nuclear weapons on the agenda. Churchill did remind Eisenhower how seriously Britons would consider any US military aid to Egypt prior to a UK–Egyptian agreement on the Suez Canal, but the old imperialist received no commitment regarding this most sensitive area.

As for Iran, news arrived on 5 December that under US prodding the Iranian government had reluctantly agreed to reestablish relations with Britain. The Americans urged Eden to send out new faces to staff the embassy in Tehran and cautioned that Britain could not go back in a controlling position over oil. Churchill assured Eisenhower they would create a consortium.[26]

After Bermuda pressure mounted within the Eisenhower administration for an early oil settlement. The NSC divided, with Humphrey and the Pentagon urging unilateral action by the United States if no agreement had been reached by April 1954. They feared that without oil revenues the shah and Zahidi would be lost. The State Department opposed this position, as it had under Truman, and Dulles succeeded in weakening the final recommendation, which said only that the situation would be reviewed in April. But Eisenhower advised Churchill that a 'prompt and completely successful arrangement with Iran' would strengthen his hand with anyone who opposed US support for Britain in Egypt. This bow and scrape in the direction of Churchill's most particular prejudice, the focus of his concern in the Middle East, seems to have had no effect.[27]

In the 14 months following the overthrow of Musaddiq, that
s up to the signing of the consortium agreement in October
1954, the only clear success for British diplomacy *vis-à-vis* Iran
was the reestablishment of diplomatic relations before oil
negotiations. On every other point, whether regarding the oil
settlement or military strategy for Iran, the British gave way
under American prodding. What was at work here, as elsewhere in the Middle East and beyond, was grudging recognition by British policymakers that the United States held the
upper hand. Without support the British were severely restricted
in what they could accomplish. Having to appeal to the Americans to stand with them, never able to proceed without consulting Washington, rankled with many people who could recall
Britain's days of glory. When young, impetuous Americans came
along to show how to put the world aright, tempers flared.
American diplomats often referred to British sensitivities; too
often, however, they paid them scant heed.[28]

For the most part, the British had handled changing circumstances gracefully, but the Conservative government had
to control a group of Tory backbenchers who insisted that
Britain should stand up to the Iranians and Egyptians regardless of what the United States advised. Their clamor intensified after the successful coup against Musaddiq. Eventually
Eden would surrender to the view that Britain must act, with
or without the United States, in its own best interests, resulting
in the tragic Suez Crisis.

One of the special difficulties that plagued Anglo-American
relations during the early Eisenhower years was a problem of
personalities. Churchill and Eden had difficulty with Dulles.
They had advised the president-elect not to appoint him secretary of state. He seemed outspoken, ideological, insensitive to
British feelings. At Bermuda he reduced Churchill to impo-
tent tears when he thwarted the prime minister's hope for a
summit with the Soviets. Herbert Hoover, Jr. had received the
blessings of Whitehall, but as the British came to know him
better, they liked him less. Makins claimed Hoover was difficult because he had little diplomatic experience and was unsympathetic toward the British.[29]

Assistant Secretary Henry Byroade, who succeeded McGhee
in 1952, also came in for censure. During the war Byroade had
served as an army engineer in India, Burma and China. In

1946 General Marshall tapped him to return to China with his mission, which tried to patch differences between the Communists and the Nationalists. Later, he worked on Germany, first in Washington then in Bonn. When Acheson asked him to resign from the army and become assistant secretary, he hesitated, knowing nothing about the region. When he questioned the secretary about the appointment, Acheson joked that because of the Arab–Israeli problem everybody who knew anything about the area had refused the job.[30]

Eden made no attempt to hide his feelings. Even before the new administration took office, the foreign secretary responded to Dulles's query on Byroade, saying, 'he is very poor.' Cables from the embassy in Washington frequently contained disparaging remarks about Byroade. At Bermuda, he challenged British Secretary of State Sir Pierson Dixon on policy in Iran and Egypt. On the former he seemed pessimistic, wondering how long the British intended to drag out negotiations. Did the British government support Zahidi? he asked. This was too much for Eden who wrote, 'Byroade is either very stupid or mischievous.' Eden gave an interview to American journalist C.L. Sulzberger in which he confided he detested Byroade, who knew absolutely nothing about the Middle East. Eden of course considered himself an expert on the area and rarely accepted any criticism of his policies there.[31]

Perhaps Byroade's undiplomatic language at Bermuda reflected not only his impatience with the British but also his frustration at having been cut out of Iran once Hoover came on board. He had been in the thick of Anglo-American discussions for months and suddenly the issue was taken out of his hands. 'Hoover wasn't interested in anything we'd done before,' Byroade remembered. As the lone, high-level holdover from the Truman administration, he suspected his days in the State Department would soon end; he could afford to be frank.[32]

The British attitude toward Byroade is reminiscent of that toward his predecessor, McGhee. Both US officials concluded that the British had made crucial mistakes in the Middle East by refusing to adjust to the rise of nationalism and changing conditions. The United States, they assumed, would support Britain if absolutely necessary, but they preferred to cut through details and solve problems before they turned into crises.

Neither showed proper respect – or so London thought –

for British experience in the region. They were young, brash and outspoken and would bring British diplomacy to grief if given rein. Whatever the justice or otherwise of British attitudes toward Dulles, Hoover and Byroade, such differences complicated negotiations for an Iranian settlement.

The larger issues of nations, it would seem, were subject to the confusions that beset individuals, and in this regard there was not much difference between the major capital of a long recognized power, London, and the dusty capital in the Middle East. The period under discussion began with the triumphal return of the shah. It turned into the shah's incessant worrying about Zahidi. London officials concerned themselves with the glories of the past and frittered away their time in spiteful remarks about American officials. Whether the latter were intelligent or unintelligent was hardly the question. It was a matter of what government in the Western world held power. The British knew that, to be sure. But they could not recognize it, and if the truth were known behaved almost as peevishly as did the shah after his triumph, if such it was, against Musaddiq.

11 Selling the Consortium

Anyone who thought an oil solution would come easily did not understand the complexities of the affair. With three governments – none speaking with a single voice – eight major oil companies, and numerous minor ones jockeying for advantage, it was little wonder negotiations dragged on long after Musaddiq's government had disappeared. At times it seemed as if the whole enterprise would come to naught, that one participant or another would pack up and go home. Although the parties came close to such a break, it never happened – there was just too much at stake. And as the shah and Zahidi slowly reestablished control, silencing if not winning over nationalist opponents, prospects for a settlement began to improve.

By the end of 1953 four months had passed since the coup and still no settlement was in sight. Matters seemed even more confused.

Musaddiq had come to trial for treason on 8 November, and only by liberal use of force had the government been able to break up a pro-Musaddiq strike in the capital. In the courtroom the former prime minister challenged the right of the military to try him, yielding nothing to the prosecution. To his fellow countrymen he gave a splendid performance; his spirited defense quickly became part of local lore. The open trial hurt the government. When the leading newspapers, *Kayhan* and *Ittila'at*, published Musaddiq's heroic courtroom speech, they were temporarily banned.[1]

What may have played well in Tehran evoked quite a different response in New York, where the unsympathetic newspapers showed how differently Americans interpreted the behavior of the former prime minister. The press ridiculed his posturing, emotional outbursts, raucous laughter. According to an Iranian observer they reduced 'the most benevolent and democratic leader we had ever had to a foolish, half-mad old man making an indecent spectacle of himself in public.'[2]

After more disturbances the government transferred Musaddiq's trial from the center of the city to the Army Officers Club north of Tehran – for his comfort, they explained. Sporadic demonstrations of students and workers continued.

Meanwhile Zahidi fended off attacks from former supporters, who believed the government had caved in to foreign
demands. On 3 December, Musaddiq's former colleagues,
Husain Makki, Muzaffar Bagha'i and Ayatollah Kashani, perhaps beginning to regret their support for Zahidi, made public statements criticizing the decision to resume diplomatic
relations. Kashani, the most outspoken, warned the shah and
Zahidi that he would lead the attack on the regime if ties were
restored prior to an oil agreement. 'That day will be a day of
mourning,' he declared.[3]

Four days later, with news of renewal of diplomatic relations, demonstrations erupted. University students led the
protest. Soldiers fired into the anti-British crowd, killing two
students and wounding many more. The government would
not risk further disturbances, not only for its own survival but
also because US Vice President Richard M. Nixon was arriving
on a goodwill visit and Prime Minister Zahidi wanted to impress him. Soldiers saturated the university; they stood guard
at the gates, along the walls, in the gardens and in corridors
and classrooms to make certain that nothing went awry.[4]

On 21 December, the court sentenced Musaddiq to three
years solitary confinement for attempted rebellion, confirming
his standing as a martyr. Publicly the shah had forgiven him,
while privately he ordered the tribunal to hand down the three-
year sentence. This dissociated the shah from responsibility
for punishing the old patriot and saddled Zahidi with any
blame. In preparation for disturbances the government appointed the ruthless General Taimur Bakhtiar military governor of Tehran.[5]

Into this maelstrom flew Nixon on his first overseas trip as
vice president, bringing American good wishes for the shah
and Zahidi. The British had opposed his visit because it would
antedate reestablishment of Anglo-Iranian relations. Nixon
promised to let them know his decision, but later announced
his itinerary, without consulting Ambassador Makins. In his
first meeting with the shah the vice president 'sensed an inner
strength in him.' Nixon scrupulously avoided the sensitive oil
question, except to remark that long-term US assistance could
not be expected before settlement of the oil dispute. A home-
town acquaintance, Whittier businessman William T. Hughes,
had warned Nixon from Tehran on 7 December to expect

political demonstrations because Iranians believed the United States showed too much favoritism toward the British. Businessmen he had met still supported Musaddiq. But the visit went off without incident. Few Iranians knew how deeply the United States had involved itself in events of the previous August. Nixon departed 12 December, trailing behind him lavish praise for Zahidi, whom he considered intelligent, wise, and having great strength of character.[6]

Little more than a week later Tehran welcomed another Western official whose mission in the short term was more important than Nixon's. Denis Wright, newly appointed chargé d'affaires of Her Britannic Majesty's Government, came with two related goals: to reestablish diplomatic relations severed in October 1952, and to determine once and for all whether the AIOC could return to Iran.

Eden had selected Wright for his intelligence and 'considerable knowledge of the oil industry.' He made a wise choice. Wright's two predecessors in the Economic Relations Department of the Foreign Office had had breakdowns, and having survived two years in that position, Wright joked, his superiors knew he was tough.[7]

In preparing Wright for his mission, the diplomats held a meeting at Britannic House to obtain the AIOC view. Using blunt language Fraser argued that Wright's sole task should be to get AIOC personnel out to Tehran to assess the position themselves and to conduct the negotiations. He did not trust the diplomats. Wright became visibly upset during the harangue but determined not to be cowed by Sir William.[8]

On the day the military court announced Musaddiq's sentence, the chargé's small plane landed at Tehran's Mehrabad Airport. Troops ringed the airport buildings, prepared for the worst. Over the next weeks Wright adopted the lowest possible profile. The Swiss had been looking after British affairs, so at midnight their brass plate was removed from atop the British plate at the embassy gate and that was it – no fanfare. Rumor circulated of bombings and assassinations, making the chargé cautious. During a skiing outing north of Tehran, he was recognized and some young men invited him to their tent for tea. He half-suspected a plot but joined them all the same to listen to Iranian music and be entertained. That proved a psychological turning-point, after which he lost his apprehensiveness.[9]

His relations with the shah did not start off amicably. The shah sent two personal representatives to explain that he expected to handle all oil arrangements directly with Wright and the British, by-passing the government. Wright refused to deal with them and reported the whole affair to Foreign Minister Intizam. Angered, the shah had nothing further to do with the embassy until the new ambassador arrived two months later.[10]

While Wright picked up the pieces in Tehran, London prepared for an oil settlement. Pressed by the Foreign Office, Fraser had agreed to invite heads of major oil companies for talks at Britannic House, but he emphasized they should not assume any kind of consortium. His letter read in part, 'Mr. Hoover has informed me that the ideal solution, in his opinion, would be for the AIOC to return to Persia alone, a view which is, of course, held by me and is, I think, shared by you.'[11]

When the oilmen gathered, 15 December, Hoover sat in because of the antitrust situation in the United States. Despite Fraser's caveat they did discuss the idea of a consortium although without any conclusion. The British government stayed away, not wishing to commit itself until Wright had made his report.[12]

The chargé's decisive dispatch arrived on 6 January. Having broadly sampled Iranian and foreign opinion in the two weeks since his arrival, he concluded that the AIOC could not come back alone. The government was not popular and a return of the company would undermine Zahidi. Eden made up his mind to support a consortium and Fraser finally agreed. On 14 January the AIOC board voted to search for agreement on the basis of a consortium in which the AIOC would have a half interest.[13]

No sooner had this hurdle been overcome than another appeared. The oilmen began to wrangle over what share the AIOC should have in the proposed consortium. Hoover thought its participation should be 35 per cent. Dulles and Humphrey agreed that 50 per cent exceeded the limit the Iranians could accept. They would never tolerate 'production and refining of the oil by a company in which the AIOC, which rightly or wrongly was still hated in Persia, occupied so prominent a position.' The American oil companies left the two governments to work out respective shares, but they were disappointed that the AIOC had demanded so much because it seemed to indicate persistent lack of realism, which had been a problem all along.[14]

Hoover returned to London to take up this issue with the Foreign Office, and in an acrimonious meeting on 29 January accused the British of dragging their feet and asking far too much for the AIOC. He recommended 40 per cent.[15]

Hoover, who the British had come to dislike intensely, could not get an agreement, and the issue simmered into February. Eden and Dulles discussed the matter at the foreign ministers' meeting in Berlin, where the foreign secretary argued forcefully. He came away thinking he had convinced the secretary of state, only to find on his return to London a US *aide-mémoire* declaring the share must be lower. According to the Americans, 50 per cent for the AIOC would lead to a weak agreement which would be subject to attacks by Iranian 'demagogues.' Until the question could be resolved, neither US oilmen nor Dulles's adviser for petroleum affairs would return to London for a second round of talks.[16]

Eden resisted American pressure as long as he could, all the while urging Fraser to accept the 40 per cent, saying that the US position was firm and could not be negotiated. Reluctantly, the AIOC accepted a 40–40–20 formula in which 40 per cent was for the AIOC, 40 per cent for US companies and 20 per cent for Shell (14) and Compagnie Française des Pétroles (6).[17]

While the two governments worked out shares, the Eisenhower administration tried to clear the way for American oil companies to participate, without violating US antitrust laws, which forbade US companies from entering into marketing and pricing arrangements. The companies already faced a suit instituted by the previous administration. They wanted a guarantee that participation in an Iranian consortium would not entail more legal problems. They had been reluctant to become involved and had agreed to do so largely under pressure from the White House, which argued that national security was the issue.

The stumbling block here was the Justice Department, more precisely its active antitrust division, which pressed Attorney General Brownell not to drop the cartel suit. Brownell stood virtually alone within the administration. In December he agreed that oil company representatives could participate in informal talks in London if Hoover appointed them special advisers.[18]

Now in mid-January, President Eisenhower took the matter out of the attorney general's hands, informing Justice that he would use his authority under section 708 of the Defense Production Act to grant exceptions to the antitrust laws in the interest of national security. He had decided to allow American companies to join the consortium. Hoover relished the victory, reporting that Justice was still wriggling on the hook. He took special delight in the fact that Leonard Emmerglick, the forceful head of the antitrust division, 'had been "slapped down" in no uncertain fashion.' On 21 January, Brownell reported to the NSC that the consortium 'would not in itself constitute a violation of antitrust laws.' The council approved the plan that day.[19]

Now, one of the problems facing the oil companies was ensuring that the reentry of Iranian oil would not destabilize world markets. Production in Iraq, Saudi Arabia and especially Kuwait had increased to make up for lost Iranian production. By 1954 there was a world oil surplus. In the short run the companies would have to limit production elsewhere to allow Iranian oil back in.

Middle East oil states cooperated; they could hardly resist when such persuasive arguments presented themselves. In Saudi Arabia the American partners in ARAMCO explained to Ibn Saud the possibility of chaos in the region without an Iranian oil settlement. The king accepted their arguments for lifting less Saudi oil, asking only that they take no more Iranian oil than necessary. Kuwait, too, proved helpful. The British diplomatic representative informed the sheikh that local production might decline somewhat in order to restore stabilty in Iran and remove the possibility of communist gains or disturbances to world oil markets. The sheikh acquiesced.[20]

Now that a settlement seemed possible, the consortium partners needed to know what conditions prevailed in Iranian oilfields three years after nationalization. They sent a delegation of experts to assess how much capital would be required to get the oil flowing again. The group returned to London on 18 February, with a report that should have surprised all those who had disparaged Iranian technical ability. They found many staff members of the National Iranian Oil Company

(NIOC) well-qualified, the physical plant in Abadan and in the fields in good working order, pilferage less than before nationalization, and harbors and jetties ready for service. Company hospitals worked full time and were neat and clean. 'On the whole the mission were agreeably surprised by what they saw.'[21]

Few Western reports about the Middle East challenged existing stereotypes, hence it was not surprising that when one did, little attention was paid to it. Evidence to the contrary appeared so overwhelming. The British had disparaged Iranian management since the beginning of the crisis. This had provided justification for AIOC insistence that any agreement with Musaddiq must leave control in Western hands. The Cox–Laird report changed few opinions. When Hoover reported to the NSC that 'the Iranians were incapable themselves of providing efficient management control' of the oil industry, no one questioned the conclusion. The British and Americans often held similar views about the incompetence of Iranians and Middle Easterners, views based either on personal, but limited, experience in Iran and the Middle East, or on second-hand tales of the natives' incapacity, the telling and retelling of which provided a pastime for Westerners in the region.[22]

Throughout February and March prospective consortium members moved closer to a working arrangement. With eight companies involved, discussions were complex. At times tempers grew short. The five American companies and Shell had responded angrily after the AIOC cavalierly offered a share to the Compagnie Française des Pétroles without consulting the others.

Compensation proved especially awkward. The AIOC put forward an exaggerated claim, which it wanted to include as part of the general consortium talks at Tehran. This would scuttle negotiation, and the other companies refused. Again the US government entered the fray. On 17 March, Dulles and Walter Bedell Smith spoke in the strongest language to Ambassador Makins, warning that the AIOC was asking too much from Iran. The United States sought to create a strong, anti-communist Iran and to preserve the rights of foreign investors. If it could not achieve both, it might have to concentrate on the first. They went on to caution that 'without agreements in Iran and Egypt, the United States might have to follow its own line in the Middle East.'[23]

The American offensive got results. Although Eden tried to defend AIOC claims, he retreated when Makins warned that if US oil companies withdrew, the AIOC would get nothing. The British government, the foreign secretary said, would negotiate separately with the Iranians for compensation and the maximum claim would be £100 million. A grim-faced Fraser agreed.[24]

This cleared the last barrier to sending a delegation. The companies signed a memorandum of understanding in which they agreed on their shares and on sums they would each pay the AIOC to buy into the consortium. They dispatched three delegates to Tehran: Orville Harden (Standard Oil of New Jersey), John Loudon (Shell) and Harold Snow (AIOC).

The new British Ambassador, Sir Roger Stevens, who had come in February, was on hand to greet them. Although recently arrived, he had analyzed the local situation carefully. He was no novice; in fact, this would be his last posting, capping a distinguished career. He warned of the delicacy of Zahidi's position, advising that any settlement must be presentable. He likened the imprisoned Musaddiq to an elderly crank 'as troublesome in death as in life,' whose will negotiators must conspire to interpret liberally while outwardly conforming to its provisions. To Whitehall he confided his concern that Hoover would not help matters but remain no doubt in the wings, 'pursuing the devious tactics he had employed earlier in London.'[25]

The negotiators received a warm official welcome with parties in their honor at which they met the members of the Iranian negotiating team. Of the six, the intelligent and energetic finance minister, Ali Amini, was the most influential. He had studied economics in Europe and been a political ally of his relative, Ahmad Qavam, in early postwar years. He served as a member of Musaddiq's first government, from which he resigned in a dispute over economic policy. Zahidi had wisely appointed him finance minister.

Following this introduction, Harden, who seemed preoccupied with his health, and Snow, a representaive of the 'former company,' avoided social events and off-the-record talks, leaving them to Loudon, who performed admirably.

Differences divided the parties, especially issues of control and management and the nationality of operating companies to be set up. On these there was little progress during the first round because the British believed they had already given so much that they had to insist on British nationality for the consortium company in order to get any settlement through parliament.[26]

Adding to these problems, the Americans had several spokesmen at Tehran – Harden, Henderson and Hoover – and no one could be certain who was saying what to whom. Harden proved secretive and because of his impatience with government interference neglected to keep Hoover and the embassy informed. Hoover sulked over this and eventually had a showdown with him. Hoover made wisecracks about the British at joint meetings, which unnecessarily increased tensions.[27]

Musaddiq and the National Front were still being stoutly defended in the Majlis by a group of supporters whose arguments frequently drew cheers from assembled deputies. There had been nothing illegal about the seventeenth Majlis, Deputy Shams Qanatabadi argued, and many agreed. The former prime minister had carried out the will of the people and although he made mistakes there was no justification for dismissing his regime as irrelevant. Another deputy, Dr Bina, defended the national movement against the company and the British, arguing that 'the Iranian people will not allow the foreigners to charge with error their sacred movement.' When pro-government deputies likened Musaddiq's regime to the reign of Genghis Khan, an uproar ensued and many deputies stormed out of the chamber.[28]

The shah was pessimistic about consortium proposals and worried how people would react. He refused to support any agreement that violated Musaddiq's nationalization law of April 1951. Hoover suggested to the NSC that it might be necessary to offer substantial military assistance 'to nail him down to the agreement.'[29]

After four weeks there seemed little prospect of an early settlement, and Harden resolved to return to London for consultations. In a farewell audience, 15 May, the shah impressed on the departing delegation the need for a settlement such that Iranian leaders 'could still be regarded as patriots and not stooges.' At the airport the Iranian negotiators handed Harden a list of demands, which relieved him of all hope of an agreement.[30]

In London most of the oil companies agreed that the task in Iran was impossible and wanted to give up, but Howard Page, the ailing Harden's replacement for Jersey, remained optimistic and became by default head of the enlarged delegation that returned to Iran in June.

Page's selection was fortuitous for he had experience negotiating in the third world and approached his task with a sensible philosophy. He tried to understand the problems confronting the other side, to approach negotiations as a mutual problem-solving matter in which one avoided snap judgments regarding opposite numbers. He worked out several approaches in advance, never assuming that he had 'the one and only answer.' Above all, he had patience. These principles served him well over the next months.[31]

Even though Page worked well with Amini, whom he respected, it required time to work out problems. The British had eased the situation by agreeing to accept Dutch nationality for any consortium company, but questions of control and management remained. The AIOC wanted to supply the top management.[32]

Page often had more difficulty with his consortium partners than with Iranian negotiators. Talks usually went on with the latter until ten or eleven in the evening, and Page would report developments early next morning to the group of oil company vice presidents. Invariably in response to Page's question, 'What do you suggest we tell them?' someone would respond, 'Tell them to go to hell!' Page would write this down very slowly and say, 'Okay, what do we tell them next?'[33]

Some AIOC representatives had learned little over the years since nationalization. One, J.M. Pattinson, reported to Fraser that not much had changed in Persia, confusion reigned as before, and 'the whole appearance of shabbiness and disrepair is just about as usual.' He assured the chairman that the Iranians were pleased to see him again. 'They have had an anxious time the last two years and no doubt are hoping for a return of the protection we used to give them when there was always one of us they could run to if in trouble.' His patronizing letters led one diplomat to quip, 'there is an air of Alice in Wonderland about these.'[34]

Despite difficulty in his own camp, Page persevered, and the breakthrough came toward the end of summer. Under the

heads of agreement signed 5 August, the NIOC retained ownership of the oil industry, but two operating companies, fully
owned by the consortium, were set up, one to explore for and
produce oil, the other to refine it. The two 'though legally
exercising their powers on behalf of NIOC were given full and
effective control of all operations.' Top management would be
Dutch, but consortium partners would determine the level of
oil production. Iran was to receive half of net profits.[35]

The final agreement was a far cry from what the nationalists
had envisioned in May 1951, or even the shah as recently as
May 1954. Yet it seemed the best Iran could obtain in light of
present world conditions of oversupply. This was the argument
that Amini and the court used in presenting the agreement to
the nation. Reluctantly, the shah gave Amini permission to
accept these terms. Boundaries of the concession were changed
slightly to satisfy the shah, who wanted the resulting concession area to look different than that of 1933.[36]

What remained was the question of Iranian compensation
to the AIOC. When Stevens separately pressed for compensation from Iran, Amini countered with claims against the AIOC.
Amini appealed to him to show a spirit of generosity and self-
sacrifice. The finance minister agreed to pay £25 million, no
more; a larger sum, he feared would set off a popular reaction.
Without US support the British had little leverage; on 30 July,
they accepted Amini's final offer.[37]

Perhaps Musaddiq could take comfort from the fact that
Britain's predominance in Iran had clearly come to an end.
The oil negotiations had shown the Americans now in control.
The American, Page, had been instrumental in their success.
He worked directly with top Iranian officials while the AIOC
representative spouted nonsense offstage about the way things
used to be. The 'former' company had to share its concession
in Iran; something it had stoutly resisted for years. The AIOC
had been the focus of British influence in Iran; now that
ownership had changed, London's power declined.

Behind the scenes the shah had taken an important part in
the search for an acceptable settlement. At first he had reacted
pessimistically toward the negotiations. After Harden and his
delegation departed for London in May, the shah suggested to
Henderson that he might dismiss Zahidi because of increasing

charges of corruption against him. Henderson urged the shah
not to take such an unhelpful action in the middle of negotiations, and the British concurred. Anglo-American firmness
seemed to impress the shah and he relented.[38]

Later he instructed Amini not to worry about parliament's
reaction to any agreement, that was his responsibility. He
dominated the Majlis elected in January–February, 1954; deputies owed their seats to his intervention. Henderson had hoped
that the shah would supervise elections in such a way that
'intelligent, broadminded, loyal patriotic Iranians' would win
seats. This expectation was doomed. Many such Iranians were
in jail with Musaddiq. Of those who had supported the *coup
d'état* and now expected their rewards, few had national reputations or standing with their countrymen. Henderson became
so disillusioned he decided to take steps to guarantee an effective parliament, but despite his intervention with the prime
minister and the court, results disappointed him. The only
surprising element in the elections for the eighteenth Majlis
was Henderson's naivete regarding the character of the anti-
Musaddiq forces in Iran, and his mistaken belief that like
Woodrow Wilson in revolutionary Mexico he could manipulate the situation so that 'good' men would be elected.[39]

Those who had loudly attacked the government in May and
June kept in contact with the shah, who apparently called them
off in July, when he became temporarily reconciled with the
prime minister. From then he did all he could to ensure Majlis
ratification. In August he sent letters to doubtful senators and
deputies, asking support for the agreement and 'equating their
opposition to it as opposition to himself.' He convinced most
of the doubters.[40]

He advised the minister of defense to tighten up security
against the nationalists and the communists who might stage
demonstrations. Partly as a result of increased surveillance and
assistance from American intelligence, the government obtained a secret list of several hundred Tudeh members serving
in the officer corps. These included the chief of Zahidi's body-
guard and the deputy chief for security of the Tehran police,
who was responsible for the shah's security and that of Nixon
when he visited. Over 400 were arrested, including some of
the most able junior officers. After a series of trials in the fall

of 1954, 27 were executed and many others given long prison sentences. This fortuitous discovery removed what might have become a grave threat to the shah's regime.[41]

Even with the shah in control, review of the agreement and the parliamentary debate that followed continued until late October. It could not be rushed for there was a small group of deputies who argued persistently that it conflicted with the nationalization law. The government used this opportunity to let people know that it also had reservations.

Debate began on 7 October with Zahidi's patriotic speech to parliament conjuring images of a glorious future for Iran. Choking with emotion, tears streaming, he could not continue, and the deputies wept with him. Ali Amini, the level-headed, coolly efficient finance minister, spoke next. He admitted that the agreement was not perfect. He had hoped that the AIOC would forgo compensation from Iran as a gesture of goodwill, but the company demanded its profits. Negotiators had done the best they could and he challenged anyone who thought he could do better to come forward and take his place. Perhaps in the future, when Iran was stronger, the agreement could be modified in its favor.[42]

The small but vocal opposition had its say. It questioned the wisdom of handing responsibility for surveying, exploiting and refining of oil to a foreign company. To do this, Muhammad Darakhshesh charged, violated the nationalization law and the interests of the nation. He refused to accept the argument that Iranians were not competent to administer their own oil industry.[43]

Ratification was probably never in doubt, but it was important to do things properly to avoid charges later of rigging the outcome. Finally on 21 October, the Majlis gave approval by a vote of 113 to 5, followed by the reconstituted senate, and the shah signed it a week later on his thirty-fifth birthday.

President Eisenhower sent an effusive message to the shah, praising his courageous efforts and steadfastness through difficult years and expressing 'the admiration of the American people for your enlightened leadership.' Churchill sent a more matter-of-fact telegram, reflecting perhaps greater British awareness of the shah's imperfections. Still, it would never do, one diplomat wrote, for him to get the impression their admiration was any less than that of the Americans. 'He has been behaving comparatively well lately,' he added, 'and deserves some praise.'[44]

Henderson, too, received high praise from Washington for his extraordinary efforts. In the midst of celebrating the oil settlement, he did not lose sight of the larger goal, reminding superiors that this was only a skirmish in the long battle with the Soviet Union. The threat of Iran being lost to the free world would continue, and the United States must not relax efforts to protect it.[45]

And so was born the consortium. The AIOC did well out of the settlement, £264 million from its partners and £25 million from Iran in addition to its 40 per cent share of the consortium. According to Shell's John Loudon, it was 'the best deal Willie Fraser ever made. . . . After all Anglo-Iranian actually had nothing to sell. It had already been nationalized.' The Iranians had settled for only slightly more than what the company offered in March 1951.[46]

The results revealed how little leverage the Iranian government exercised over the oil companies. As one Majlis deputy lamented, 'How can we get powerful oil companies to bend to our ideas on selling price when we cannot even get the fruit and vegetable vendors of Tehran to do this?' The world market was temporarily glutted, and the oil cartel would not allow Iran to sell its own oil and risk depressing prices. The cartel controlled most of the tanker fleet and had established sophisticated marketing procedures; it alone would decide when and how much Iranian oil could enter the world market. Furthermore, the Zahidi government depended on the United States for assistance, and this became critical if the regime hoped to control the opposition and show internal progress. Washington showed no evidence of supporting an agreement more favorable to Iran. Such a document would have taken longer to negotiate and would have required leaning harder on London and the oil companies, the latter of which had shown little interest in the consortium.[47]

Not surprisingly, Iranian response to the settlement was unenthusiastic. One paper summed up the prevailing attitude: 'Do not let us kid ourselves and say that the agreement with the consortium fully conforms to the nationalization law. . . . As we see it Iran has ceded every point to the Consortium.'[48]

In the long run people would judge the agreement by the

benefits it provided Iran. Would the Zahidi government use
the oil revenues effectively? Now that Iran had drawn closer to
the West, what benefits would accrue from this more open
association?[49]

Partly to reassure them, the Zahidi government conceived
of a grand project that might enhance government prestige.
This was building a magnificent dam at Karaj not far from
Tehran to supply water and electricity to the rapidly growing
population of the capital. The dam became a symbol of progress
and, hence, a priority for Zahidi. Prodded by Henderson, officials in Washington came to appreciate how important the
dam would be for strengthening the government. It helped to
know that the American engineering firm, Morrison-Knudsen,
had won the contract for the project. Even skeptics such as
Treasury Secretary Humphrey and International Bank President Eugene Black, who questioned the Export–Import Bank's
involvement in long-term loans, were won over. On 1 November, the United States announced a $127.3 million package of
grants and loans for the dam. This auspicious news reached
the shah as he was preparing for his second trip to Washington.[50]

This seemed to the shah a propitious time for a return visit
to the capital of the Western alliance. The oil settlement had
been approved and Iranian oil had begun to flow again into
world markets. Musaddiq was safely behind bars along with
hundreds of his supporters and members of the Tudeh party.
The United States had agreed to support the Karaj Dam project
and, most important, the United States had accepted a build-
up of Iran's military. What more favorable time for a royal
visit? The trip would announce to observers at home and abroad
that the regime had achieved such stability that the shah could
journey overseas for extended periods.

London and Washington were not so confident and tried to
discourage the shah, claiming there were too many problems
needing his attention at home. Nothing could dissuade him.[51]

Henderson advised him not to expect any major commitments from the Eisenhower administration while in Washington. The British were not so sure. They worried that their
allies might give too much away as they had threatened earlier
under Musaddiq. But talks were largely exploratory. They
agreed to send American military training teams to Tehran in
1955 to assess Iran's needs and capabilities.[52]

The shah's two-month informal visit was a success. He did not need to press the American government because it had given him so much. The administration tactfully played down any mention of US help to overthrow Musaddiq the previous year. The architect of that assistance, Kim Roosevelt, who had secretly been awarded the president's medal of honor, attended the White House dinner for the royal guests, but his secret was locked away. The royal couple spent their remaining weeks in the United States in the Florida sun.[53]

Shortly before his departure for Britain the shah received a rousing reception at city hall in New York. The great liberal, Mayor Robert Wagner, extolled one who 'knew the secret of democracy and had done so much to promote the kind of world in which we believe.' Not to be outdone, the shah called upon the Almighty to 'grant the American people more and more strength to invigorate the prosperity of freedom-loving nations and to fortify the altruistic spirit that animates the American people.' On that happy if unrealistic note the royal party set sail for London.[54]

Thus closed what was arguably the most important chapter in US–Iranian relations. Iran had been 'saved.' The threat from extremists had been beaten back, containment had registered a major success. Oil would continue to flow in predictable amounts at reasonable prices. The success of clandestine action in Iran, moreover, provided a model for the Eisenhower administration, which it employed again in Guatemala and then later in Cuba.

12 Emerging Patterns

In the years following Musaddiq's overthrow, everything seemed quiet in Iran, especially compared with conditions of the previous decade. Yet it was a critical time. The shah worked to eliminate all opposition to his increasingly dictatorial rule. The Eisenhower administration established a pattern of relations with the shah that would last until the revolution.

Despite the shah's increasing power and prestige, there can be no doubt that the shadow of Musaddiq hung over US relations with Iran in the decades after August 1953. It seems difficult to believe, but such was the case. In times of crisis, American officialdom remembered this man who had defied both them and their British opposites, who did not seem to have much physical strength, and mentally speaking seemed at the least odd, but somehow managed to find his way, and not only in local politics. Policymakers could not escape the vision of the former prime minister and his National Front supporters as harbingers of chaos in Iran, lords of misrule, so they thought; hence their reluctance to deal with them. Strangely, as Musaddiq's rule receded, its lingering impressions remained, the shadow remained, so that whenever a new American official innocently suggested pressing the shah to liberalize his regime, the old hands conjured terrifying images of 'Mosadeqist' demagogues. And so the years passed and with them the desire for change. Although newcomers might remember little about Musaddiq, the idea became fixed that there could be no alternative to the shah.[1]

At first the Americans needed no convincing that they had acted wisely in helping overthrow the prime minister. As the shah became more autocratic, officials sought reassurance that they had done the right thing, and found it in the retelling of half-truths and misunderstandings that presented Musaddiq as a demon of the cold war, a symbol of dangers that might befall naive national leaders anywhere. Until the eve of the revolution, references to Musaddiq as bogeyman peppered official correspondence, especially in times of crisis. As late as 1975, Secretary of State Henry Kissinger reported to President Gerald

Ford that 'Mossadegh, in alliance with the Iranian communists, tried to overthrow the shah.'[2]

The shah had a vested interest in the view that Musaddiq
had been responsible for Iran's ills. He retained horrifying
memories of Musaddiq throughout his reign, accusing him of
'infantile xenophobia' and 'negative demagoguery.' According to the shah, his fall represented 'the routing of alien forces
that came within a hair's breadth of extinguishing our independence.' The shah confided his bitterness to an adviser:
'The worst years of my reign, indeed of my entire life, came
when Mosaddeq was prime minister. The bastard was out for
blood and every morning I awoke with the sensation that today might be my last on the throne.' For years the monarch
suspected American diplomats of secret meetings with his followers. Even in death Musaddiq haunted the shah, who refused his last request to be buried among the martyrs of the
July 1952 uprising. When he died in March 1967, the prime
minister was quietly laid to rest at his country home, where he
had spent a decade under house arrest.[3]

After Musaddiq's defeat, the shah set out to tighten his hold
on the country. He busied himself with strengthening the army.
He wanted more than a glorified police force maintaining
internal security; he envisioned a military capable of delaying
a Soviet advance. Such a force would safeguard Iranian independence. He told Vice President Nixon and other officials
that he planned to cooperate with Iran's neighbors in a regional association, but it was too soon to talk about that because Iran's army was too weak and could contribute little to
regional defense. Before his eyes must have flashed scenes of
the collapse of his father's precious military before British and
Soviet forces in 1941.[4]

The Eisenhower administration responded approvingly to
the shah's request for a build-up of Iranian armed forces. The
shah appeared the linchpin of Iran's attachment to the West,
and the monarch relied on the military to maintain his power
and national stability. To keep Iran within the Western camp,
the NSC readily concluded, the army must be improved to
cement its loyalty to the shah.[5]

One difficulty was that Britain did not agree with the new

American policy. London preferred a small Iranian military to maintain internal security. Acheson and Truman had planned that, too, before Korea. London doubted whether Iran, even if strengthened, would be able to delay a Soviet force. The British took a more disparaging view than the Americans based on their experience with Iranian military forces in the nineteenth century and more recently during the Anglo-Soviet invasion of 1941, when Riza Shah's modern army crumpled before the invaders. In addition, Britain had long planned to defend the Middle East against Soviet invasion along the Zagros Mountain line in southwestern Iran, turning over most of the country – but not the oil fields – to the invader at the start of hostilities. The allies had kept this plan from the shah, but London remained convinced it offered the only strategically sound defense of the region. During winter 1954, US officials worked on Britain to accept an expanded role for Iran's military, and as on so many other issues, London eventually gave way.[6]

In the two years after Musaddiq's overthrow, the US government encouraged a regional alliance. Since 1946, Washington had worked to keep out the communists, and with Musaddiq out of the way policymakers thought increasingly in terms of regional defense for the northern tier. This was a subject associated with Secretary Dulles, who set up the Southeast Asia Treaty Organization in September 1954, and who had in mind a complementary defense pact, with Pakistan as the hinge, to close the gap in Western defenses between Southeastern Europe and South Asia.[7]

A Middle East defense scheme had been under discussion intermittently since 1951. Conceived as a Middle East Command (MEC), including Egypt, the United States and the United Kingdom, whose combined forces would replace the British along the Suez Canal, by 1953 it was apparent that Egypt would have no part in such an arrangement – nor, for various reasons, would any other Arab state except Iraq. There, Nuri al-Said, conservative prime minister and principal source of power in the kingdom of young Faysal II, had close ties with Britain. London had bases in Iraq and supplied the nation with most of its materiel. So close was this association that Egypt's Gamal Abdul Nasser routinely attacked Nuri as a British stooge.

With the demise of the notion of a Middle East Defense Organization, policymakers in Washington began to think seriously about a northern tier arrangement along the southern borders of the Soviet Union that would include Turkey, Iraq, Pakistan and, eventually, Iran, and they welcomed Turkish and Iraqi moves to create a regional defense pact early in 1955 and the accession of Pakistan and Britain a few months later.[8]

It was of such an arrangement that the shah had spoken when Nixon visited Tehran in December 1953, but the United States, Britain and Turkey agreed that it would be premature for Iran to consider entering such a regional pact. The Iranian press seemed to agree. 'Iran will remain neutral so long as its neutrality is respected,' said *Kayhan*. 'It is in our interests to remain neutral and preserve our independence,' wrote the editor of *Dad*. 'By remaining neutral we shall not antagonize either bloc.'[9]

Despite this apparent consensus, at least some members of the Eisenhower administration encouraged the shah to seek early admission to the Baghdad Pact. Shortly after Nixon's visit, Henderson advised him that congressional approval of further military aid would be influenced not only by a country's requirements but also by consideration of its contributions to regional defense. Dulles, too, pushed for Iranian participation, even though Secretary of Defense Charles E. Wilson and his own brother, CIA chief Allen Dulles, advised waiting until US advisers could assess Iran's military requirements.[10]

By summer 1954, Turkey had concluded that the United States was trying 'to inveigle' Iran into a regional defense agreement. In November, Iranian Foreign Minister Intizam told the British undersecretary in charge of Middle Eastern affairs, Evelyn Shuckburgh, that the United States seemed in a hurry for Iranian participation. The British considered Iran's adherence of only marginal benefit, to be offset by increased Soviet hostility, and set out their attitude plainly: 'If Iran wants to join, fine, but don't press them.' But it was too late. The shah had made up his mind, almost certainly reasoning that by joining he could increase the flow of American arms.[11]

The first indication of a policy change came in late September 1955 when Prime Minister Ala suggested to the Majlis that cooperation and friendship with other like-minded states would prevent Iran from being isolated. 'This will make those who might want to attack us think twice.' Editorials followed, supporting the regional pact, arguing that Iran's neutrality in World War I and in World War II had not protected it from invasion. Finally, in his address opening the Senate on 8 October, the shah confirmed what everyone had expected. Iran would indeed join the Baghdad Pact. Matters moved quickly, and within two weeks both the Majlis and the senate had approved the government's bill with only minimal opposition.[12]

Although the shah's sudden adherence took Washington by surprise, Dulles was not unhappy, for the result accorded with his strategic plans for the Middle East.

The shah would regret his hasty decision, for he expected the United States to join the pact, but it refused, preferring to limit its participation to committee deliberations. The Americans concluded that full membership would antagonize the Soviet Union, the Arab states – especially Egypt and Saudi Arabia – and Israel. Nasser, who had earlier rejected participation in any military association with Western powers, saw the Baghdad Pact as nothing more than a British attempt to reimpose its hegemony in the region. The Saudis had a longstanding feud with the Hashemite rulers of Iraq, which precluded their adherence, and, of course, American oil companies depended on the goodwill of King Ibn Saud. As for Israel, the Americans worried that Washington's formal adherence would bring forth a demand that they extend a security guarantee to Tel Aviv. All in all, it seemed wiser for the United States to stay out.

This policy of non-membership was not popular with everyone in the Eisenhower administration. At the time of the Suez crisis in 1956, and again after the Iraqi revolution in 1958, the Defense Department urged adherence, in part because it feared the pact might fall apart otherwise. Diplomats in pact nations also favored US membership. But Dulles remained firmly opposed, arguing that after Suez support for the alliance in Iraq and Pakistan had seriously weakened and that the Soviet Union, using non-military measures, had 'hopped over the northern tier line,' raising doubt about the pact's effectiveness. Later, he strangely added that the United States had never wanted Baghdad in the Baghdad Pact and for that reason Washington had not joined at its formation. Despite repeated requests from members and pressure from within the administration, the United States stayed out.[13]

The shah was troubled by another problem. In his view the United States had failed to contribute the military assistance he had expected and Iran deserved, and throughout the 1950s his discussions with officials in Tehran and in Washington revealed a series of requests for more sophisticated arms. The shah rarely missed an opportunity for special pleading. In July 1956 Eisenhower wrote to congratulate him on the success of his first state visit to the Soviet Union, and to praise his 'courageous foreign policies,' which had, he said, gained the respect of the world. In reply the shah referred to his nation as 'the shield of the Middle East' and pointed out the difficulty of providing for regional defense as well as maintaining a strong economy. He asked the United States to increase assistance 'at this critical juncture.'[14]

The United States was not niggardly in what it gave Iran. By mid-1958 it had provided equipment for 12 infantry divisions, well over 100 000 men, as well as aircraft for four air squadrons and six ships. The shah wanted more. At times he threatened to withdraw from the pact unless his demands were satisfied.[15]

Eisenhower and Dulles found themselves in a dilemma respecting policy toward Iran. The shah wanted more weapons than the Americans considered wise; indeed it had become apparent that they could never satisfy all his demands. They had to decide how much materiel would keep the shah committed to the West. If they miscalculated, they feared reorientation of Iran's foreign policy toward neutralism, maybe even closer cooperation with the USSR.[16]

At times they gave a little more here, a little more there, to keep the shah happy; other times they told him bluntly that the United States could not provide an inexhaustible supply of weapons. It became a kind of game, at which the shah got progressively better as the years passed. He used the new apparent friendliness of the Soviet Union to press Washington, hinting that he must have assistance from whatever source. Dulles seemed especially sensitive to these threats, admitting to Ambassador Selden Chapin in late 1957, when US–Iranian relations were at a low point, that although the shah was likely bluffing, he did not want to force him to take action he would later regret.[17]

As the decade progressed the policymakers became more aware of the need for social and economic change, realizing that many Iranians put little value on what the Americans did for the army. They began to worry that the shah might be overthrown without reforms, but dared not push him too hard. Again the question arose: how much would be *just* enough?[18]

There was little of that reform mentality among Eisenhower's bureaucrats that would figure so prominently under his successor. Reform did not preoccupy American officials. Yet they had to admit that the Iranian government had done little to cope with fundamental social and economic causes of discontent that had contributed so much to Musaddiq's strength. They did not mention political reform, which was anathema to the shah and to many US policymakers as well. Rather than encouraging broader political participation, the embassy focused on establishing close personal relations with the shah, which it assumed would provide the best means of encouraging reform.[19]

In the middle years of the decade Iranians became increasingly frustrated with the shah's regime, and most of those interviewed by American diplomats agreed that the shah was steadily losing support, especially among the urban middle class. After he ousted Zahidi in April 1955, the shah had begun to rule as well as reign, and in a government made up increasingly of sycophants, he could no longer pass off responsibility for the regime's corruption and inefficiency.[20]

American officials worried what might happen when Musaddiq became a free man in August 1956. Hoover, now undersecretary of state, wondered if the United States should try to influence or assist the Iranian government in deciding what precautions to take. But the shah, taking no chances, had decided what to do. General Bakhtiar staged an attack by a group of thugs on Musaddiq's village residence outside Tehran, giving the government an excuse to station police in the village to 'protect' Musaddiq. The elderly nationalist would remain under house arrest until his death 11 years later.[21]

The government finally ended martial law in Tehran in March 1957 but only because the creation – with American assistance – of the new internal security agency, SAVAK, made the former unnecessary.[22]

It was difficult to know how accurate a picture the shah had of deteriorating conditions. He would speak to Ambassador Chapin of popular dissatisfaction reaching the danger point, but then assure close advisers he was well loved and that it would be easy to assemble 500 000 Tehranis for a royalist rally. What probably saved the shah during these difficult times was the fact that the opposition was divided and could not or would not support a single leader. No one arose who had Musaddiq's charisma, and with the nationalist leader still alive, there was awkwardness in selecting a successor. Allahyar Salih, a likely candidate, seemed unworldly, with little sense of how to ignite a popular movement. In early April 1956, for example, he briefly sought sanctuary in the parliament building, announcing that he was embarking upon a hunger strike to protest conditions. His surprising action could have become the nucleus of a serious nationalist protest, but he bungled it, failing to make preparations. A day later he changed his mind and without explanation returned home. The shah might have difficulty making progress on reform, but he had no problem dealing with enemies and rivals. Time after time he had proven himself an excellent tactician, a master at dividing the opposition, and he showed his skill again in the 1950s.[23]

In fall 1957 relations between the embassy and court deteriorated, for the shah considered American officials there unsympathetic to his requests for military and economic assistance. The chief of the military mission, Major General J.F.R. Seitz, was said to be 'openly contemptuous of Iran and Iranians.' By early 1958 the situation had become critical. The shah was not responding as predicted; he seemed more difficult to work with, more reluctant to take American advice. This had happened before. Since the end of World War II, American diplomats had frequently overestimated their influence on the shah, and Ambassadors Chapin (1955–8) and Edward Wailes (1958–61), neither of whom had experience in the Middle East, were only the latest. To be fair, however, one must recognize that the shah had changed from the early days of his reign; he no longer sought relationships with foreign diplomats as he had once done.[24]

In some ways the shah appeared the same – vacillating, indecisive, inclined to meddle, and unable to delegate authority – but a new-found confidence, based on the successful counter-coup of August 1953 made the task of American diplomats more challenging than before.[25]

The crisis came to a head in February 1958 when SAVAK uncovered a plot led by the vice chief of staff of the Iranian

army, Major General Valiollah Qarani, who had met frequently
with embassy officials, and the shah accused Americans of
having assisted the plotters. The embassy denied this, but the
incident did nothing to improve relations. Washington began
to wonder how long the shah could continue to serve as the
stabilizing force for his country.[26]

So displeased was the monarch with what he termed lack of
sympathy from American officials in Tehran that he undertook a special trip to Washington to convince policymakers of
Iran's urgent needs. In discussion with Eisenhower he carefully restrained his demand for assistance, saving it for others,
and spoke instead of geopolitics and threats in the Middle
East. Aside from the Soviet menace he identified Nasserism as
the most unsettling factor. Earlier he had warned that Nasser
had to be put in his place to forestall Musaddiq-style nationalistic uprisings. Now he and the secretary of state proceded to
make common cause against the Egyptian leader, equating
Nasserism with communism, comparing pan-Arabism to Hitler's
pan-Germanism. Israel, the shah said, served well the purpose
of limiting Arab expansionism. Egypt, he told the president,
was 'nothing but a few million unhappy and impoverished
beggars.'[27]

Eisenhower was impressed, but responded with the restraint
he often displayed on Middle East questions. Where Nasser
was concerned he spoke with none of Dulles's passion, arguing rather reasonably the need for nationalism in the region
as a counter to communism as long as it was 'constructive,'
that is, identified with freedom and other free world ideals.[28]

In Washington the shah obtained little more than vague
promises of additional aid, but events conspired to guarantee
immediate delivery of all that he desired. On 14 July, just days
after his departure, came news of the bloody coup in Iraq,
which swept aside leaders on whom Washington had relied for
stability in the troubled region. The revolution came without
warning, catching the CIA and embassy staff by surprise; Eisenhower heard the first fragmentary reports over the radio. The
president must have recalled the shah's prescient comments
two weeks before when he had wondered whether Iraq could
be trusted as a firm ally 'since Nasser is more popular with the
Iraqi people than the Iraqi government.' The president trusted

the monarch's views on the Middle East, and this recent obser-vation seemed to justify confidence.[29]

The coup came as a reprieve for the shah, showing how inextricably bound together was the United States and the Iranian monarch. It marked an end – temporarily – to at-tempts to limit assistance. Two days after the uprising Eisen-hower told Dulles 'to make Turkey and Iran of first priority.' That was 'the cheapest way' to maintain the *status quo*. On 18 July, the president and secretary of state decided to send 'con-crete encouragement' to the shah, including details of how the United States would help in the months ahead. Eisen-hower personally informed Chairman of the Joint Chiefs of Staff General Nathan Twining that he wanted no delay at the Pentagon.[30]

As a sweetener for better relations, the United States had already recalled Chapin, replacing him with Edward Wailes, who proved more sympathetic toward the shah. The new ambassador did all he could to maintain friendly ties.

As Iranian troops deployed along the border with Iraq, the Soviet ambassador warned that an attack would bring invasion from the north. In such a situation speed seemed essential. By August, Washington had committed itself to increased deliver-ies for an expanded Iranian army and to consideration of economic needs caused by the build-up.[31]

But if the coup augured well for increased military aid, it also raised anew questions about the stability of the shah's regime. The shah, who was visiting Ankara, cabled his security chief asking whether he should return under cover of dark-ness. General Hasan Kia advised him to come back in the broad light of day. He crept back into Tehran a few days after the coup. Tanks ringed the palace, and the shah kept an eye on key officers. Newspapers faced censorship for reporting that the new Iraqi regime had brought down the price of bread, and the monarch became furious when the *New York Times* published articles pointing to unrest in his kingdom.[32]

Developments in Baghdad had a liberating effect on the Iranian opposition, especially on former supporters of Musad-diq, who took heart, expecting something similar might hap-pen in Tehran, where according to American reports conditions were worse than in Iraq before the revolution. The funeral in

Tehran of Senator Abulfazl Lesani, outspoken opponent of both the oil consortium agreement and Iran's membership in the Baghdad Pact, attracted the biggest crowd in years. The embassy thankfully concluded that Washington's decisive action in sending troops to Lebanon might have saved the shah by proving American determination if a crisis should arise.[33]

Prodded by these developments, Washington authorized Wailes to raise with the shah the issue of popular dissatisfaction and the need for reforms. Surprisingly the shah listened, to what doubtless echoed advice from Asadollah Alam and other advisers. More important, he initiated minor changes: holding press conferences, abolishing feudal dues on peasants, establishing a complaints bureau, and introducing legislation to end nepotism and favoritism in government. Although none of these represented major reforms, they seemed promising. The Americans were optimistic.[34]

Before long, however, the shah returned to business as usual, failing even to push the reforms he had so recently introduced. He just did not have the will or interest. Throughout his reign, whenever threats receded he would abandon reform. Uppermost in his mind was the desire for a strong military. Ultimately, he determined, this instrument would decide the fate of his throne, the success of his dynasty. Reformers had not fared well in recent Iranian history. The great landowning families had distanced themselves from any suggestions of land reform or of broader political participation. The shah's father had introduced changes, but they were all designed to produce a more efficient state – better transportation and communication, more schools, settlement of the tribes, weakening of provincial authority – not a more democratic one. The present shah could see little advantage in a program of land reform or in encouraging a more open political process.

The shah complained that American performance, too, had fallen short. Before the year was out he began to negotiate with the Soviet Union on a non-aggression pact. In the face of some opposition, Premier Nikita Khrushchev supported these talks and the Soviets 'gave in on virtually everything.' The shah's motives were difficult to discern. Perhaps he wanted to see how far the Russians would go toward normalizing relations. Certainly he could use the talks as leverage to pry assistance out of the United States. He had developed a skill in turning international developments to advantage. Wailes panicked at the thought that the shah might abandon his pro-Western orientation, and urged Eisenhower to persuade the shah how dangerous could be the Soviet embrace. Wailes informed the shah that he was praying for a breakdown of the talks. His prayers seemed answered when the shah suddenly broke them off and accepted the president's offer of a bilateral defense agreement and reinstitution of budget assistance, discontinued in 1956. The Soviets packed up and went home in high dudgeon. Propaganda commenced at once with personal attacks on the shah by Khrushchev, who had been badly embarrassed in the affair.[35]

Eisenhower put Tehran on his itinerary for his world trip in December 1959. During his short stay in the Iranian capital he discussed military and economic developments, and the shah seemed more realistic, favoring quality of equipment over quantity. Eisenhower came away convinced that the shah had matured considerably in his military thinking since their last meeting. Later, to the president's surprise, the shah reported that Eisenhower had endorsed his plans 'to build up Iran's strategic defenses against the Soviets,' including a greatly expanded air force.[36]

In the waning months of the administration as the concerns of 1958 faded, American officials again became frustrated with the shah's appetite for military hardware. In June 1960 the White House rejected Tehran's latest request for $600 million in military aid.[37]

Perhaps these demands were fueled not by concern for Soviet threats but by the ugly public debate between the shah and Nasser, which reached a crescendo in July, 1960, with the severing of diplomatic relations. At that time the semi-official Egyptian newspaper, *Al-Ahram*, cast the shah as a pariah in the Middle East, adding insultingly that next time he would not be restored to his throne 'with the help of bayonets to take barbarous revenge upon free Iranian patriots.' Iran's recognition of Israel, which Nasser charged had been dictated by the shah's imperial bosses, triggered this torrent of abuse. Beware, the Egyptian leader warned, 'imperial stooges are falling like autumn leaves.'[38]

Not only could the Americans not convince the shah to plan realistically with regard to Iran's military requirements, but neither could they overcome his inertia regarding reform. By the mid-1950s embassy reports were occasionally warning of what might happen without social and economic reform. They spoke of a deteriorating internal situation; the self-delusion of the monarch; his reluctance to antagonize vested interests; SAVAK's role in driving liberal opponents from the regime; and court and royal family involvement in financial operations and corruption. In the aftermath of events in Iraq and Lebanon the reports even suggested that it might be necessary to cut ties with the shah's regime in order that American interests not go down with the dynasty.[39]

Yet when internal conditions deteriorated in late 1959, Iranian and American observers concluded the shah would be able to keep everything under control, not because he had won any more support but because he had shown himself more skillful in playing enemies off against each other. As long as they failed to unite, the shah would survive.[40]

This suited the pundits at the embassy who conjured images of what would happen should a 'Mosadeqist' come to power in the wake of uncontrolled reform. Either the West would become a scapegoat or 'some innocent minority such as the Jews or Bahais. Anti-Western demagogery [sic] with increasing communist influence possibly at its heels. . . . The end result would probably be danger to the lives of Americans and a setback for American interests.' Better to support the *status quo* than to risk destabilizing that strategically important nation.[41]

Such was the pattern of US–Iranian relations during the latter years of the 1950s, a pattern that continued with only minor interruptions to the end of the regime.

13 New Frontier and White Revolution

The one break in the prevailing pattern of US–Iranian relations came in the early months of the Kennedy administration when it appeared for a short time that the whiz kids of the New Frontier might transform ties with the shah.

The New Frontiersmen predicted revolutionary change in the third world, and 'to inoculate conservative regimes' against the threat of violent upheaval they strove to replace US military assistance to developing nations with greater support for reform and orderly development. They rarely understood the complexity of local problems and the limits of American influence, however. In Iran they toyed with political reform, attempting to turn the shah into a constitutional monarch, but when he proved more resistant to manipulation than they expected and crises elsewhere distracted President Kennedy, they turned to economic and social reform. The shah subsequently convinced President Kennedy that he, too, favored reform, that he represented tomorrow rather than yesterday, and the Kennedy administration belatedly endorsed his regime.[1]

If to the casual observer the shah's position in the late 1950s appeared strong, careful observation betrayed weaknesses. Although no Iranian openly challenged the shah or blamed him for inflation, salary freezes, or election rigging, criticism was rising; press attacks on parliament and on the succession of lackluster governments amounted to indirect attacks on the throne. For several years oil revenues had failed to meet the cost of the ambitious seven-year development plan and growing military expenditure. Iran resorted to deficit financing through foreign borrowing. The deficit, made worse by a bad harvest in 1959–60, led to a rapid rise in the cost of living. Depletion of foreign currency reserves forced the shah to ask for emergency assistance from the International Monetary Fund (IMF) and the US government. The IMF insisted on austerity measures, so the Iranian government froze wages and salaries. The strikes that ensued brought confrontations between workers and the army. The election campaign for the twentieth

Majlis in 1960 produced so many charges of corruption that
the shah halted the voting and replaced Prime Minister Manu-
chihr Ighbal with another courtier, Ja'far Sharif Imami.[2]

At one point in the autumn of 1960 the shah, apparently at
a loss as to how to restore calm in Iran, tried liberalizing his
policies. He allowed the National Front, banned since 1957, to
operate openly; one of its leaders, Allahyar Salih, won a parliamentary seat in the rescheduled elections of February 1961
and became an outspoken critic of the new government. The
shah dismissed the ruthless and ambitious chief of SAVAK,
General Bakhtiar. If the purpose of these steps was to bring
about a rapprochement between the shah's regime and the
National Front, they were a failure. The National Front only
called more insistently for free and honest elections and demanded freedom of the press and the dissolution of SAVAK.[3]

This was the unsettled situation in Iran when President John
F. Kennedy entered the White House. Kennedy's views on the
third world had begun to take shape in 1951 during a seven-
week trip through Asia and the Middle East. Visiting Indochina,
he became convinced that the French could not hang on to
that 'remnant of empire.' Talks with Prime Minister Nehru
persuaded him that India's non-aligned policy did not threaten
US interests. Everywhere he saw the need for a vigorous American diplomatic presence.

At home in Massachusetts Senator Kennedy came into contact with a group of economists and political theorists from
Harvard and the Massachusetts Institute of Technology, including John Kenneth Galbraith, Edward S. Mason, and Walt
Rostow. They introduced him to the idea of staged development, which they offered as a remedy for international political instability. Soon Kennedy was accusing the Eisenhower
administration of 'grave errors' in the Middle East, where, he
said, the United States had given its support 'to regimes instead of to people' and had too often tied its future 'to the
fortunes of unpopular and ultimately overthrown governments
and rulers.' Americans mistakenly believed, wrote Kennedy,
that governments that were 'friendly' to the United States and
'hostile' to the communists 'were therefore good governments.'[4]

This critique seemed particularly appropriate for Iran, and
when Kennedy became president the shah was not pleased.
Kennedy's enthusiasm for change in American foreign policy

did not bode well for the Iranian monarch. If the administration really intended to judge each government on the basis of its 'responsiveness to the vital economic, political, and social concerns of its people,' the shah might fall out of favor.[5]

The shah especially worried that the new administration might interrupt US assistance, and he sent a letter to Kennedy defending the *status quo* in his country. Iran, he wrote, was 'the one country that enjoys a democratic regime with all the freedoms except freedom to commit treason and to betray the interests of the Fatherland. We have no need here to strangle public opinion or resort to political incarcerations.' He reminded the president that the people had risen up in a patriotic fervor in 1953 to restore the monarchy. This self-serving letter could not have accomplished much in Washington, except to reveal to Kennedy and his staff the troubled mind of its author.[6]

The shah's fears were realized: Kennedy did indeed delay aid to Iran. The shah sent a representative to Washington to explain the need for assistance; he also pointed out that the arms program for Iran compared unfavorably with those for Iraq and Afghanistan. Kennedy was awaiting a report from his task force on Iran, but to reassure the shah and to get a clearer picture of what was happening in Iran he sent Ambassador W. Averell Harriman, the veteran trouble-shooter of 1944 and 1951, to Tehran.[7]

Many officials in the Kennedy administration did not share the president's enthusiasm for forcing development in the third world. Opposition was strong within the State Department, where conservatives continued to support cold war policies that would strengthen military alliances and advised the president to move cautiously on reform. Secretary of State Dean Rusk, Iran desk officer John Bowling, outgoing ambassador to Iran Edward Wailes, and Ambassador-designate Julius Holmes were among this group. They opposed intervention in Iran's internal affairs, fearing that Iran might become unstable as a result and that instability could create an advantage for the Soviets.[8]

The Eisenhower administration had faced the same dilemma regarding Iran. The shah's opponents would likely overthrow the monarchy unless reforms were instituted soon, officials admitted, yet too much American pressure on the shah would push him toward a neutralist foreign policy. The Suez crisis, the Iraqi revolution, and the shah's flirtations with the Soviets had prevented the Republicans from resolving the dilemma.[9]

The traditionalists in the State Department and the Defense Department did not want the Democrats to resolve this dilemma either, for they were satisfied with the *status quo* in Iran. John Bowling, whose personal influence within the department was extraordinary, admitted that he and his fellow traditionalists intended 'to change or dilute' the president's decision to demand reform 'through delay or bureaucratic misdirection.' With that end in mind they provided the same advice to President Kennedy that they had to Eisenhower. Their influence seemed substantial, and President Kennedy magnified their importance when he ignored channels to telephone them directly, asking questions and requesting written reports. In one such early report to the White House, Bowling pessimistically dismissed one alternative after another for Iran, expressing the fear that the United States might end up having to deal with someone worse than the shah and that the communists might benefit from any change. Rather weakly he concluded that the United States must continue to be on the lookout for 'competent and creative alternate leadership.'[10]

Actually the situation within Iran was open to reform. The Second National Front offered a viable alternative to the shah. It represented a broad alliance of autonomous organizations whose members came from the urban middle class – teachers, engineers, journalists, and university students – and it had some support among bazaar merchants and clerics as well. National Front leaders such as Allahyar Salih, Mihdi Bazargan, Karim Sanjabi, Dariush Furuhar and Khalil Maliki, all of whom had served under Musaddiq a decade earlier, retained support among articulate Iranians. When not in prison or forbidden to speak out, they called for constitutional rule, free elections, freedom of the press, and non-alignment, and they looked to President Kennedy, who had criticized US support for unrepresentative regimes, to press the shah for political reform. The diverse membership of the National Front made concerted action difficult, however, and US policymakers belittled the notion that it could govern effectively.[11]

Department officials also claimed that they did not want to anger the shah by contacting the urban middle-class leaders of the National Front. But in fact, they viewed the urban middle class no more favorably than did the shah. To them it represented a threat to both Iranian and American goals. They assumed its members were radical, dogmatic, and incompetent. This assumption was largely a product of the Musaddiq years, 1951–3, when the department had watched in dismay as the intransigent prime minister and his fractious supporters had provided the conditions for a communist takeover. Now, amidst talk of reform, department officials warned that a Musaddiqist government would contribute to the break-up of the Central Treaty Organization (CENTO), enable communists to infiltrate the Iranian government, and challenge arrangements with the Western oil companies. The shah, they said, possessed the brains and cunning to establish ties with this group and take charge of it; the United States should leave well enough alone.[12]

Many administration officials disagreed with the State Department's conclusions. One of the most persistent of these officials was Assistant Director of the Bureau of the Budget Kenneth Hansen. Hansen came to Washington after several years in Iran as chief of the Harvard Advisory Group, and he had close ties to the Charles River economists. To counter traditionalists at the State Department, he drafted a memorandum to National Security Adviser McGeorge Bundy, stressing that the US aid program seemed uninspired, a tired leftover from the 1950s. The United States had become too closely allied with the shah and his single-minded emphasis on the military, he argued, and the new administration urgently needed an aid program that paid more attention to 'the vital areas of productivity and social and institutional change.'[13]

The New Frontiersmen in the White House were intrigued by Hansen's argument. Bundy's assistant for Middle East affairs, Robert Komer, allowed Hansen to sit in on meetings of the president's task force on Iran, chaired by Assistant Secretary of State Phillips Talbot. The task force included representatives from several agencies. The State Department sent Bowling and Iranian Ambassador-designate Julius Holmes. Komer represented the National Security Council (NSC). From the Agency for International Development (AID) came William Gaud, and from the Defense Department, Peter Solbert. There was also a representative from the Treasury Department, and when the importance of the discussions became known, the CIA and US Information Agency sent representatives as well.[14]

As the spring of 1961 wore on, developments in Tehran outpaced the deliberations of Talbot's task force. In April the National Front, sensing Washington's coolness toward the shah, organized teachers, students, and government workers to demonstrate against rigged elections, economic mismanagement, and corruption. From the safety of the Majlis, Deputy Salih attacked the Sharif Imami government, while outside in Baharistan Square crowds of teachers and students gathered to protest inadequate salaries. The demonstrations gained public sympathy. Then, without warning, police opened fire, killing a teacher. Thousands of Tehranis joined the funeral procession. Sharif Imami resigned. Outgoing US Ambassador Edward Wailes cabled the president that the next day, 6 May, would be critical for the government. 'Should major demonstrations occur and should the security forces refuse to fire in the event of need, the outcome may gravely threaten the shah's regime.'[15]

At this juncture the shah turned to Ali Amini to save the throne. After negotiating the 1954 oil consortium agreement and winning the respect of British and American representatives, the shah had shipped him off in 1955 to be ambassador to the United States. Amini won the admiration of many prominent Washingtonians, including then Senator Kennedy.

Amini took office in May 1961. He received broad powers, and much was expected of him. The leading Tehran daily claimed that Iranians were 'thirsting for reform' and declared that 'the more drastic' Amini became, the greater would be his popularity.[16]

If anyone outside the National Front could restore order, it was Amini; on this everyone in Washington agreed. To modernizers like Hansen, he offered the prospect of reform; to traditionalists, rule by a member of the old guard. Looking back on the situation, John Bowling wrote that everyone 'assumed' that Amini would be able to 'withstand the shah' better than he did.[17]

Influenced by events in Iran, the president's task force argued in its final report that the United States should support the Iranian government more and the shah less. 'Profound political and social change in one form or another is virtually inevitable,' it concluded. Encouraging Amini might be the last best chance for peaceful change.[18]

The report coincided with President Kennedy's preparations to meet Soviet Premier Nikita Khrushchev in Vienna in June. Washington officials expected the Soviet leader to bring up Iran, as in the past, and he did not disappoint them. Khrushchev cited the regime as reactionary and undemocratic and criticized the United States for supporting it. The president parried by saying that 'if the shah did not improve conditions for the people, change would be inevitable.'[19]

Distracted by the crisis that arose that summer in Berlin, the president took no immediate action on the task force report. American officials waited for Kennedy to set policy on Iran, but they were not overly concerned about the delay, because the appointment of the capable Amini as prime minister of Iran encouraged them to believe the situation there was under control.

Meanwhile the Iranian people assumed that Amini would persuade the United States to increase its assistance to Iran. When no assistance materialized, they began to criticize the United States, claiming that in the past American loans had been used to enrich a few officials and to saddle the Iranian people with a large foreign debt. Communist states like Yugoslavia and neutral nations like India and Egypt, they said, had received far more assistance than Iran, which had allied itself with the West. Newspapers criticized American diplomats for snubbing ordinary Iranians and maintaining ties only with a wealthy elite. One editor charged that 'the Americans have in practice done much damage to freedom in our country.' Criticism continued even after the United States announced a $48 million grant to Iran in November 1961.[20]

Undoubtedly, the regime generated some of this criticism to try to persuade the Kennedy administration not to cut military aid or make economic assistance contingent on reform. Being anticommunist was no longer enough to ensure assistance, as it had been in the Eisenhower–Dulles years. Yet criticism was so widespread that much of it has to be considered genuine. Books, journal articles, and editorials presented complaints that articulate Iranians had been repeating since the early 1940s, complaints that US administrations had ignored.[21]

It remained for a group of American scholars to voice the deep concerns of the middle-class opposition in Tehran. At the end of 1961, American experts on Iran, many of whom frequently advised the State Department, including T. Cuyler Young, George Baldwin, Richard Cottam and Manfred Halpern, suggested that the administration did not pay enough attention to political reform in its planning for Iran and that economic reform without political reform would be self-defeating, for 'organized development depends on the achievement of a political consensus.' They did not advocate democracy, only a more broadly based government. The United States had to find a way of 'maneuvering the shah into the role of constitutionally limited monarch.' Aware of the difficulties of tinkering with Iran's political system, they nevertheless suggested using American aid as leverage.[22]

The State Department quickly buried their assessment. It came at an awkward time, only a few days after the 'Thanksgiving Massacre,' when President Kennedy had eased Undersecretary of State Chester Bowles, a close associate of Senator Hubert Humphrey and United Nations Ambassador Adlai Stevenson, into a position as ambassador-at-large. Bowles had struggled to bring new men and ideas into the policy process, but Secretary of State Rusk and the 'Achesonians' had stymied his efforts and the president considered him a visionary. He might have gotten a broader hearing for the concerns of the academics, but by December he was on the outside.[23]

In any case, Bowles had become more interested in economic and social matters than in political reform. In February 1962, while on a tour of trouble spots in the Middle East, he visited Iran and encouraged the shah to promote land reform. He also sought to convince the shah that the United States was unlikely to grant his request for increased military aid, especially sophisticated jets. Ambassador Holmes protested; like his predecessor, he wanted to bring in planes to please the shah. Nevertheless, Bowles thought he had convinced the monarch to accept more economic and less military aid. This pleased President Kennedy, and he prepared a new aid package to present to the shah, who was tentatively scheduled to visit Washington in April. The administration would urge the monarch to decrease his armed forces from 200000 to 150000 and to accept the end of defense support funds to the Iranian budget.

In return Kennedy would offer the shah a five-year package of military assistance.[24]

The shah and Empress Farah arrived as scheduled in April 1962. They were hailed by the press as symbols of a better day in Iran, but a hostile demonstration by Iranian students disturbed the shah. He told a sympathetic Rusk that the United States should arrest the students and ship them back to Iran.[25]

The shah was reluctant to reduce his armed forces. Over the years he had resisted similar suggestions, and he thought he could resist these proposals as well. He pointed to the threat from President Nasser and from the Arab left. But the Kennedy administration remained determined. Reduction of military assistance was an issue on which the White House and State Department were in full agreement. Modernizers thought that a reduction in military aid would mean a smaller, more efficient army and more money for development projects; traditionalists thought a smaller army would encourage the shah to rely more on the landowning, commercial, and religious classes and believed that closer ties with those classes would give him long-term stability.[26]

During this period the Amini government appeared to be making progress. In January 1962 Amini and his minister of agriculture, the outspoken Hasan Arsanjani, a former journalist, newspaper editor, and Musaddiq supporter, introduced a bill for land reform that promised drastic changes in Iranian society. The prime minister and his able colleague intended to press for more change than the shah probably thought wise. But land reform was naturally popular among the peasants, and by endorsing it the shah might gain their support. Although he would lose the backing of landlords, winning the support of the peasants might help compensate for his failure to attract the urban middle class.[27]

The shah withheld the support needed to make land reform work, however, and on 17 July Amini resigned in frustration, placing part of the blame for his defeat on the United States, which, he claimed, had provided too little economic assistance. Within Iran few mourned his passing. The National Front considered him a renegade, the landlords a traitor to his class.[28]

The shah gradually took hold of the situation. By working out an understanding with the Soviet Union, he distracted the opposition, which had been calling for rapprochement with the Soviets for many years. In 1959 the monarch had broken off negotiations with the Soviets and had signed a bilateral defense agreement with the United States. The Soviets had then launched a barrage of anti-shah propaganda from clandestine transmitters across the border. Better relations would put an end to these broadcasts and might also pressure policymakers in Washington to reconsider their plans for Iran. The shah may have believed that Iran could play the United States against the Soviet Union and accept help from both sides as Nehru and Nasser had done so effectively.[29]

Tehran announced the agreement with the Soviets in the fall of 1962. As part of the accord, Iran promised not to allow foreign missile bases on its soil. The nationalists were pleased; as one editor wrote, 'two neighbors that have nearly 1500 kilometers of common border must of necessity remain friends.' The shah had informed the Americans of the negotiations, but few in Washington seemed concerned. At the height of the Cuban missile crisis President Kennedy did instruct the State and Defense departments to prepare for the worst in Iran, but as that crisis faded, fears of an emergency in Iran subsided. Soviet–Iranian relations continued to improve. Anti-shah propaganda ceased, and Soviet economic aid began to flow into Iran.[30]

The shah continued to take the initiative. He introduced what became known as the White Revolution, proposing a six-point reform program for Iran, with land reform as its centerpiece. He allowed Arsanjani to convene a peasants' congress in early January 1963 and put his reform program to the test by submitting it to a national referendum. The royal program received an overwhelming endorsement.[31]

The shah was fully aware that the Kennedy administration would applaud any land reform initiatives. Therefore he was confident that the White Revolution would impress credulous policymakers in Washington even as it strengthened his position at home. Kennedy, who had supported the shah's regime reluctantly, sent him an enthusiastic congratulatory telegram after the referendum. Although there was evidence of rigged returns, the president interpreted the referendum as a stunning success for the shah and concluded that the White Revolution was in keeping with the spirit of the New Frontier.[32]

Within the State Department officials 'shamelessly led JFK

to believe that the shah's White Revolution was the greatest thing since cellophane,' believing, as did the shah, that the president 'would never dare cut support to a regime identified with "land reform".' Traditionalists at the State Department would have been happier if the shah was weaker, or more of a figurehead, but criticizing him might have helped the modernizers bring in a supporter of Musaddiq, or so they feared, and they opted for the lesser evil. US support for the shah's White Revolution was thus the by-product of a bureaucratic compromise between those who would have preferred a middle-class planner to govern Iran and those who preferred the traditional elite.[33]

Although the Americans had served as catalysts for change, the new prime minister, Asadollah Alam, a close friend of the shah who came to power in July 1962, undertook to curtail American influence in his government, dismissing American-trained economists and planners. Other changes followed. Minister of Agriculture Arsanjani, the driving force behind land reform, resigned, claiming lack of cooperation from the cabinet. The real reason behind his resignation was that he had become too popular in the Iranian countryside, outshining the monarch. Alam appointed an ineffective general in his place, and the land reform program slowed. The press did not easily accept Arsanjani's departure. The influential *Kayhan* wondered whether Alam could bring him back. 'It is ironic comment on the workings of our political machinery,' wrote the editor, 'that we have lost an astute, even brilliant, leader precisely at the moment when the nation requires him most.' Alas, the press could say no more for fear of antagonizing the court.[34]

Although the shah did want to reform agriculture, he was not prepared to invest the needed capital, skills, and energy. Reform, so enthusiastically embraced by land-hungry peasants, petered out after Arsanjani's departure. Many of the poorest farmers may have become worse off under the new system. Arsanjani was not blameless; he had rushed to turn over land without providing credit and advice for new landholders. One expert has interpreted his resignation as an admission of failure, arguing that the minister of agriculture knew that there would be problems ahead and decided to leave with his reputation intact.[35]

Washington ignored these early signs of trouble. Following the president's telegram in January, the administration lined up in support of the shah. William Gaud, assistant administrator of AID, explained that the shah's commitment to reform had alienated powerful forces in Iran, especially landowners, and suggested that the United States should support development there with loans because of lost investment from wealthy Iranians. William Brubeck, executive secretary of the NSC, summed up the shah's accomplishments. The shah, he said, had 'launched and pushed with boldness and determination a reform program which is drastically and irrevocably altering the political situation and prospects of Iran.' His unprecedented experiment was aimed at 'building the peasant masses into the fundamental pillar of a radically different and new Iranian society.' Secretary Rusk was equally convinced that the shah was on the right track. Responding to Kennedy's request for a review, he stated that 'support and encouragement of the shah and his reform program is correct. . . . The shah remains a linchpin for the safeguarding of our basic security interest in Iran.'[36]

Kenneth Hansen, who had supported policy change in 1961, pointed to backsliding. He reminded the NSC staff that the task force had urged support for a reform-minded government, with the shah acting as a constitutional monarch, yet the Amini government had succumbed, and now Rusk was suggesting that the United States revert to its role as friendly adviser to a regime that dealt in 'short-term expediency.' The shah had raised hopes in the countryside, but reform was losing steam and administrative problems were emerging. If reform failed the shah might have to rely on the military to keep him in power. Hansen rejected the 'largely passive and fatalistic' views of Ambassador Holmes and the State Department and called for more vigorous American intervention.[37]

McGeorge Bundy agreed. He wrote to the members of the task force in preparation for a decisive meeting on Iran and asked them whether the United States should take a more active role in Iranian reform. He cited Rusk's suggestion that the United States should let things happen at a Persian tempo but declared that he thought 'perhaps the time has arrived when the US should again press harder.'[38]

A majority of the standing group, however, disagreed. On 21 May they concluded that 'the shah has substantially satisfied US pressure for reform by his unilateral program of January 1963.' They recommended that the shah limit his military so as not to eat into money earmarked for economic reform, but they advised against taking any action. The White Revolution had coopted the New Frontier.[39]

Events in Iran soon reached a turning-point. Opposition to the shah had increased. Religious leaders joined landowners and the National Front in speaking out against the government. Not all religious leaders opposed the regime; those aroused, however, were formidable. The ulama, or religious class, often attracted masses of people when they preached. No single development had antagonized the clergy, but actions of the government and the shah had signaled unacceptable trends. Some clerics opposed the decision to reform lands belonging to religious foundations. Many more opposed allowing women to vote and to campaign for office. Ayatollah Ruhollah Khomaini came to national attention. He 'revealed a masterful grasp of mass politics,' hammering on concerns that raised popular indignation: the autocratic methods of the shah; foreign influence (especially American and Israeli) in Iran; widespread corruption; and the muzzling of the press.[40]

Considerable violence ensued. On 23 March 1963 in the holy city of Qum, south of Tehran, government forces attacked the Faiziyih Theological School, killing a cleric and wounding several students. The most active ulama urged their colleagues to use the mourning month of Muharram to encourage antigovernment demonstrations. On the eve of Ashura (3 June), the day Shi'ism commemorates the martyrdom of Imam Husain, preachers castigated the shah, some likening him to the Caliph Yazid who centuries earlier had had Husain put to death. To Shi'ites there is no more meaningful event than the death of Husain, and no more dastardly villain than Yazid. To a vast crowd at Qum, Khomaini delivered an emotional sermon, warning the shah to change his ways before it was too late.[41]

The shah could hardly ignore the agitation. On 4 June he had Khomaini and several clergymen arrested and brought to Tehran. Throughout the country mourning processions turned into antigovernment riots. In Tehran demonstrations continued for five days, supported by ulama, students, teachers, shopkeepers, office employees, wage workers and the unemployed. The shah tried to control the demonstrations with his security forces, which were rotated so that no man would have too much contact with the crowds, but on 5 June he gave the army the order to shoot to kill. Hundreds, perhaps thousands, died before rioting ended three days later.[42]

The National Front had no power to protest against the shah's actions, for he had imprisoned many of its overconfident leaders. Its largely secular membership, surprised by the intensity of popular feeling against the shah and unwilling to give the appearance of opposing reform, had remained aloof from the antigovernment demonstrations. Only a splinter group led by Mihdi Bazargan and some liberal clerics had joined them. If the National Front had cooperated with the ulama, the two groups together might have toppled the regime, but they were divided, and the shah's troops reasserted control.[43]

Like August 1953, June 1963 was a turning point for the shah. He managed to assert control once again, but after this later crisis he moved toward outright dictatorship. Still, he had little trouble deflecting American criticism from his regime. In Tehran the government press blamed the disturbances on 'black reactionaries.' The American press repeated the charge, attributing the demonstrations to reactionaries incensed because the shah's reforms threatened to break their power and impoverish them.[44]

The significance of the Tehran riots of 1963 escaped American officials, to whom the Shi'i mind remained *terra incognita*. President Kennedy summarized the American reaction to the demonstrations when he wrote to the shah:

> I share the regret you must feel over the loss of life connected with the recent unfortunate attempts to block your reform programs. I am confident however that such manifestations will gradually disappear as your people realize the importance of the measures you are taking to establish social justice and equal opportunity for all Iranians.

This assessment of the events of June 1963 was simplistic, to say the least, for the rioters were not all fanatics whipped into a frenzy by reactionary mullas. Many of them were rebelling against an increasingly oppressive regime. Kennedy's assessment, which concluded, in effect, that the shah was good and the opposition evil, contained the seeds of disaster for American policy in Iran.[45]

When the shah called for parliamentary elections, the Kennedy administration applauded, even though there was only a single slate of candidates. The editor of a leading Tehran daily pointed out that such elections did not constitute democratic process. Reporting on the subsequent twenty-first parliament (1963–7), the CIA claimed that most of its deputies were political unknowns; only 18 of them had been members of previous parliaments. According to the agency report, 'Some oddities were elected, a national wrestling champ . . . a movie and TV actor who specialized in country bumpkin parts; he was probably the most authentic peasant in the widely heralded peasants' parliament.' Many of the new members were beholden to the shah, and there was no deputy who had an independent following or was likely to develop one.[46]

For the first time since 1941 there were no obstacles between the shah and autocracy. But with increased power came greater responsibility and a greater burden of accountability, for as the shah humbled all rivals, he left no one to aid him in time of crisis. In earlier years he had called on military men like Generals Ali Razmara and Zahidi or on members of the old aristocracy like Qavam and Amini to act as lightning rods for popular discontent. In the future he would stand alone.

All the talk within the Kennedy administration about changing American policy had yielded little. American goals remained the same: to contain the Soviets and to guarantee oil supplies. There would be no liberalization in Iran, and for lack of planning and royal support economic reforms would prove ephemeral. As the shah brushed aside the old elites, he would depend ever more on the military.[47]

Ironically, John F. Kennedy was the only American president to press seriously, if only briefly, for political reform in Iran, yet it was during his administration that Muhammad Riza Pahlavi swept away all opposition to his regime. The New Frontiersmen contributed to the elimination of the opposition by pressing the shah for change and then accepting his credentials as a reformer, without bothering to investigate the status of the reform program in Iran. Those experts in the State Department who led the president to believe that the shah's opponents offered an unacceptable alternative also contributed to the defeat of the opposition.[48]

14 As the Shah Goes

With the administration of Lyndon B. Johnson, US officials became increasingly reluctant to criticize or challenge the shah's policies. Up to this point in the bilateral relationship, the scales had been tipped in favor of the United States because the shah depended on American economic and military assistance, but as Iran's oil revenues grew and the United States, mired in Vietnam, faced an increasingly hostile world, the balance began to shift in favor of the Iranian monarch.

The shah quickly established a good relationship with Johnson, whom he had met earlier during a vice-presidential visit. Johnson admired the shah's apparent toughness and was greatly pleased by his support of the US mission in Vietnam at a time when Washington had few friends in the third world. Chief adviser Walt Rostow reported directly to Johnson from Tehran that 'the shah made heart-warming remarks re the bravery and discipline of American soldiers in Vietnam, noting that the rest of the world had thought they [were] only interested in "ice cream and television".'[1]

However much he admired some American leaders, the shah could not refrain from criticizing aspects of their society. These criticisms, only hinted at in Rostow's message, grew more forceful and direct over the years. As his power and influence increased, the Iranian monarch lectured his people more about the need to avoid the excesses of the West – social, economic and political. He decried its lack of discipline and rampant materialism, which provided no model for Iran.

US administrations tolerated his undiplomatic observations and his preachiness, in part because they had too much at stake to do otherwise. For example, the shah allowed overflights of American aircraft and the setting up of electronic listening posts along the border with the Soviet Union. By late 1965, however, officials recognized a new independence in the shah. This was rooted in rapidly increasing oil revenues, which meant that he could now do without American aid, and in his apparent success at coopting or silencing all domestic opposition. SAVAK, the secret police organization set up in the late 1950s with American encouragement and assistance, was developing into an effective instrument of control. Americans asked few questions about the shah's internal policies, convincing themselves that Iran needed a tough leader to guarantee stability. Drawing on an imperfect understanding of recent Iranian history they concluded that the shah had 'to let people know who was boss . . . that was the Iranian mentality.'[2]

Although the challenge of the National Front weakened as the 1960s progressed, policymakers still kept an anxious eye on Musaddiq, whom they recognized as the symbol of radical nationalism in Iran. They knew the shah had an almost 'psycopathic fear of the National Front as a political force,' and thus they praised him without stint when he coopted many of Musaddiq's followers with government programs and jobs and cowed those who could not be bought.[3]

After years on the throne more than a touch of megalomania affected the shah's thinking, leading him to conclude that a tragic end awaited anyone who dared cross swords with him. 'Nasser is no more, John and Robert Kennedy died at the hands of assassins, their brother Edward has been disgraced, Khruschev was toppled, the list is endless,' he explained. 'And the same thing goes for my enemies at home; just think of Musaddiq.'[4]

Ambassador Armin Meyer (1965–9), who became a strong supporter of the Iranian regime, counseled Washington that it could no longer dictate policies to the shah, but that it could maintain considerable influence as long as it kept in dialogue with him. What this meant in practical terms soon became apparent. The shah was unhappy with the high cost of US arms and their slow delivery, and he sent officers to Europe to look for better buys. The Soviets offered to sell him SAM missiles. These threats started wheels turning more quickly in Washington, where officials soon offered lower prices and interest rates. Rostow advised Johnson that most of the president's advisers thought the shah foolish to spend so much money on advanced weapons but 'if we cannot dissuade him, no point in losing a good sale.' For good measure, Johnson wrote a soothing letter, expressing how much he wanted to hear directly from the shah 'about the heartening economic and social progress Iran has made under your skillful leadership.'[5]

This uncritical endorsement of the Iranian regime reached its apogee under Presidents Richard Nixon and Gerald R. Ford.

Although the shah got along well with Johnson, nothing could have gladdened him more than Richard Nixon's election in 1968. These two men had become personal friends. They had kept in close contact even after Nixon's defeat for the governorship of California in 1962. They visited each other, exchanged letters, and held lengthy telephone conversations. The shah welcomed the 1969 Nixon Doctrine, which encouraged the expansion of Iranian power in the Persian Gulf 'as the key pillar of support for American interests in an increasingly important part of the world.' This came at a time when Americans were war-weary and disillusioned, and 'marked the triumph of the shah's own long-held view of a proper role for himself over twenty years of State Department reservations.'[6]

In May 1972 Nixon and National Security Adviser Henry Kissinger made a special stopover in Tehran after their Moscow summit meeting with Leonid Brezhnev. Iranian media used the occasion to hail the shah's growing international stature. 'The highest of the world's leaders,' said the state-owned radio, 'come to our capital to pay tribute to our wise and beloved King of Kings.' During this brief visit the president gave the shah a blank check to purchase any conventional American weapons in whatever quantity, without bureaucratic review. Gone was any thought that such purchases might prove unwise or destabilizing. On the heels of this decision the shah indulged in several billion-dollar shopping sprees. To pay for his new arsenal, he took a consistently hard line at meetings of the Organization of Petroleum Exporting Countries (OPEC), helping thereby to quadruple oil prices in 1973–4. He insisted that prices should reflect the true value of that scarce and essential commodity, and he refused to back down even when high-ranking American officials such as Kissinger visited him in Tehran. The secretary of state later advised the president against 'trying to argue with the shah that prices were raised too far and too much, inasmuch as he is utterly convinced of the correctness of what was done and easily takes umbrage at suggestions to the contrary.'[7]

The shah must have been saddened to see his old friend Nixon hounded from office, especially for offenses which counted little in the monarch's opinion. 'He had little time for American ideals and ideas. He often mocked the American way of life and ridiculed the system of government by consent

that gave every Johnny-come-lately on Capitol Hill the power
"to hold even the president to ransom, in the name of the
people".' But he could rest assured that President Ford, with
Secretary of State Kissinger at his side, would carry on the
policies of his predecessor. Ford even continued the one-on-
one meetings that the shah had initiated with Nixon. When
his old and close friend, Nelson Rockefeller, became vice president, the shah could hardly have imagined a more favorable
turn of events.[8]

Preparations for a royal visit in May 1975 indicated just how
little American policy had changed. The secretary of state
shared with Ford his admiration for the shah, telling the president that Muhammad Riza Pahlavi had every reason to be
'confident and pleased with the dynamism of his foreign policy,
his domestic position, his growing military power and the sig-
nificant increase in his own prestige in the world.' The only
doubt expressed in the Kissinger memorandum was whether
they could convince the shah that the United States was still an
ally worth having. The shah questioned the reliability of American commitments overseas, in light of recent events in Cambo-
dia, Vietnam and Cyprus, and the weakness the administration
showed in its relations with Israel and with the American
Congress. He might well wonder whether the United States
would move toward isolationism and what that would mean
for Iran. According to Kissinger 'he will relate what we can do
for him to what he assesses as our stamina and capacity for
leadership in the world arena.' The Americans depended on
the shah not only to maintain security in the Persian Gulf
region but also to provide investment opportunities for US
firms at a time when the US economy was in deep trouble.
Good relations seemed more essential than ever before.[9]

Testimony of American ambassadors to Iran in the 1970s
also indicates how much their relationships with the shah had
altered since the days of John Wiley, who thought he could
instruct the monarch how to do good. The shah had once
sought the company of US representatives; now he kept his
distance. Douglas MacArthur III (1969–73) stood rather in
awe of the shah. One scholar claimed that MacArthur seemed
to him almost obsequious toward the shah, never registering
any dissent from what he had to say. 'We didn't control the
shah,' admitted the ambassador, 'he made it quite clear to

everybody that if he couldn't get [what he wanted] from us, he would turn to them [Europeans].' Richard Helms (1973–7), former director of the CIA, testily reported that 'on the question of human rights, the shah held the conviction that he was running his country and that if there was any rough stuff it was necessary and that was the end of that.'[10]

From a supercilious response to President Ford's reassurances early in 1976, one senses the shah's own awareness of just how much his relationship with the United States had been transformed. 'I greatly appreciate the deep and sympathetic interest with which you look upon the special relationship between the USA and Iran,' wrote the shah. Then he added, 'In view of your profound understanding of what is at stake, I do not expect your attitude to be otherwise.'[11]

The Nixon and Ford administrations had let the shah have his way. They staked American interests in the region on his continuing success and paid scant attention at the highest levels to any other domestic forces in Iran. 'As the shah goes, so goes Iran' became a principle of US policy. During the early 1970s there were some rumblings in the lower ranks of the State Department. The files contained occasional reports from Tehran warning of a recent alliance between religious leaders and the middle-class opposition. But none of this made an impression at the White House, where the same official response was repeated over and over: 'It's not our country; the shah is in control; we don't know enough about what could happen if he lost control – the communists might take over.'[12]

Behind this rationalizing lay fears of a return to the disorder associated with Musaddiq. In the hazy memories of American officials, the former prime minister had become the archetype of the communist puppet, who 'resorted to repressive, strong-arm tactics to silence his critics . . . and sought to prop up his position by dismissing parliament. When the shah tried to remove him . . . he called crowds into the streets to demonstrate in his favor and he deposed the shah.' Even Secretary of State Kissinger, who ought to have known better, repeated these distortions. Ambassador MacArthur admitted that we knew 'Musaddiq was being manipulated by the Soviet Union.'[13]

NSC Middle East specialist Gary Sick would no doubt agree with these sentiments. Referring to his work during the Carter years, Sick has emphasized how little American policymakers remembered of events associated with the overthrow of Muhammad Musaddiq. 'In Washington by 1978,' he wrote, 'the events of 1953 had all the relevance of a pressed flower.' Yet to Iranians, he maintains, 'the memory (or mythology) of 1953 was as fresh as if it had happened only the week before.' Neatly skirting the rights and wrongs of the coup, he quickly proceeds to more recent developments, leaving the impression of Iranians as political dreamers with a tenuous hold on reality. And yet one might reasonably write of an American 'mythology' that surrounded the events of Musaddiq's government and have remained part of official understanding. Sick, himself, subscribes to this mythology when he observes that Musaddiq 'felt secure enough to dismiss the Majles altogether,' which of course he had no intention of doing. American policymakers might not remember much about Musaddiq, less and less as the years passed, but what they (or their advisers) did remember was full of similar inaccuracies. Such distortion led every president from Eisenhower through Carter to conclude they could only trust the shah.[14]

Ironically the shah's success in influencing Washington worked against him. His insistence that American diplomats not contact opposition leaders, for example, left them relatively uninformed and unable to give the State Department a balanced picture of what was happening inside the country. This situation denied the shah the kind of sensible and spirited advice he might otherwise have received from his ally. As one diplomat sagely observed, the US position *vis-à-vis* the shah came to reflect his confidence or lack of confidence so one could almost identify US policy toward Iran with the moods of the shah. At the end of the 1970s when the shah's health deteriorated and he became deeply depressed, US policymakers could not decide what to do. Their uncritical acceptance of the shah's regime had isolated them from the changing political realities of Iran, and with the coming of the revolution this isolation spelled disaster for American policy.[15]

Through all these developments the Americans remained loyal to the shah. They supported his regime with economic and military aid during the vulnerable years of the 1950s, when profits from oil were small and opponents dared speak out. They had doubts, especially during the Kennedy years, but the shah's apparent move toward reform silenced critics. Each successive administration appeared trapped in the policy Eisenhower and Dulles had devised. Officials could see no alternative; any successor, they concluded, would face the same problems. They foresaw no grassroots revolt against the monarch, and as for the politically conscious, educated Iranians, they were opportunists, who were easily controlled from above. The only source of effective action would be the military, hence they applauded the shah's determination to satisfy his officers. These were the comforting conclusions American policymakers arrived at again and again. They could not break the thinking that bound the United States and the shah. Policy centered on the shah; they would rise or fall together.[16]

This was a legacy of the Musaddiq years, which had confirmed American officials in the belief that nationalists could not be trusted. As late as August 1978 the Tehran embassy could caution Washington that 'those familiar with the Mossadeq period (1949–53) see no evidence that many of the opposition leaders have changed their own authoritarian coloration despite their rhetoric today about constitutional principles.'[17]

Admittedly, successors to Musaddiq and the National Front did little to encourage confidence at home or abroad. They argued endlessly among themselves. Their best opportunity came in the early 1960s, but they never offered effective opposition to the oppression of the regime.

Only with the shah's regime visibly crumbling in late 1978, did Washington reluctantly turn to the aging survivors of Musaddiq's long-departed government, Karim Sanjabi, Mihdi Bazargan, Gholam Husain Sadiqi, Shahpour Bakhtiar, Dariush Furuhar, to save the situation. Even then, Ambassador William Sullivan insisted that the National Front would have to retain the shah 'as both king and commander-in-chief.' That was the 'reality' of the situation as he saw it. By then, of course, it was too late. Religious leaders had taken the vanguard against the shah, and they had very different solutions for Iran's ills.[18]

At first the new rulers of Iran embraced the memory of Musaddiq. 'Oppositionists from across the political spectrum – Marxists, leftists, liberals and rightists, both secular and religious – invoked his name and example, cherished his picture, and found appropriate quotations from him to support their views.' They considered themselves at one with Musaddiq because of a shared desire to lessen foreign control and increase

Iran's independence. On 5 March 1979, the twelfth anniversary of Musaddiq's death, thousands of mourners made the pilgrimage to Ahmadabad to hear Ayatollah Mahmud Taliqani, one of the most respected ulama, deliver an oration in his honor. Such ceremonies were repeated across the country. In Tabriz, capital of Azarbaijan province, where Ayatollah Khomaini faced considerable opposition, one speaker rose to his defense by likening him to Musaddiq who was 'a champion of the disinherited against the imperialist aggressors.'[19]

The takeover of the American embassy in November 1979 could be linked to the legacy of Musaddiq. President Carter's decision to allow the ailing shah to enter the United States for medical treatment looked ominous viewed from Tehran. Perhaps this signaled a conspiracy between the Great Satan and the Pahlavis to restore the dynasty as they had done in August 1953. This time the Iranians would take no chances. Only days after the shah's arrival in New York City, students seized the US embassy and its 66 American occupants, demanding the return of the shah and his plundered wealth. The memorable hostage crisis followed.

By early 1981, however, as divisions within the revolutionary movement became more apparent, the regime began to distance itself from the late prime minister, as it rejected the concept of a secular, democratic state that he symbolized. They had no wish to breathe new life into the middle-class supporters of Musaddiq. On the anniversary of the popular uprising of 21 July 1952 that had restored Musaddiq to power, they chose to praise the role of one of their own in that event, Ayatollah Abulqasim Kashani. As the political crisis between President Abul-Hasan Bani Sadr and the Islamic Republican Party deepened, officials became more hostile, allowing accounts to be published that discredited the former prime minister, charging him with responsibility for the failure of the nationalist movement and with being a British stooge. The more Mihdi Bazargan and his successor, Bani Sadr, drew on his memory to bolster their demands for open politics and a lessened role in government for the ulama, the more the latter felt obliged to erase from Iranian minds any favorable image of Musaddiq. After a brief rehabilitation, Musaddiq had again become *persona non grata*, but this regime had been no more successful than its predecessor in sullying his memory.[20]

Despite all the recent drama in US–Iranian relations, and the vilification of Musaddiq's memory in Iran, one looks in vain for any indication that American officials have reviewed the events of the early 1950s, to wonder whether they or their predecessors might have made mistakes with Musaddiq, that they judged him too harshly, that they might have given him more support. On the contrary some officials, including Richard Helms, former CIA director and US ambassador to Iran, have derived a certain satisfaction from the turn of events in Tehran. In a 1985 interview Helms ridiculed American scholars who had supported the National Front as the salvation of Iran. 'Well, sure enough they got their wish and it lasted just a matter of weeks,' he observed. 'When it was all over they were just as wrong as everybody else.'[21]

But this failure to reevaluate should not surprise us. Even now, rather than reassessing relations with Tehran, Washington waits for the Iranians to come around. Thinking in the State Department and the White House apparently has changed little. The rest of the industrialized world has made its peace with the Islamic Republic, while the United States remains aloof. We might well ask: what kind of diplomacy is this? Does it befit the leader of world order?

Appendices

APPENDIX A

Nationalization Act of 15 March 1951

In the name of the prosperity of the Iranian nation and with a view to helping secure world peace, we, the undersigned, propose that the oil industry of Iran be declared as nationalized throughout all regions of the country without exception, that is to say, all operations for exploration, extraction and exploitation shall be in the hands of the government.

APPENDIX B

Nine-point Bill of 28 April 1951

1. With a view to arranging the implementation of the law of 15 and 20 March 1951, concerning the nationalization of the oil industry throughout Iran, a joint committee composed of five senators and five deputies elected by each of the two houses and of the minister of finance or his deputy shall be formed.

2. The government is required to dispossess at once the former Anglo-Iranian Oil Company under the surpervision of the joint committee. If the company refuses to hand over at once on the grounds of existing claims on the government, the government may, by mutual agreement, deposit in the National Bank of Iran or in any other bank up to 25 per cent of current revenue from the oil after deduction of exploitation expenses in order to meet the probable claims of the company.

3. The government is required to examine the rightful claims of the government as well as the rightful claims of the company under the supervision of the joint committee and to submit its proposals to the two houses of parliament in order that they may be implemented after approval by the two houses.

4. Inasmuch as from 20 March 1951, when the Senate also approved the nationalization of the oil industry, all revenues from oil and oil products are the unquestioned right of the Iranian nation, the government is required to audit the company's accounts under the supervision of the joint committee. The joint committee must also supervise closely matters relating to the exploitation as from the date of the implementation of this law until the appointment of a board of management.

5. The joint committee must draw up as soon as possible and submit to the two houses for their approval the statutes of the National Iranian Oil

Company, in which provision is to be made for a board of management and a board of supervision composed of experts.

6. For the gradual replacement of foreign experts by Iranian experts the joint committee is required to draw up regulations for the sending of a number of students to foreign countries annually on a competitive basis to engage in the various branches of study and practical experience connected with the oil industry, the said regulations to be implemented by the ministry of education after approval by the cabinet. The expenses connected with the studies of these students shall be met out of the oil revenues.

7. All purchasers of the products of the oil deposits recovered from the former Anglo-Iranian Oil Company may purchase hereafter annually at the current international price the same quantity of oil that they purchased annually from the beginning of 1948 up to 20 March 1951. For any surplus quantity they shall have priority in the event of equal terms of purchase being offered.

8. All proposals formulated by the joint oil committee and submitted to the Majlis for its approval must be referred to the special oil committee.

9. The joint committee must complete its work within three months from the date of the ratification of this law, and must submit a report on its activities to the Majlis in accordance with article 8. Should an extension of the period be required, it must submit an application for extension, giving valid reasons. Until the extension of time is for any reason disapproved by the two houses, the joint committee may continue its activities.

Notes

Preface

1. Robert Jervis, *Perception and Misperception in International Politics* (Princeton, 1976); Deborah Welch Larson, *Origins of Containment: A Psychological Explanation* (Princeton, 1985); William O. Walker III, 'Decision-making Theory and Narcotic Foreign Policy: Implications for Historical Analysis,' *Diplomatic History* 15 (Winter 1991); Richard Cottam, 'Nationalism in Twentieth-Century Iran and Dr. Muhammad Musaddiq.' in *Musaddiq, Iranian Nationalism and Oil,* eds James A. Bill and William Roger Louis (Austin, 1988), 36.

1 The American Experience

1. Franklin Walker, *Irreverent Pilgrims: Melville, Browne and Mark Twain in the Holy Land* (Seattle, 1974), 223, 42, 83. Mark Twain, *Notebook* (New York, 1935), 93, 97; *Innocents Abroad* (Boston, 1895), 2: 559, 407.
2. See Emily S. Rosenberg, *Spreading the American Dream: American Economic and Cultural Expansion, 1890–1945* (New York, 1982), 59–62.
3. M.E. Yapp, *The Making of the Modern Near East, 1792–1923*, A History of the Near East (New York, 1987), 196–7, 202.
4. James Goode, 'A Good Start: The First American Mission to Iran, 1883–1885,' *The Muslim World,* 74 (1984): 100–18.
5. James Henry Breasted, 'The University of Chicago Expedition to the Near East, 1919–1920,' *The University Record,* 7 (1922): 6, 7, 14, 18; T. Callander to Kelsey, 14 March 1924, Box 1, Francis W. Kelsey Papers, Bennett Library, University of Michigan, Ann Arbor. This referred to President Theodore Roosevelt (1901–9) and British foreign secretary Lord Curzon (1919–24), both of whom had reputations for wielding the 'big stick.'
6. Goode, 'A Good Start,' 116–17.
7. Edward Said, *Orientalism* (New York, 1978), 156–7.
8. Arthur Millspaugh, *Americans in Persia* (Washington, D.C., 1946); Berry to Robert Douglas Cole, 11 April, 8 May 1935, Box 1: Correspondence, Burton Y. Berry Papers, Lilly Library, Indiana University, Bloomington.
9. Homa Katouzian, *The Political Economy of Modern Iran, 1926–1979* (New York, 1981), 85–91; Farhad Diba, *Mohammed Mossadegh: A Political Biography* (London, 1986), 41.
10. Mohammad Musaddiq, *Musaddiq's Memoirs,* ed. Homa Katouzian (London, 1988), 236.
11. Diba, *Mossadegh,* 57–8.
12. *Musaddiq's Memoirs,* 11–12, 108.
13. Ibid., 174, 196, 212–13, 217–18, 220, 225. Diba, *Mossadegh,* 14–28.
14. *Musaddiq's Memoirs,* 12.

15. Author's translation from copy.
16. Ervand Abrahamian, *Iran Between Two Revolutions* (Princeton, 1982), 189, 204–5.
17. *Musaddiq's Memoirs*, 221–2.
18. Abrahamian, *Iran Between Two Revolutions*, 189.
19. Ibid., 211, 216.
20. James Goode, *The United States and Iran, 1946–51: The Diplomacy of Neglect* (London, 1989), 114, 138.
21. *Tulu'* (Bushihr) [The Sunrise] 18 September 1950. *Khavar* (Tehran) [The East] 10 February 1948.
22. Rood to Grady, 12 February 1951, 321.1 Neutrality, Tehran Post Files (TPF), Record Group 84, National Archives, College Park, MD.
23. Jernegan to Hare, 21 September 1948, 711.911, RG 59, NA, College Park, MD.
24. Husain Kayustuvan, *Siyasat-i Muvazinih-ye Manfi dar Majlis-i Chahardahom* [The Policy of Negative Equilibrium in the Fourteenth Majlis] (Tehran, 1951), 233.
25. Abrahamian, *Iran Between Two Revolutions*, 262.
26. Wiley to H. Freeman Matthews, 8 March 1951, Box 1, John Wiley Papers, Franklin Delano Roosevelt Library, Hyde Park, NY.
27. Grady to SS, 25 September 1950, 788.00, RG 59, NA.
28. General Robert W. Grow diary, 1 April 1947; Grady to SS, 15 January 1951, 788.00, RG 59, NA.
29. Wagner to SS, 25 September 1950, 788.00, RG 59, NA.
30. *Khavar*, 23 December 1947. Report of conditions in Iran [May 1950], Box 1, Wiley papers, FDR Library. Grady to Secretary of State (SS), 24 July 1950, 321 Middle East Command 1950/51/52, TPF, RG 84, NA. Somerville to SS, 24 February 1949, 891.011, RG 59, NA.
31. Martin F. Herz, ed., *Contacts with the Opposition: A Symposium* (Lanham, MD, 1986), 17–18, 26–27.
32. Joseph Wagner to SS, 25 September 1950, RG 59; 'The Current Crisis in Iran,' 16 March 1951, Intelligence File, CIA, President's Secretary's File, Papers of Harry S. Truman, Harry S. Truman Library (HSTL), Independence, MO.; Undersecretary's Meeting, N-336, 25 April 1951, RG 59, NA.
33. Herz, *Contacts with the Opposition*, 4.

2 Background to Crisis

1. Sattareh Farman Farmaian, *Daughter of Persia* (New York, 1992), 84.
2. J.H. Bamberg, *The History of the British Petroleum Company. The Anglo-Iranian Years, 1928–1954* (Cambridge, 1994), 328.
3. Goode, *Diplomacy of Neglect*, 59, 68; Razmara to Grady, 7 July 1950, 788.00, RG 59; *Diplomacy of Neglect*, 84–102.
4. Wolfgang Lentz, *Iran, 1951/52* (Heidelberg, 1952), 30. Grady to SS, 29 April 1951, box 32, RG 84, NA. The shah understood that power equalled responsibility and if Musaddiq should falter, his popular support would wither and he would have to resign. In fact, Court Chamberlain Hormuz Pirnia had assured Ambassador Grady that at

age 71 Musaddiq was too old to run for a seat in the Majlis and thus once out of office his career would be over. Grady to SS, 7 May 1951, 350 Iran-Internal Affairs, RG 84, NA.

5. *Bakhtar-i Imruz*, 10 May 1951.
6. 17 July 1951, box 3508, 741.00, RG 59.
7. Kenneth Younger diary (KYD), 25 February 1951, Open University.
8. Sir Robert Scott, oral history transcript, London School of Economics, 1; Bernard Donoughue and G.W. Jones, *Herbert Morrison: Portrait of a Politician* (London, 1973), 513. To add to his worries, Morrison learned in April that his wife had cancer. KYD, 28 March 1951; *Herbert Morrison*, 510–12; 24 May 1951, box 3508, 741.00, RG 59.
9. D.A. Logan, 21 May 1951, Foreign Office (FO) 371, 91459/EP1015/204, Public Record Office (PRO), Kew; Habib Ladjevardi, *Labor Unions and Autocracy in Iran* (Syracuse, 1985), 120–1; 14 March 1949, Diary, Papers of Robert Garner, HSTL.
10. *Spectator*, 25 May 1951.
11. Goode, *Diplomacy of Neglect*, 46.
12. KYD, 28 August 1951; 23 May 1951, FO 371, 91537/EP1531/426, PRO; US House Committee on Foreign Affairs, *Selected Executive Session Hearings of the Committee, 1951–1956: The Middle East, Africa and Inter-American Affairs* (Washington, 1980), 16: 27–31, 41–3; 28 June 1951, Research and Analysis Report 5563, RG 59.
13. US Senate. Armed Services Committee. *Military Situation in the Far East.* Part 2 (Washington, 1951), 1005, 1822–6; 12 March 1952, Senator Brewster to Burton Y. Berry, 350: Alpha by Countries, box 28, RG 84, NA; US Congress, Senate, *Congressional Record*, 82nd Cong., 1st sess., 10: pt. 8, 10564–5, pt. 10, 12978.
14. Arthur Krock, *Memoirs: Sixty Years on the Firing Line* (New York, 1968), 262; Henry Villard, oral history transcript, HSTL.
15. *Parliamentary Debates*, Commons, 5th series (1909–) 489: 763, 776, 796.
16. 29 March 1951, FO 371, 91184/E102; 30 June 1951, FO 371, 91562/EP1531/980.
17. Grady to SS, 13 May 1951, 888.2553, RG 59; 3 May 1951, FO 371, 91530/EP1531/264.
18. Grady to Basil Jackson, 24 April 1953, Grady papers, HSTL; 14 August 1951, Diary, Iran special correspondence, Box 293, Harriman papers, Library of Congress (LC); 7 June 1951, FO 371, 91545/EP1531/602.
19. 12 May 1951, FO 248, 1528/1531; 12 May 1951, FO 371, 91533; 14 May 1951, FO 371, 91534/EP1531/321.
20. 15 May 1954, Princeton Seminars, Acheson papers, HSTL; Gulf Oil on situation in Kuwait, 10 April 1951, 788.00, RG 59.
21. 25 June 1951, Thomas I. Woolard to Chairman, Iranian National Oil Board, 11 July 1951, B.M. Lee to President Truman, Official File, Harry S. Truman papers, HSTL.
22. 29 May 1951, FW661.88, Policy Planning Staff, RG 59.
23. 20 June 1951, Annex to NSC 107/1, RG 273 (Records of the National Security Council), NA; 21 June 1951, 888.2553, RG 59; 1 May 1951, FO 371, 91531/EP1531/284; 11 May 1951, FO 371, 91535/EP1531/365; 12 May 1951, FO 248, 1528/1531.

24. *Cahier de l'orient contemporain* (Paris), 18–19 May 1951.

25. *Ittila'at* (Tehran), 20 May 1951; *Shahid* (Tehran), 21 May 1951.

26. 25 May 1951, FO 371, 91551/EP1531/410; 20 June 1951, Annex to NSC 107/1, RG 273; 26 May 1951, FO 371, 91537/EP1531/420.

27. L.P. Elwell-Sutton, *Persian Oil: A Study in Power Politics* (1955; reprint ed., Westport, CT, 1975), 228.

28. Truman to Attlee, 30 May 1951, President's Secretary's File (PSF): NSC, HSTL; 5 June 1951, FO 371, 1541/EP1531/516; Attlee to Truman, 5 June 1951, PSF: Subject file/Foreign Affairs, HSTL.

29. Despite Foreign Office reluctance, Herbert Gass, author of the supplementary oil agreement and a favorite of Fraser, went along as well.

30. 18 June 1951, Cabinet Minutes, CAB/130/67, GEN 363/7th, PRO.

31. 1 June 1951, Foreign Broadcast Information Service (FBIS); 6 June 1951, FO 371, 91541/EP1531/526; 6 June 1951, 320 Iran and Other Countries, RG 84, NA. To the delight of the Foreign Office, the State Department reprimanded Grady for his outspokenness. 12 June 1951, FO 371, 91541/EP1531/629.

32. 13 June 1951, FO 371, 91547/EP1531/655; Alan W. Ford, *The Anglo-Iranian Oil Dispute, 1951–52* (Berkeley and Los Angeles, 1954), 65; Levy to SS, 14 September 1951, 788.00, RG 59.

33. 21 June 1951, State Department Briefs: Daily Briefs, Naval Aide Files, Papers of Harry S. Truman, HSTL.

34. Mehdi Sami'i, oral interview, London, March 1983. One of Sami'i's fellow delegates was Mihdi Bazargan, a youthful engineer at the time, and later president of the Islamic Republic.

35. Muhammad Ali Murtazavi, *Yak mah mamuriyyat-i tarikhi dar Khuzistan barayi ijrayi qanun-i milli shudan-i san'at-i naft* [One Month's History-making Assignment in Khuzistan to Implement Nationalization of the Oil Industry]. (Tehran, n.d.) 21, 23, 53. Bamberg, *The Anglo-Iranian Years*, 428.

36. Sami'i, oral interview.

37. The Shatt al-Arab begins at the confluence of the Tigris and Euphrates rivers. 1 May 1951, FO 371, 457/EP1015/169/34.

38. Minutes of meeting, 16 May 1951, DEFE4/42, COS(51)81.

39. Minutes of meetings, 21, 23 May 1951, DEFE/4/42, COS(51)84, 86; 2 July 1951, Hugh Dalton Diary, London School of Economics; 11 May 1951, *Foreign Relations of the United States, 1951* (*FRUS*), 5: 679, 699; *Parliamentary Debates*, 20 May 1951, 489: 524.

40. 17 May 1951, NSC minutes, 788.a, box 4107 RG 59.

41. 29 June 1951, FO 371, 91553/EP1531/802; 29 June 1951, Cabinet Minutes, CAB130/67, GEN363/12th; Fakhreddin Azimi, *Iran: The Crisis of Democracy, 1941–53* (New York, 1989), 264–70.

42. 29 June 1951, FO 371, 91559/EP1531/914; 25 June 1951, FO 371, 91551/EP1531/736; 26 June 1951, FO 248, 1527/G15301/848/51; *FRUS, 1952–1954* (Washington, 1989), 10: 67; Acheson to Senator Robert Kerr, 29 June 1951, Memoranda of Conversations, box 66, Acheson papers, HSTL.

3 Peacemaker

1. 1 July 1951, Grady to SS, Confidential file, 1950–2, RG 84, NA.
2. 7 July 1951, memorandum of conversation, Acheson papers, HSTL.
3. 7 July 1951, FO 371, 91559/EP1531/913; 11 July 1951, FO 371, 91486/EP1112/43.
4. 14 July 1951, FO 371, 91562/EP1531/987.
5. 9 July 1951, FO 371, 91450/EP1013/29; FO 248, 1528/G15301/1221A/51.
6. 12 July 1951, FO 371, 91564/EP1531/1049.
7. 19 July 1951, folder 6, and unpublished mss., box 5, Grady papers, HSTL; Vernon Walters, *Silent Missions* (New York, 1978), 246.
8. 17, 19 July 1951, Subject file, Iran-Harriman, PSF, HSTL; 16 July 1951, box 5505A, RG 59; 19 July 1951, Iran Special Correspondence, box 293, Harriman papers, LC.
9. 24 July 1951, Subject file, Iran-Harriman, PSF; 9 August 1951, Harriman to Eisenhower, Iran Special Correspondence, box 293, Harriman papers, LC.
10. 24 July 1951, Subject file, Iran-Harriman, PSF.
11. Ibid.
12. 25, 27 July 1951, Subject file, Iran-Harriman, PSF.
13. 27 July 1951, CAB130/67, GEN363/16th.
14. 30 July 1951, Subject file, Iran-Harriman, PSF.
15. Elwell-Sutton, *Persian Oil: A Study in Power Politics* (London, 1955), 251; 25 August 1951, 888.2553, RG 59.
16. *Parliamentary Debates*, 491: 30 July 1951; 29 July 1951, FO 371, 91573/EP1531/1236; 7 August 1951, FO 371, 91573/EP1531/1259.
17. 31 July 1951, Iran Special Correspondence, box 293, Harriman papers, LC. *Some Documents on the Nationalization of the Oil Industry in Iran* (Washington: Iranian Embassy, 1951), 37.
18. 13 August 1951, Subject file, Iran-Harriman, PSF.
19. Bamberg, *The Anglo-Iranian Years*, 444, 449.
20. 14 August 1951, Subject file, Iran-Harriman, PSF.
21. 19 August 1951, Subject file, Iran-Harriman, PSF. *Some Documents on the Nationalization*, 40–2, 46.
22. 22 August 1951, Treasury T236/2828; 23 August 1951, Subject file, Iran-Harriman, PSF.
23. 22, 23 August 1951, Subject file, Iran-Harriman, PSF; 23 August 1951, FO 371, 91580/EP1531/1398; 24 August 1951, CAB130/67, GEN363/20th.
24. 23 August 1951, FO 371, 91580/EP1531/1409.
25. Walters, *Silent Missions*, 258–9; 31 August 1951, State Department correspondence, folder 28, White House Central Files, HSTL.
26. 28 August 1951, Attlee papers, box 124, Bodleian Library, Oxford; 1 September 1951, FO 371, 91586/EP1531/1500.
27. 28 August 1951, box 124, Attlee papers; 30 August 1951, 6 September 1951, FO 371, 91621.
28. 31 August 1951, Notes on cabinet meetings, Post-presidential file, HSTL.
29. 30 August 1951, FO 248, 1528/G15301/1381/51; 6 September 1951, FO 371, 91586/EP1531/1511.

4   Changing the Guard

1.   September 1951, FO 248, 1515.
2.   FO 371, 91614/EP1531/2226; 28 August 1951, Subject file: Iran-Harriman, PSF, HSTL; 12 December 1951, Herbert Morrison file, box 22, Stokes papers, Bodleian Library, Oxford.
3.   4 September 1951, FO 371, 91462/EP1015/302, 7; 11 September 1951, FO 371, 91463/EP1015/307, 309.
4.   22 September 1951, FO 248, 1529/G15301/1542/51; 27 August 1951, FO 248, 1515/G10103/91/51.
5.   18, 19 September 1951, FO 371, 91463/EP1015/333, 326; 7 September 1951, 788.00, RG 59.
6.   20 September 1951, FO 371, 91589/EP1531/1588; 18 September 1951, FO 371, 91589/EP1531/1594; 22 September 1951, box 22, Stokes papers.
7.   21 September 1951, FO 371, 91591/EP1531/1633; 22 September 1951, FO 371, 91595/EP1531/1736.
8.   12 December 1951, Herbert Morrison file, box 22, Stokes papers.
9.   30 August 1951, box 31, Stokes papers; Clement Attlee, *Twilight of Empire* (London, 1960), 250.
10. 16 July 1951, FO 371, 91493/EP11345/15; 12 September 1951, FO 371, 91493/EP11345/122; 3 October 1951, Harriman to Gross, Iran Special Correspondence, box 293, Harriman papers, LC; 11 September 1951, Confidential file, box 36, TPF, RG 84; 11 September 1951, FO 371, 91472/EP1024/1; Iran: International agreements, 1950–1, Box 237-B, RG 166 (Dept. of Agriculture), NA.
11. Unpublished Mss., 42–8, box 5, Grady papers, HSTL; 27 August 1951, 888.10, RG 59.
12. 11 September 1951, 501: Iran, TPF, RG 84; 16 July 1951, folder 10, Grady papers; 'What Went Wrong in Iran,' *Saturday Evening Post*, 224 (1952): 58. 19 January 1954, FO 371, 109998/EP1051/4.
13. For a book-length study of Henderson, see H.W. Brands, *Inside the Cold War: Loy Henderson and the Rise of the American Empire, 1918–1961* (New York, 1991).
14. 27 June 1951, FO 371, 91555; 9 July 1951, FO 371, 91563/EP1531/1022.
15. 16, 18, July 1951, CAB130/67, 363/9, 14.
16. 5 June 1951, FO 371, 91460/EP1015/234; 29 June 1951, FO 371, 91461/EP1015/264; 3 July 1951, FO 371, 91462/EP1015/280.
17. 5 September 1951, FO 371, 91587/EP1531/1532; 27 September 1951, Dalton diary, LSE; 27 September 1951, FO 371, 91591/EP1531/1662.
18. 2 October 1951, Middleton to Shepherd, FO 248, 1529/G15301/1727/51; 27 September 1951, FO 371, 91591/EP1531/1647; 28 September 1951, Naval Aide files, box 23, HST papers, HSTL.
19. 21 May 1951, FO 371, 91436/EP1531/373; 27 September 1951, CAB128, CM(51)60.
20. 28 September 1951, FO 371, 91592/EP1531/1656, 1663.
21. 28 September 1951, FO 371, 91591/EP1531/1629; 30 September 1951, FO371, 91592/EP1531/1665, 1666; 1, 5 October 1951, FO 371, 91598/EP1531/1815, 1817.

22. 26 September 1951, Minutes of Undersecretary's meeting-399, RG 59; 6 October 1951, FO 371, 91596/41612.
23. KYD, 3 October 1951.
24. *Foreign Relations of the United States*, 1951 (Washington, 1981) 3, pt. 1: 1180–4.
25. David Butler, *British General Election of 1951* (London, 1952), 100; *Daily Telegraph*, 4, 6, 10 October 1951.
26. Henry M. Pelling, *The Labour Governments, 1946–51* (New York, 1984), 256–9. Butler, *British General Election of 1951*, 118, 121–3; KYD, 14 October 1951.

5 Man of the Year

1. George Middleton, oral interview, London, March 1983; 24 March 1952, Basil Bunting to Ezra Pound, Ezra Pound Mss II, Lilly Library, Bloomington, IN.
2. Robert Rhodes James, *Anthony Eden: A Biography* (New York, 1987), 183. John Colville, *The Fringes of Power: 10 Downing Street Diaries, 1939–1955* (New York, 1985), 731.
3. James, *Anthony Eden*, 87.
4. Robert Scott, oral interview transcript, LSE.
5. 2, 5 October 1951, 350: Iran, Internal political affairs, TPF, RG 84.
6. US House of Representatives, Committee on Foreign Affairs, *Selected Executive Session Hearings of the Committee, 1951–56: The Middle East, Africa, and Inter-American Affairs*, History series, number 16 (Washington, 1980), 89–91.
7. 2 October 1951, Gross to Hickerson, Iran Special Correspondence, box 293, Harriman papers, LC; United Nations, Security Council: *Official Records, 1951*, 19. Fuad Ruhani, *Tarikh-i Milli Shudan San'at-i Naft-i Iran* [The History of the Nationalization of the Iranian Oil Industry] (Tehran, 1973), 223.
8. Stokes and Hartley Shawcross, president of the Board of Trade, had urged Morrison to send one of them immediately to New York to negotiate, but the foreign minister refused, arguing that there was not time before the election nor would Musaddiq negotiate seriously in New York City. 8 October 1951, FO 371, 91600/EP1531/1865.
9. Acheson, *Present at the Creation* (New York, 1969), 510–11.
10. George McGhee, *Envoy to the Middle World: Adventures in Diplomacy* (New York, 1983), 393–404. Vernon Walters was much less sanguine about the possibility of an agreement with Musaddiq. *Silent Missions*, 259–63. 24 October 1951, Memorandum of Conversation, Acheson papers, HSTL.
11. 30 October, 3 November 1951, FO 371, 91607/EP1531/2032, 2032G.
12. 31 October 1951, FO 371, 91608/EP1531/2061.
13. For a fine example of this sometimes difficult relationship see, Evelyn Shuckburgh, *Descent to Suez: Diaries, 1951–56* (New York, 1987), 152–3.
14. September–October 1951, T236/2825, 5–11; 1 November 1951, FO 371, 91608/EP1531/2045.

15. 4, 5, 6 November 1951, FO 371, 91608/EP1531/2056, 2058, 2059, 2065.

16. According to Robert Scott, Eden tried to carry his advisers along with him. Bevin would listen to their views and then say, 'I heard what you say. I don't accept it. We'll do it my way.' Eden would more likely reply, 'Well, Scott, I don't know. You may be right. I think so and so. Don't you agree?' Scott, oral interview transcript, LSE. Shuckburgh, too, commented on this characteristic. 'AE still shows signs of indecision over Egypt. . . . He is like a sea anemone, covered with sensitive tentacles all recording currents of opinion around him. He quivers with sensitivity to opinion in the House, the party, the newspapers.' Shuckburgh, *Descent to Suez*, 148; 7 November 1951, FO 371, 91610/EP1531/2124.

17. Shuckburgh, *Descent to Suez*, 76; Peter J. Hahn, *The United States, Great Britain and Egypt: Strategy and Diplomacy in the Early Cold War* (Chapel Hill, 1991), 175.

18. 7, 9 November 1951, FO 371, 91609/EP1531/2082, 2083; 10 November 1951, Subject file: Iran, PSF, HSTL.

19. Shuckburgh, *Descent to Suez*, 27; 14 November 1951, 888.2553, RG 59.

20. 15 May 1954, Princeton seminars, Acheson papers, HSTL; 16 November 1951, Subject file: Iran, Truman papers, HSTL.

21. 9 November 1951, Musaddiq to Truman, Official file, White House Central file, Truman papers, HSTL; 17 November 1951, 888.2553, RG 59.

22. Yonah Alexander and Allen Nanes, eds, *The United States and Iran: A Documentary History* (Frederick, MD, 1980), 223; *Selected Executive Session Hearings of the Committee, 1951–56*, 106–7. Brands, *Inside the Cold War*, 266; Daniel Yergin, *Shattered Peace: The Origins of the Cold War and the National Security State* (Boston, 1978), 26–7, 38–9; 7 November 1951, FO 371, 61472/EP1024/8; *FRUS, 1952–54*, 10: 236–40.

23. Fereidun Keshavarz, *Man motaham mikonam* [I Confess] (Tehran, 1977), 139, 146. *Central Asian Review*, 4 (1956): 392.

24. Osamu Miyata, 'Khalil Maleki During the Oil Nationalization Period in Iran,' *Jusur* 1 (1985): 51–3. Khalil Maleki, *Niruy-i sivum piruz mishavad* [The Third Force Will Win] (Tehran, 1951), 16–18, 20.

25. *FRUS, 1951*, 5: 264; Foreign Agricultural Service, narrative reports, 1950–54, box 232, RG 166; Homa Katouzian, 'Oil Boycott and the Political Economy: Musaddiq and the Strategy of Non-oil Economics,' in Bill and Louis (eds), *Musaddiq, Iranian Nationalism, and Oil*; Hossein Mahdavy, 'Patterns and Problems of Economic Development in Rentier States: The Case of Iran,' in M.A. Cook (ed.), *Studies in the Economic History of the Middle East* (London, 1970).

26. 350 Iran: Internal Political Affairs, 1951, box 29, TPF, RG 84.

27. Iran-Agriculture, summary report, May–July 1951, box 232, RG 166; Husain Kayustuvan, *Siyasat-i Muvanzinih-ye Manfi dar Majlis-i Chahardahom* [The Policy of Negative Equilibrium in the Fourteenth Majlis] (Tehran, 1951), 233.

28. Ruhani [Nationalization of Iranian Oil Industry], 238; *Al-Ahram* (Cairo), 22 November 1951; 1 December 1951, 788.13, RG 59.

29. Azimi, *Crisis of Democracy*, 271; 12 December 1951, 350: Iran, box 29, TPF, RG 84.
30. 30 September 1951, box 35, TPF, RG 84; 17 December 1951, FO 371, 91466/EP1015/435, Azimi, *Crisis of Democracy*, 269.
31. *Bakhtar-i Imruz* (Tehran), 25 November 1951.
32. 12 December 1951, 361.2 Cabinet: General, 1951–52, TPF, RG 84; Ruhani [Nationalization of Iranian Oil Industry], 242.
33. 12 December 1951, 350: Iran, TPF, RG 84.
34. Ibid.
35. 12 December 1951, 361.2 Cabinet: General, 1950–52, TPF, RG 84.
36. *Time*, 7 January 1952.
37. *Times of India*, 14 October 1951.
38. Bunting to Pound, 24 March 1952, Ezra Pound Mss. II, Lilly library.
39. Bunting to Pound, 24 March 1952, Ezra Pound Mss. II, *Speech by Musaddiq to Representatives of the American Press, 18 March 1952* (Lima). Even today it is common to find scholarly authors, who insert the obligatory paragraph or two about Musaddiq in their general studies of the period, adopting the caricature of Musaddiq as a buffoon that so delighted his enemies more than 40 years ago.
40. *New York Times*, 14 October 1951, 7 December 1951, 25 July 1952.
41. Ruhani [Nationalization of Iranian Oil Industry], 237.

6 Failed Plot

1. Acheson, *Present at the Creation*, 599
2. 4, 9 January 1952, General file: Churchill, PSF, HSTL. Hahn, 132–9.
3. 13 August 1952, Dept. of Air Force Intelligence Memo, 092 Iran, Records of the Joint Chiefs of Staff, 1951–3, RG 218, NA; 4, 9 January 1952, General file: Churchill, PSF, HSTL.
4. 12 January 1952, 611.88, RG 59; Acheson, *Present at the Creation*, 599–600.
5. Ibid., 600; 7 January 1952, Memoranda of Conversations, Acheson papers, HSTL.
6. 5 January 1952, General file: Churchill, PSF, HSTL.
7. 16 October 1952, Memoranda of Conversations: Camille Gutt, Acheson papers, HSTL; Goode, *The Diplomacy of Neglect*, 44, 79; 12 December 1952, IBRD file, TPF, RG 84.
8. 26 December 1951, 888.2553, RG 59. Ruhani [Nationalization of Iranian Oil Industry], 254.
9. 13 February, 4 March 1952, FO 371, 98608/EP1022/7, 19; *Musaddiq's Memoirs*, 45.
10. 30 January 1952, (Ministry of Fuel and Power) POWE 33/1929; 22 May 1952, POWE 33/1934; 1 March 1952, T236/3670.
11. 14 February 1952, FO 371, 98608/EP1022/22; 9 April 1952, FO 371, 98677/EP1538/4.
12. 5 May 1952, box 29, TPF, RG 84.
13. 7 April 1952, FO 371, 98667/EP15314/103; 13 February 1952, FO 371, 98608/EP1022/21.
14. Ford, *The Anglo-Iranian Oil Dispute, 1951–52*, 158–9. *New York Times*, 26

April 1952; 092 Iran (4–23–48) section 5, Joint Chiefs of Staff, 1951–3, RG 218, CD 091.3 (Iran) 1952, Records of Office of Secretary of Defense, RG 330, NA; 25 April 1952, notes on cabinet meetings, Post-presidential file, HSTL.

15. 28 April 1952, FO 371, 98636/EP1192/7; 28 April 1952, 440: General, 1952, TPF, RG 84.

16. Richard Cottam, *Nationalism in Iran* (Pittsburgh, 1964), 153–4, 274–7; Habib Ladjevardi, 'Constitutional Government and Reform under Musaddiq,' in Bill and Louis (eds), *Musaddiq, Iranian Nationalism and Oil*, 70–2.

17. 8 July 1952, FO 248, G19401/35.

18. 24, 28 May 1952, 350: Iran, TPF, RG 84; 6 July 1952, FO 371, 98690/EP15314/166.

19. A vote of inclination indicated which candidate the Majlis preferred. There was much debate as to whether or not such a vote was binding on the shah. 31 December 1953, FO 371, 109988/EP1016/1; 9 July 1952, 350: Iran, TPF, RG 84.

20. Ahmad Alizadeh, *Shuhadayi Siyum-i Tir Mah 1331* [The Martyrs of 21 July 1952] (Isfahan, 1952), 22; Diba, *Mossadegh*, 153–7; Abrahamian, *Iran Between Two Revolutions*, 270–1.

21. Alizadeh [The Martyrs of 21 July 1952], 22.

22. *FRUS, 1952–54*, 10: 239; 11 June 1953, Richards to Byroade, 788.5, RG 59.

23. Azimi, *Crisis of Democracy*, 303–4.

24. 12 July 1952, 788.13, RG 59; 24 May 1952, 350: Iran, TPF, RG 84; House Committee on Foreign Affairs, *Selected Executive Session Hearings*, 16: 119; 28 June 1952, FO 371, 98690/EP15314.

25. 14 June 1952, FO 371, 98690/EP15314/160.

26. 7, 14 June, 8 July 1952, FO 371, 98690/EP15314/158, 160, 175.

27. 18 July 1952, 001 Iran, Foreign Broadcast Information Service (FBIS).

28. Ali Shayegan, 'Faja'i siyyom-i tir,' [The tragedy of the Twenty-first of July] *Yaghma* 5 (September 1952): 303–10.

29. 18 July 1952, 350: Iran, July demonstrations, TPF, RG 84.

30. 21 July 1952, FO 371, 98601/EP1015/179.

31. Abrahamian, *Iran Between Two Revolutions*, 271; Yann Richard, 'Ayatollah Kashani,' in Nikki R. Keddie (ed.), *Religion and Politics in Iran: Shi'ism from Quietism to Revolution* (New Haven, 1983), 111.

32. The shah suggested that Qavam save him a place in France. 22 July 1952, 350: Iran, TPF, RG 84; *Ittila'at*, 7 August 1952.

33. Mahmud Sakha'i, *Musaddiq va Rastakhiz-i Millat* [Musaddiq and the Resurrection of the Nation] (Tehran, 1953), 80–4. The senate had come into existence only in 1949. Of its 60 members, the shah appointed 30. It was correctly viewed as a locus of royal power. Ruhani [Nationalization of Iranian Oil Industry], 294.

34. 29 July 1952, Daily briefs, Naval Aide files, Harry S. Truman papers, HSTL.

35. 13 August 1952, Loy Henderson file, 123, RG 59.

36. 30 July 1952, FO 371, 98603/EP1015/217; 20 November 1952, NSC 136/1, RG 273 (Records of the National Security Council), NA.

37. 24 August 1952, box 27, TPF, RG 84.
38. 8 July 1952, FO 248, 1531/287; 28 July 1952, FO 371, EP15314/189; 7 August 1952, FO 371, 98602/EP1015/198.

7 Britain Departs

1. 31 July 1952, FO 371, 98691/EP15314/198; *FRUS, 1952–54*, 10: 445.
2. 7 August 1952, CAB128/25, CC(52)76; 2 August 1952, FO 371, 98692/EP15314/212.
3. 11 August 1952, Secretary of State, 8/52–1/53, Acheson papers, HSTL; 12 August 1952, FO 371, 98693/EP15314/225, 230A.
4. 16, 18 August 1952, FO 371, 98706/EP15316/3, 5.
5. 20 August 1952, FO 371, 98694/EP15314/254.
6. 23, 24 August 1952, FO 371, 98694/EP15314/259, 260.
7. Colville, *The Fringes of Power*, 654; 25 August 1952, FO 371, 98694/EP15314/256.
8. 27, 28 August 1952, FO 371, 98695/EP15314/282, 282a, 282w, 294.
9. 9, 20 August 1952, 611.88, RG 59; 27 September 1959, Acheson 167, notecards, HSTL; 1 September 1952, FO 371, 98697/EP15314/331.
10. Ibid.
11. Ruhani [Nationalization of Iranian Oil Industry], 301; *FRUS, 1952–54*, 10: 437; Freidoune Sahebjam, *L'Iran des Pahlavis* (Paris, 1966), 262; 4 September 1952, FO 371, 98706/EP15316/13. The most recent volume of *The History of the British Petroleum Company* does not mention the British embargo, referring only to Iran's inability to sell its oil abroad. Bamberg, *The Anglo-Iranian Years*, 459–60.
12. *Oil Forum* (February 1954): 59–60; *FRUS, 1952–54*, 10: 478–9.
13. 9 October 1952, FO 371, 98700/EP15314/429; *FRUS, 1952–54*, 10: 493, 496.
14. 9, 11 October 1952, FO 371, 98700/EP15314/431, 435; 3 October 1952, FO 371, EP15314/404.
15. 13 October 1952, FO 371, 98701/EP15314/450.
16. 2 October 1952, 501.6 Banks: IBRD, TPF, RG 84; 27 August 1952, FO 371, 98695/EP15314/299; 26 August 1952, FO 371, 98695/EP15314/273.
17. George Middleton, interview, London, 8 March 1983.
18. 31 October 1952, FO 371, 98718/EP1691/1–6.
19. November 1951, FO 371, 91612/EP1531; Office of Naval Intelligence, *Review* (July 1951): 270, Naval Historical Center.
20. David S. Painter, *Oil and the American Century* (Baltimore, 1986), 179–81; Petroleum Administration Weekly Summary, Office files of Secretary of the Interior Oscar Chapman, Records of the Office of Secretary of Interior, 1933–53, RG 48; Shoshana Klebanoff, 'Oil for Europe: American Foreign Policy and Middle East Oil' (Ph.D. dissertation, Claremont Graduate School, 1974), 88–9; Acheson, *Present at the Creation*, 681–4.
21. 5 November 1951, 888.2553, RG 59; 16, 21 August, 24 October, 12 November 1952, CD 092 (Iran), RG 330; 13 August, 15 October 1952,

(4–23–48) 092 Iran, section 6, 7, JCS 1951–3, RG 218; 1 January 1952, 888.2553, RG 59.

22. David S. McLellan, *Dean Acheson: The State Department Years* (New York, 1976), 391; 18 February 1955, PPF: Memoirs file, Acheson papers, HSTL; 4 November 1952, CD 092 (Iran) 1952, RG 330.

23. Burton I. Kaufman, *The Oil Cartel Case: A Documentary Study of Antitrust Activity in the Cold War Era* (Westport, Conn., 1978), 44–7; 8 October 1952, Memoranda of Conversations, Acheson papers, HSTL.

24. 14, 20 October 1952, POWE33/1936; 20, 25, 27 October 1952, FO 371, 98702/EP15314/460, 465, 479.

8 Time Runs Out

1. 4 December 1952, Memo of Conversation, Box 67a, Papers of Dean Acheson, HSTL.

2. Acheson, *Present at the Creation*, 700–1; James, *Anthony Eden*, 352–3; Shuckburgh, *Descent to Suez*, 50–1.

3. Shuckburgh, *Descent to Suez*, 54.

4. Walters, *Silent Missions*, 259; 18 November 1952, 'Briefing for Eisenhower,' Acheson papers, HSTL; 20 November 1952, FO 371, 98703/EP 15314/503G; Shuckburgh, *Descent to Suez*, 55.

5. 22 November 1952, FO 371, 98703/EP15314/493; Shuckburgh, *Descent to Suez*, 55; Acheson, *Present at the Creation*, 683–4.

6. 27, 29 November, 5 December 1952, FO 371, 98703/EP15314/501, 506, 508; 20 December 1952, FO 371, 98704/EP15314/538.

7. 12 December 1952, FO 371, 98704/EP15314/513.

8. 15 May 1954, Princeton seminar, Acheson papers, HSTL; 12 April 1952, Memoranda of Conversations, Acheson papers, HSTL.

9. Kaufman, *The Oil Cartel Case*, 45–7; 15 May 1954, Princeton seminars, Acheson papers, HSTL; *FRUS, 1952–1954* (Wash., 1983), 1, pt. 2: 1338–45; 3 December 1952, Classified material, Subject series, John Foster Dulles papers, Dwight D. Eisenhower Library (DDEL), Abilene, Kansas.

10. Colville, *Fringes of Power*, 660, 662–4.

11. 8–15 January 1953, FO 371, 104607/EP1531/34. At one point Musaddiq had suggested that arbitration could be guided by Britain's own principles of nationalization.

12. 7 January 1953, FO 371, 104606/EP1531/15; 16 January 1953, FO 371, 104612/EP1531/148.

13. Anthony Eden, *Full Circle* (Boston, 1960), 232; Shuckburgh, *Descent to Suez*, 75. Eden had agreed to discuss with the Egyptians the withdrawal of British troops from the Suez Canal Zone, a move that Churchill vehemently opposed.

14. 8–15 January 1953, FO 371, 104607/EP1531/34; 15 January 1953, FO 371, 104609/EP1531/69.

15. 17, 19 January 1953, FO 371, 104609/EP1531/70, 84; 10 November 1952, 611.88, RG 59; 15 May 1954, Princeton seminars, Acheson papers, HSTL; Barry Rubin, *Paved with Good Intentions: The American Experience and Iran* (New York, 1980), 76–7. Churchill refused to sanction the sending of the five technicians. 6, 26 January 1953, FO 371,

104610/EP1531/107, 108. See also on Jones's activities, Farman Farmaian, *Daughter of Persia*, 182–95.

16. 27 November 1952, General correspondence, Grady papers, HSTL.
17. James A. Bill, 'America, Iran, and the Politics of Intervention, 1951–1953,' in Bill and Louis (eds), *Musaddiq, Iranian Nationalism, and Oil*, 271.
18. Bamberg, *The Anglo-Iranian Years*, 471, 521.
19. 'Expropriated Oil: Mexico and Iran,' *The Reporter*, 7 August 1951, 26.
20. 28 August 1951, FO 371, 91582/EP1531/1442; October 1951, FO 371, 908381/AM1531/5; 7 November 1951, 888.2553, RG 59; *Newsweek*, 22 October 1951, 45; 1 October 1951, 888.2553, RG 59.
21. Stephen H. Longrigg, *Oil in the Middle East: Its Discovery and Development* (New York, 1954), 277, 279–80.
22. *Times of India*, 14 October 1951.
23. December 1952, Research and analysis report 6126, RG 59; Ruhani [Nationalization of Iranian Oil Industry], 401, 404. For an assessment of Iran's economy under Musaddiq, see Homa Katouzian, 'Oil Boycott and the Political Economy: Musaddiq and the Strategy of Non-Oil Economics,' in Bill and Louis (eds), *Musaddiq, Iranian Nationalism, and Oil*, 203–25.
24. Abrahamian, *Iran Between Two Revolutions*, 252.
25. Richard Cottam, 'Nationalism in Twentieth-Century Iran and Dr. Muhammad Musaddiq,' in Bill and Louis (eds), *Musaddiq, Iranian Nationalism and Oil*, 33–4.
26. Shahrough Akhavi, 'The Role of the Clergy in Iranian Politics, 1949–1954,' in Bill and Louis (eds), *Musaddiq, Iranian Nationalism and Oil*, 100; Abrahamian, *Iran Between Two Revolutions*, 234.
27. 15 January 1953, FO 371, 104562.
28. *Tehran Press Review* (US Embassy, Tehran), 22 January 1953; *Ittila'at*, 15 January 1953.
29. Akhavi, 'The Role of the Clergy,' 100–7.
30. Albion Ross, *Journey of an American* (Indianapolis, 1957), 278; Fakhreddin Azimi, 'The Reconciliation of Politics and Ethics, Nationalism and Democracy,' in Bill and Louis (eds), *Musaddiq, Iranian Nationalism, and Oil*, 65, Shahpour Bakhtiar, *Ma fidelité* (Paris, 1982), 54, 61, 76; Azimi, 'Reconciliation,' 63–5; Miyata, 'Khalil Maliki,' *Jusur*, 49.
31. See especially Musaddiq's speech to the Majlis, December 1952, box 233, RG 166, NA.
32. 16 May 1952 R&A report 5915, December 1952, R&A report 6126, 16 February 1952, 788.00, RG 59; Loy Henderson, Columbia Oral History Project, 9.
33. Akhavi, 'Role of the Clergy,' 106; Ladjevardi, 'Constitutional Government,' 78; Katouzian, *Musaddiq and the Struggle for Power in Iran*, 267.
34. Cottam, 'Nationalism in Twentieth-Century Iran,' 36–7.

9 Coup

1. Henry Byroade, oral interview, Potomac, MD, June 1989. 2 January 1953, Subject series, box 8, JFD papers, DDEL.

2. 18 February 1953, FO 371, 104612/EP1531/162.
3. 4 February 1953, FO 371, 104612/EP1531/149, 153.
4. 28 January 1953, FO 371, 104610/EP1531/117; 10, 18 February 1953, FO 371, 104012/EP1531/152, 162; Rose L. Greaves, *History of British Petroleum in Iran* (London, 1970) [Privately published], 3: 69.
5. *The Oil Forum* (February 1954): 60; Painter, *Oil and the American Century*, 189. In opening negotiations after Musaddiq's overthrow, the British agreed not to seek more than £100 million compensation.
6. 14 April 1953, FO 371, 104615/EP1531/243; 31 May 1953, FO 371, 104616/EP1531/269.
7. 19 February 1953, NSC series, box 4, Dwight D. Eisenhower papers [Ann Whitman file], DDEL; 4 February, 1953, FO 371, 104612/EP1531/ 149; 4 March 1953, Chronological series, JFD papers, DDEL; 7 March 1953, FO 371, 104614/EP1531/197.
8. 4 March 1953, NSC 135th meeting, RG 273.
9. 6 March 1953, FW788.00, RG 59.
10. 19 March 1953, International series, box 16, AWF, DDEL; Shuckburgh, *Descent to Suez*, 82; Ibid., 99; Lord Butler, oral interview transcript, 24, LSE.
11. 21 May 1953, FO 371, 104659/EP1943/1.
12. Jalil Buzurgmihr, *Taghrirat-i Musaddiq dar zindan* [Musaddiq's Conversations in Prison] (Tehran, 1980), 145.
13. 26 February 1953, NSC series, box 4, AWF, DDEL; 4 March 1953, NSC 135th meeting, RG 273.
14. 23 February 1953, 788.00, RG 59; 24 February 1953, FO 371, 104562/ EP1015/46.
15. Mihdi Mir-Ashrafi, *Qiam dar rah-i sultanat* [Uprising on the Road to Monarchy] (Tehran, 1954), 9. Recent research has indicated that operatives of BEDAMN, a CIA project to undermine Musaddiq's regime, were probably involved in these disturbances as well. Mark Gasiorowski, 'The 1953 Coup D'état in Iran,' *International Journal of Middle East Studies* 19 (1987): 268–71.
16. 2 March 1953, FO 371, 104563/EP1015/61E; 7 April 1953, FO 371, 104564/EP1015/101; 24 April 1953, FO 371, 104567/EP1015/157.
17. Bakhtiar, *Ma fidelité*, 68; Buzurgmihr, *Taghrirat-i Musaddiq dar zindan*, 127–8; Mir-Ashrafi, *Qiam dar rah-i sultanat*, 19; Katouzian, ed., *Musaddiq's Memoirs*, 62.
18. Buzurgmihr, *Taghrirat-i Musaddiq dar zindan*, 133; Mahmud Sakha'i, *Musaddiq va rastakhiz-i millat*, 111–12.
19. *Musaddiq's Memoirs*, 63; Abrahamian, *Iran Between Two Revolutions*, 278–9.
20. 1, 6 March 1953, 788.00, RG 59.
21. Gasiorowski, 'The 1953 Coup D'état in Iran,' 277; 12 March 1953, FO 371, 104563/EP1015/71; Loy Henderson, oral interview transcript, Columbia Oral History project, 12; Ibid., 11; 23 May 1953, Dulles– Herter series, box 1, AWF, DDEL.
22. William Warne, oral interview transcript, HSTL; 1 June 1953, NSC series, 147th meeting, AWF, DDEL.
23. Ruhollah K. Ramazani, *Iran's Foreign Policy, 1941–1973: A Study of*

Foreign Policy in Modernizing Nations (Charlottesville, 1975), 236, 240; Abrahamian, *Iran Between Two Revolutions*, 322, 377, 382.

24. Ramazani, *Iran's Foreign Policy*, 234; Katouzian, *Musaddiq's Memoirs*, 167; Abrahamian, *Iran Between Two Revolutions*, 322, 338.
25. Katouzian, *Musaddiq's Memoirs*, 167; James A. Bill, *The Eagle and the Lion: The Tragedy of American–Iranian Relations* (New Haven, 1988), 91. Ruhani [Nationalization of Iranian Oil Industry], 380.
26. 4 June 1953, FO 371, 104659/EP1943/2G. A second note from Churchill, overtaken by events, was not delivered. In it the prime minister used characteristically strong words to prompt the shah to act, saying, 'It is the duty of a constitutional monarch or president when faced with violent tyrannical action by individuals or a minority party to take the necessary steps to secure the well-being of the toiling masses and the continuity of an ordered state.' 5 June 1953, FO 371, 104659/EP1943/3G.
27. Kim Roosevelt, *Countercoup: The Struggle for Control of Iran* (New York, 1979); 7–8, 26 June 1953, FO 371, 104616/EP1531/276; Brian Lapping, *End of Empire* (New York, 1988), 218.
28. Stephen Ambrose, *Eisenhower*. vol 1. *Soldier, General of the Army, President Elect, 1890–1952* (New York, 1983), 105–6.
29. 13 February, 5, 23 May 1953, FO 371, 104581/EP10345/5; 11 April, 5 May 1953, FO 371, 104581/EP10345/7; 10, 19 May 1953, FO 371, 104616/EP1531/269.
30. Husain Bihniya, *Pardih-hay-i siyasat: Naft, nihzat, Musaddiq, Zahidi* [Behind the Scenes: Oil, Resurgence, Musaddiq, Zahidi] (Tehran, n.d.), 90.
31. Cottam, *Nationalism in Iran*, 281.
32. 4 June 1953, FO 371, 104659/EP1943/2G.
33. Mir-Ashrafi, *Qiam dar rah-i sultanat*, 118, 124–5; Cottam, *Nationalism in Iran*, 276.
34. House Committee on Foreign Affairs, *Selected Executive Session Hearings*, 16: 145, 150.
35. 24 July 1953, Minutes of telephone conversations, Dulles papers, DDEL.
36. 2 July 1953, box 2853, 611.88, RG 59; Walter W. Krause, *Soraya, Queen of Persia* (London, 1956), 111.
37. 18 August 1953, 788.00, RG 59; 17 August 1953, FO 371, 104659/EP1943/4.
38. 18 August 1953, Iran, *FBIS*; 14 September 1953, Brigadier General Robert McClure to Jackson, C.D. Jackson papers, DDEL.
39. *Shahid*, 15 August 1953. *Dad* (Tehran), 18 August 1953.
40. 18 August 1953, FO 371, 104570/EP1015/213; Gasiorowski, 'The 1953 Coup D'état in Iran,' 273–4. Lapping, *End of Empire*, 220.
41. Henderson, oral interview transcript, Columbia, 15–18; John J. Harter, 'Mr. Foreign Service on Musaddiq and Wristonization,' *Foreign Service Journal* (November, 1980): 17–18; *FRUS, 1952–1954*, 10: 748, 752.
42. 18 August 1953, *FBIS*; *Bakhtar-i imruz*, 16, 17 August 1953.
43. Abrahamian, *Iran Between Two Revolutions*, 324–5. Keshavarz, *Man motaham mikonam*, 143.
44. Bakhtiar, *Ma fidelité*, 71.

45. 19 August 1953, *FBIS*.
46. Andrew F. Westwood, 'Politics of Distrust in Iran,' *Annals of the American Academy* 358 (March 1965): 123–35; Gasiorowski, 'The 1953 Coup D'état in Iran,' 277. For an account that plays down the importance of the CIA role, see Homa Katouzian, *The Political Economy of Modern Iran*, 179–82.
47. Cyrus Ghani, ed. *Yaddashtha-yi Duktur Qasim Ghani* [The Notebooks of Dr. Qasim Ghani] (London, 1982), 9: 635.

10 Second Chance

1. *FRUS, 1952–1954*, 10: 773.
2. 20 August 1953, Australian High Commissioner London to Canberra, A5954, box 2260, Australian Archives, Belconnen, ACT; 21 January 1954, 788.00, RG 59; 14 September 1953, McClure to Jackson, C.D. Jackson papers, DDEL; 17 September 1953, NSC series, 162nd meeting, AWF, DDEL; 25 August 1953, 092 Iran (4–23–48), section 10, JCS 1951–53, RG 218.
3. 27 August 1953, 611.88, RG 59, 24 August 1953, FO 371, 104570/EP1015/221. Homa Katouzian has argued persuasively that, contrary to what Zahidi wanted the United States to believe, the Musaddiq government was in good financial shape in August 1953. 'Oil Boycott and the Political Economy,' in Bill and Louis (eds), *Musaddiq, Iranian Nationalism and Oil*, 203–27.
4. 24 August 1953, FO 371, 104570/EP1015/221; 21 August 1953, FO 371, 104517/EP1024/1; 29 August 1953, FO 371, 104659/EP1943/9.
5. 30 September 1953, FO 371, 104584/EP1051/8; 28 August 1953, FO 371, 104589/EP1114/1; 25 August 1953, CAB128/26 CC(53)50.
6. 1 September 1953, FO 371, 104640/EP15316/9.
7. 9 September 1953, FO 371, 104577/EP1024/10; 6 May 1953, FO 371, 104616/EP1531/266; 4 September 1953, FO 371, 104640/EP15316/5, 8.
8. 25 August, 8 September 1953, Minutes of telephone conversations, Dulles papers, DDEL; 27 August, 17 September 1953, NSC series, 160th, 162nd meetings, AWF, DDEL.
9. 1953 Far East Trip, series 366, box 2, Iran I, Richard Nixon Pre-presidential papers, National Archives Pacific Southwest, Laguna Niguel, CA.
10. 5 September 1953, FO 371, 104640/EP15316/13.
11. Greaves, *History of British Petroleum, 1952–54*, 3: 88.
12. 29 September 1953, FO 371, 104641/EP15316/41.
13. 14, 18, 25, 28 September 1953, FO 371, 104641/EP15316/32, 33, 24, 34.
14. 30 September 1953, FO 371, 104641/EP15316/36.
15. 8, 20 October 1953, FO 371, 104642/EP15316/44, 64.
16. 17 September 1953, FO 371, 104571/EP1015/237; 16 September 1953, 611.88, RG 59. Office of Naval Intelligence *Review*, 8: 533, Naval History Center, Washington Naval Yard (WNY); Mohammed Reza Shah Pahlavi, *Mission For My Country* (New York, 1961), 58; 28 September 1953, B.L. Austin to Secretary of Navy, Strategic Plans Division, Office

of the Chief of Naval Operations, box 288, EF (foreign countries), WNY; *FRUS, 1952–54*, 10: 786; 20 October 1953, FO 371, 104642/EP15316/64.

17. 1 September 1953, FO 371, 104571/EP1015/233.
18. 26 September 1953, FO 371, 104572/EP1015/252.
19. 24 November 1953, FO 371, 104572/EP1015/264.
20. 1 November 1953, FO 371, 104616/EP1531/281; 5 November 1953, FO 371, 104642/EP15316/77.
21. 5 November 1953, FO 371, 104642/EP15316/77; *FRUS, 1952–54*, 10: 820; 7 November 1953, FO 371, 104642/EP15316/72.
22. Ibid., 10 November 1953, FO 371, 104642/EP15316/75.
23. 19 November 1953, Strategic Plans Division Office of Chief of Naval Operations, box 288, EF, WNY.
24. 26 October 1953, FO 371, 104642/EP15316/66, 12 December 1953, POWE 33, 2089.
25. 27 November 1953, 'Memorandum on Relative US–UK Roles,' 2 December 1953, Pre-Bermuda Conference report, Int. meetings series, AWF, DDEL.
26. 9 December 1953, 'Results of Bermuda Conference' C-9(1), Office of Staff Secretary: Cabinet series, White House Office files, DDEL.
27. 30 December 1953, NSC series, 178th meeting, AWF; 28 December 1953, series xvi, op-30s/op-60s subject and serial files, box 291, Strategic plans division records, CNO, WNY; 23 December 1953, President to Churchill, International series, box 17, AWF, DDEL.
28. April 1951, Personal correspondence: Greece, box 3, Francis F. Lincoln papers, HSTL; 29 July 1952, US naval attaché, Baghdad, box 275, EF, Strategic plans division, CNO, WNY.
29. Martin Gilbert, *Winston S. Churchill* (London, 1988), 8: 936.
30. Byroade, oral interview, 1989.
31. C.L. Sulzberger, *A Long Row of Candles: Memoirs and Diaries, 1934–54* (Toronto, 1969), 934; 8 December 1953, FO 371, 104644/EP15316/119.
32. Byroade, interview, 1989.

11 Selling the Consortium

1. Roy Mottahedeh, *The Mantle of the Prophet* (New York, 1986), 133; 13 November 1953, 988.64, RG 59.
2. Farman Farmaian, *Daughter of Persia*, 196.
3. 5 December, 30 November 1953, FO 371, 104586/EP1051/55D, 71; Yann Richard, 'Ayatollah Kashani' in Nikki R. Keddie (ed.), *Religion and Politics in Iran*, 117.
4. 12 November 1953, 788.00, RG 59.
5. Mottahedeh, *Mantle of the Prophet*, 133; 4 January 1954, FO 371, 109986/EP1015/4.
6. 23 December 1953, FO 371, 104581/EP10345/24; 1953 Far East trip, series 366, box 2, Iran I, Richard Nixon, Pre-presidential papers, NAPS; Richard Nixon, *Memoirs* (New York, 1978), 133.
7. Eden, *Full Circle*, 240; Denis Wright, oral interview, London, March 1983.

8. 12 December 1953, POWE 33, 2089.
9. Wright, oral interview.
10. Ibid.
11. 27 November 1953, FO 371, 104643/EP15316/102; Greaves, *History of British Petroleum in Iran*, 3: 99. This was just the opposite of Hoover's advice!
12. 14 December 1953, FO 371, 194644/EP15316/118B; Charles W. Hamilton, *Americans and Oil in the Middle East* (Houston, 1962), 59.
13. Greaves, *British Petroleum*, 3: 104, 106, Shuckburgh, *Descent to Suez*, 125–6.
14. 22 January 1954, FO 371, 110047/EP1531/48.
15. Greaves, *British Petroleum*, 3: 110.
16. 18 February 1954, FO 371, 110047/EP1531/74; 19 February 1954, FO 371, 110047/EP1531/77, 78.
17. Greaves, *British Petroleum*, 3: 116. Iranian officials considered Shell a British company, thus, according to them, 54 per cent of the consortium was under Britain's control; 25 February 1954, FO 371, 110047/EP1531/91.
18. 9 December 1953, Results of Bermuda Conference, box 1, Office of Staff Secretary, Cabinet series, White House Office, DDEL.
19. 1 January 1954, POWE 33, 2089/PD230/94/4/28; *FRUS, 1952–54*, 10: 888. Although Brownell reserved the right to prosecute the existing cartel suit, the government's case was greatly weakened. Painter, *Oil and the American Century*, 192–8. Bennett H. Wall, *Growth in a Changing Environment: A History of Standard Oil Company (New Jersey) Exxon Corporation, 1950–1975* (New York, 1988), 485–9.
20. 8 August 1954, FO 371, 110071/EP1534/327. Senate Subcommittee on Multinational Corporations [Church Committee]. *Multinational Oil Corporations and U.S. Foreign Policy* (Washington, DC, 1975), pt. 7: 304.
21. 23 February 1954, FO 371, 110051/EP1532/9. The money set aside for rehabilitating the Iranian oil industry proved unnecessary. Hamilton, *Americans and Oil in the Middle East*, 60.
22. 28 May 1954, Minutes of 199th meeting, box 5, NSC series, AWF, DDEL.
23. Greaves, *British Petroleum*, 3: 117; 17 March 1954, FO 371, 110048/EP1531/127, 128.
24. Greaves, *British Petroleum*, 3: 118, 121; 22 March 1954, FO 371, 110049/EP1531/133; 26 March 1954, FO 371, 110048/EP1531/144; 26 March 1954, FO 371, 110049/EP1531/141; 24 March 1054, Dulles to Humphrey, Minutes of telephone conversations, Dulles papers, DDEL. A year earlier when Musaddiq had insisted that Britain state its compensation demands before negotiations could begin, his suggestion was rudely dismissed.
25. 13 March 1954, FO 371, 110060/EP1534/49; 3 April 1954, FO 371, 110050/EP1531/184.
26. 23 April 1954, FO 371, 110061/EP1534/74, 75.
27. May 1954, FO 371, 110063/EP1534/128; 21, 28 April 1954, FO 371, 110061/EP1534/83, 88; 27 April 1954, FO 371, 110062/EP1534/105.
28. 28 April, 5, 10, 16, 19, 25 May 1954, Iran, *FBIS*.

29. 28 May 1954, Minutes of 199th meeting, box 5, NSC series, AWF, DDEL.
30. Greaves, *British Petroleum*, 3: 129; 26 April 1954, FO 371, 110061/EP1534/78, 79.
31. Wall, *Growth in a Changing Environment*, 491–2. Howard Page, 'Notes on Negotiating,' [n.d.] (copy in possession of author).
32. Greaves, *British Petroleum*, 3: 130; 28 May 1954, minutes of 199th meeting, box 5, NSC series, AWF, DDEL.
33. Howard Page, oral interview transcript (conducted by Bennett Wall), June 1975.
34. 14 May 1954, FO 371, 110062/EP1534/103.
35. Painter, *Oil and the American Century*, 197.
36. Greaves, *British Petroleum*, 3: 136.
37. Ibid., 138, 142, 144.
38. 28 May 1954, FO 371, 109986/EP1015/26; 29 May 1954, FO 371, 109987/EP1015/28.
39. 3 July 1954, FO 371, 110066/EP1534/199; *FRUS, 1952–1954* (Washington, 1989), 10: 891–92, 896, 899.
40. 22 July 1954, FO 371, 109987/EP1015/35; 13 August 1954, FO 371, 110072/EP1534/331; 20 August 1954, FO 371, 110073/EP1534/355.
41. 3 July 1954, FO 371, 110066/EP1534/199. Kennett Love, box 152, Allen W. Dulles Papers, Princeton University, Princeton, NJ; 30 August 1954, 788.00, RG 59.
42. Ramazani, *Iran's Foreign Policy, 1941–1973*, 269; 10 August 1954, FO 371, 110071/EP1534/310; 3 December 1954, 888.2553, RG 59; *FRUS, 1952–54*, 10: 1053.
43. 7, 11, 12, 15, October 1954, Iran, *FBIS*.
44. 3, 6 August 1954, FO 371, 110070/EP1534/286, 298, 299.
45. 9 August 1954, Henderson to Dulles, Dulles-Herter series, AWF, DDEL.
46. Bamberg, *The Anglo-Iranian Years*, 510–11. Daniel Yergin, *The Prize: The Epic Quest for Oil, Money and Power* (New York, 1993), 478.
47. 19 October 1954, Iran, *FBIS*.
48. Brian Lapping, *End of Empire*, 224. *Setareh Islam* (Tehran), 11 August 1954.
49. 3 December 1954, 888.2553, RG 59.
50. 23 September, 7, 8, 12 October 1954, 888.10, RG 59, 8 January, 31 March, 24 November 1954, 888.2614, RG 59.
51. 16 October 1954, FO 371, 110092/EP1941/16.
52. 16 November 1954, FO 371, 110093/EP1941/38. 8 December 1954, FO 371, 109998/EP1051/38A. 22 December 1954, FO 371, 110093/EP1941/50.
53. 8 December 1954, Allen Dulles to JFD, Minutes of telephone conversations, Dulles papers, DDEL.
54. *New York Times*, 9, 12 February 1955.

12 Emerging Patterns

1. James F. Goode, 'Reforming Iran During the Kennedy Years,' *Diplomatic History* 15 (Winter, 1991): 15.

2. May 1975, Memorandum for the President, 'Iran, Briefing Book for Visit of Shah,' Edward J. Savage files, Gerald R. Ford Library, Ann Arbor.
3. Mohammad Reza Shah Pahlavi, *Mission for My Country*, 302, 127, 110. Asadollah Alam, *The Shah and I* (New York, 1992), 318.
4. 28 December 1953, 788.00, RG 59; 23 December 1953, FO 371, 104581/EP10345/24.
5. 21 December 1953, NSC 175, Annex to NSC 175; 2 January 1954, 'U.S. Policy toward Iran,' NSC 5402, RG 273.
6. 28 July 1954, 641.88, RG 59; 26 November 1953, FO 371, 104662/EP2231/1; 21 December 1953, Annex to NSC 175, RG 273; 8 December 1953, FO 371, 109998/EP1051/38A. In February 1957 the Eisenhower administration agreed to move Iran's first line of defense northward to the Elburz Mountains. This represented a victory for the shah because the Americans could now justify providing Iran with more sophisticated weapons. *FRUS, 1955–57*, 12: 893.
7. 7 December 1953, 788.5, RG 59.
8. Hahn, *The United States, Great Britain and Egypt*, 182–6; *FRUS, 1952–54*, 10: 1076.
9. *Kayhan* (Tehran), 15 February 1955; *Dad*, 23 February 1954.
10. 29 March 1954, 'Progress report on NSC 5402,' Central File series, Operations Coordinating Board, NSC Staff papers, White House Office, DDEL; 26 November 1957, 611.88, 31 January 1955, Jeffrey Kitchen to Abbas Aram, 788.00, RG 59; *FRUS, 1955–57*, 12: 685, 745–6, 756, 780–1.
11. Clifford Matlock, Oral interview transcript, 176, DDEL; 7 March 1956, Australian High Commissioner London to Canberra, A5954/1, box 1409, Australian Archives, Belconnen, ACT.
12. 21 September, 10, 24 October 1955, *FBIS*.
13. 6 April 1955, 'Progress Report on NSC 5428,' RG 273; 18 July 1958, Cabinet minutes, box 5, Cabinet series, Office of Staff Secretary, WHO, DDEL.
14. 20 November 1956, Hoover to Eisenhower, Dulles-Herter series, AWF; 4 December 1956, Wilson to Eisenhower, Department of Defense subseries, Subject series, Office of Staff Secretary, WHO, DDEL; 16 August 1956, 611.88, RG 59.
15. 9 June 1958, Memo for Secretary of Defense, International series, box 28, AWF; 25 January 1958, Dulles-Herter series, box 7, AWF.
16. *FRUS, 1955–57*, 12: 898, 963.
17. Ibid., 869, 948, 952, 958.
18. 3 July 1956, NSC 5610, Policy papers, NSC series, Office of Special Assistant for National Security Affairs, WHO; *FRUS, 1955–57*, 12: 955.
19. 21 August 1957, NSC 5703, RG 273; *FRUS, 1955–57*, 12: 878.
20. 1 November 1957, 788.00, RG 59.
21. 27 July, 5 September 1956, 788.00, RG 59.
22. 8 April 1957, 788.00, RG 59.
23. 28 February 1959, 788.00. 26 November 1957, 611.88. 14 April 1956, 788.00. 4 February 1959, 788.00, RG 59.
24. 2 April 1958, NSC 5703/1, Policy papers, NSC series, Office of Special Asst. NSA, WHO, DDEL; *FRUS, 1955–57*, 12: 913.

25. Ibid., 914, 928.
26. Mark Gasiorowski, 'The Qarani Affair and Iranian Politics,' (Paper delivered at the Middle East Studies Association meeting, Washington, DC, 23 November 1991).
27. *FRUS, 1955–57*, 12: 842–43; 1 July 1958, Memorandum of Conversation, International series, box 29, AWF, DDEL.
28. Ibid.
29. 28 June 1958, International series, box 28, AWF, DDEL.
30. 16 July 1958, Eisenhower to Dulles, Minutes of telephone conversations, Dulles papers; 18 July 1958, Greene to Rountree, Special assistant's chronological series, box 13, Dulles papers, DDEL.
31. 19–22 July 1958, Department of Defense subseries, box 4, Subject series, Office of Staff Secretary, WHO, DDEL; 5 September 1958, Operations Coordinating Board report, Briefing notes subseries, NSC series, Office of Special Assistant for NSA, WHO, DDEL.
32. General Hasan Kia interview, Iranian Oral History Project, Harvard University. 14 August 1958, 788.00. 20 August 1958, 788.00, RG 59.
33. 14 August, 4 September 1958, 788.00. 15 January 1959, 788.00. 13 January 1959, 788.00, RG 59.
34. 29 August 1958, 788.00. 27 October 1958, 788.00.
35. 25 February 1959, International series, box 8, Office of staff secretary, WHO; 31 January, 23 February 1959, International series, box 28, AWF, DDEL; 11 December 1959, NSC 5821/1, RG 273.
36. 14 December 1959, International meetings series, box 4, AWF; 31 December 1959, International series, box 28, AWF; 16 December 1959, Subject subseries, Special assistant series, box 9, Office of Special Assistant for NSA, WHO, DDEL.
37. 8 June 1960, NSC 6010, Policy papers, NSC series, Office of Spec. Asst. NSA, WHO, DDEL.
38. *Al-Ahram*, 26 July 1960; *Al-Akhbar* (Cairo), 31 July 1960. See also *Al-Gomhouria* (Cairo), 26 July 1960; and *Egyptian Gazette* (Cairo), 27 July 1960.
39. 30 August 1958, Christian A. Herter papers, box 19, 8 October 1958, OCB Report on Iran, Policy papers, NSC series, Office Spec. ASST. NSA, WHO; 8 October 1958, 8 June 1960, Policy papers, NSC series, Off. Spec. Asst. NSA, WHO; 10 November 1958, CIA Estimate, Briefing notes subseries, box 11, NSC series, Office Spec. Asst. NSA, WHO, DDEL.
40. 4 February 1959, 788.00.
41. 4 September 1958, 788.00.

13 New Frontier and White Revolution

1. Douglas Little, 'From Even-Handed to Empty-Handed: Seeking Order in the Middle East,' in Thomas G. Paterson (ed.), *Kennedy's Quest for Victory: American Foreign Policy, 1961–1963* (New York, 1989), 168. For critical views of the 'can do' attitude of the New Frontiersmen see Robert A. Divine, 'The Education of John F. Kennedy,' in Frank J. Merli and Theodore A. Wilson (eds), *Makers of American Diplomacy:*

From Benjamin Franklin to Henry Kissinger (New York, 1974), 625–7; Midge Decter, 'Kennedyism,' *Commentary* 49 (January 1970): 21; and Jim F. Heath, *Decade of Disillusionment: The Kennedy-Johnson Years* (Bloomington, 1975), 61, 162–3.

2. Abrahamian, *Iran Between Two Revolutions*, 421–2. The shah turned again to the ineffectual Sharif Imami in 1978.

3. The shah had an interesting personality. Usually firm and even stubborn, he would decide upon a course and stick to it. But occasionally a setback would throw him into a dark mood, and he would become indecisive and sink into despair. The government, which he had made completely dependent upon him, would then be leaderless. See McGhee, *Envoy to the Middle World*, 326–7; and Parviz C. Radji, *In the Service of the Peacock Throne* (London, 1983), 252, 274–5, 283; Cottam, *Nationalism in Iran*, 300–2. The dismissal of Bakhtiar also removed a possible rival. See Rubin, *Paved with Good Intentions*, 108–9; Abrahamian, *Iran Between Two Revolutions*, 424, and *Akhbar-i Jabhay-'i Milli-i Iran* [News of the Iranian National Front] (Tehran), 29 July, 7 September 1962.

4. Arthur M. Schlesinger, Jr., *A Thousand Days: John F. Kennedy in the White House* (Boston, 1965), 586–91; Seyom Brown, *The Faces of Power: Constancy and Change in United States Foreign Policy from Truman to Reagan* (New York, 1983), 154; John F. Kennedy, *The Strategy of Peace*, ed. Allan Nevins (New York, 1960), 107–8.

5. Brown, *The Faces of Power*, 154, 184. In the 1960 campaign, the shah's sympathies had been with Richard Nixon. President Eisenhower reassured him that regardless of who won the election, the United States would continue to be concerned about Iran's welfare. See Bill, *Eagle and the Lion*, 130; and Eisenhower to shah, September 1960, Ann Whitman Files, International Series, box 28, DDEL.

6. Shah to Kennedy, 26 January 1961, National Security Files, Countries: Iran, box 119, John F. Kennedy Library, Boston, Massachusetts (hereafter NSF, with filing information). David Lilienthal shows how troubled the shah was in February 1961. See *The Journals of David E. Lilienthal: The Harvest Years, 1959–1963* (New York, 1971), 5: 258.

7. Summary of President's Meeting with Teymour Bakhtiar, 1 March 1961, NSF, Iran, box 115. The administration did not have confidence in the embassy's reporting. See John Kenneth Galbraith, *Ambassador's Journal: A Personal Account of the Kennedy Years* (Boston, 1969), 38.

8. Lilienthal, *Harvest Years* 5:230, 258–9; John Bowling, letter to author, 28 March 1988.

9. NSC 5821, 31 October 1958, White House Office: Office of Special Assistant for National Security Affairs, NSC Series, Policy Papers, box 23, DDEL.

10. Richard Cottam, letter to author, 8 June 1987. Bowling had served in Tehran from 1955 to 1959. According to Assistant Secretary Phillips Talbot, Bowling supplied whatever information the department needed on Iran and also argued forcefully for his policy recommendations. Phillips Talbot, telephone conversation with author, 26 September 1989; Bowling, letter to author. Herbert S. Parmet, *JFK: The Presidency of John F. Kennedy* (New York, 1983), 102. On Kennedy's inclination to

ignore channels, see Edward Weintal and Charles Bartlett, *Facing the Brink: An Intimate Study of Crisis Diplomacy* (New York, 1967), 114; and Thomas G. Paterson, 'Introduction: John F. Kennedy's Quest for Victory and Global Crisis,' in Paterson (ed.), *Kennedy's Quest for Victory*, 17. Bowling received a number of these calls, which could make life difficult at the department; in his telephone conversation with me on 26 September 1989 Phillips Talbot spoke about the awkwardness of informing superiors about such calls. NEA to McGeorge Bundy, 'Current Internal Position in Iran,' 11 February 1961, NSF, Iran, box 115.

11. Abrahamian, *Iran Between Two Revolutions*, 460–1; Cottam, *Nationalism in Iran*, 304–5. For Musaddiq's continuing influence on the National Front, see *Musaddiq's Memoirs*, 79. Many members of the Second National Front, such as Sanjabi and Barzargan, were still active when the revolution began in the late 1970s. In fact, the shah turned to them to save his throne, but it was too late.

12. J. W. Bowling, 20 March 1961 (*Declassified Documents Reference Systems*, Washington, Carrollton Press, 1978), 81A. Phillips Talbot would come to believe that the United States should not push the shah too hard and risk throwing power to the Musaddiqists. Telephone conversation with author, 26 September 1989.

13. 'Some Notes on the Situation in Iran,' Bureau of the Budget, 20 March 1961, NSF, Iran, box 115. Hansen's views contrasted sharply with the cautious views at the State Department. See Schlesinger, *A Thousand Days*, 414, 416.

14. Robert W. Komer, telephone conversation with author, 25 June 1987. A South Asia specialist, Talbot did not arrive in Washington from India until April and immediately faced the problem of Iran. He initially adopted a policy position closer to that of the modernizers than the traditionalists, finding the upbeat mood of the administration, the feeling that it was all right to try things, immensely stimulating. He became convinced that development in Iran would increase stability. As time passed, however, he became more cautious, concluding that there was no alternative to the shah. He still believed that economic change might help win over the opposition, but he was no longer interested in pressuring Iran for social and institutional change. Phillips Talbot, telephone conversation with author, 26 September 1989.

15. Abrahamian, *Iran Between Two Revolutions*, 460; *Kayhan* (Tehran), 29 April, 3 and 8 May 1961; Wailes to Kennedy, 5 May 1961, NSF, Iran, box 115; 'Basic Facts, Report of President's Task Force on Foreign Economic Assistance: Iran,' 22 May 1961 (*Declassified Documents*, 1982), 1774.

16. *Ittila'at*, 21 May 1961. Front members considered Amini a turncoat because he had abandoned Musaddiq and joined Zahidi's government in 1953, and Amini did nothing to redeem himself in their eyes when, shortly after taking office in 1961, he dismissed the Majlis without calling for new elections – an act that violated the constitution. A later interview with Amini seems to indicate that he had no intention of seeking the National Front's support in 1961, preferring instead to further his government's goals via the more traditional use of personal influence. Richard Cottam, letter to author, 8 June 1987.

17. Bowling, letter to author, 28 March 1988.
18. 'Iranian Task Force Recommendations,' Talbot to Chester Bowles, 16 May 1961, NSF, Iran, box 115. For why the United States favored Amini see Abrahamian, *Iran Between Two Revolutions*, 422–3.
19. 'The President's Meeting with Khrushchev,' Department of State Position Paper, 25 May 1961 (*Declassified Documents*, 1976), 124B; Theodore Sorensen, *Kennedy* (New York, 1965), 546–7; Schlesinger, *A Thousand Days*, 363.
20. *Azarin* (Tehran), 28 August 1961, *Mehr Iran* (Tehran), 22 June 1961; *Ittila'at*, 19 December 1961; Husain Ramtin, *Amrika'iha dar Iran* [Americans in Iran] (Tehran, 1962), 107, 109; *Melliyun* (Tehran) 14 August 1961; *Iradeh-yi Azarbaijan* (Tabriz), 27 August 1961 and 3 September 1961; *Peigham Imruz* (Tehran), 11 November 1961.
21. For some diplomatic views on this problem see Herz, *Contacts with the Opposition*, 17, 27.
22. Memorandum: Harold Saunders to Robert W. Komer, 2 December 1961, NSF, Iran: General, box 115.
23. Schlesinger, *A Thousand Days*, 442–5; Sorensen, *Kennedy*, 287–90; Chester Bowles, *Promises to Keep: My Years in Public Life, 1941–1969* (New York, 1971), 360–7. For Dean Acheson's views on Kennedy's conduct of foreign policy see Lilienthal, *Harvest Years* 5: 214–17; and Schlesinger, *A Thousand Days*, 444.
24. C.D. Carr, 'The United States–Iranian Relationship, 1948–78: A Study in Reverse Influence,' in Hossein Amirsadeghi (ed.), *The Security of the Persian Gulf* (New York, 1981), 68–9. To Bowles's chagrin, the sophisticated aircraft he had recommended against were included in the new aid package. See *Promises to Keep*, 369–71. The shah and Ambassador Holmes did not give up easily. In September 1962 Assistant Secretary Talbot passed on a request from Tehran for frigates, prompting Komer, who favored giving Iran no more than what was necessary to meet internal security requirements, to write: '*Where do we draw the line?* I'd like to tell Bill and Phil that President personally says "hell no."' Komer Memo for McGeorge Bundy, 15 September, 1962, NSF, Country Files, Iran: General, box 116.
25. *New York Times*, 10 April 1962; Dean Rusk, interview with author, Athens, Georgia, 18 October 1984. For more on the American press's attitude toward the shah see William A. Dorman and Mansour Farhang, *The U.S. Press and Iran: Foreign Policy and the Journalism of Deference* (Berkeley, 1987). Rusk wanted to send some Iranian students home, claiming they were communists. William Douglas, Oral Interview Transcript, 8–9, RFK Oral History, Kennedy Library. One of the students demonstrating against the shah was Sadegh Ghotbzadeh who became foreign minister in the Islamic Republic and was executed in 1984 for allegedly plotting a *coup d'état*.
26. C.D. Carr, 'US–Iranian Relationship,' 69; Robert W. Komer, letter to author, 8 May 1987. The shah's concern about Nasser and the Arab left was not taken seriously in Washington, which is not surprising, considering the friendly relations between the president and Nasser. See 2 April 1962 (*Declassified Documents*, 1982), 1762; and Douglas

Little, 'JFK, Nasser and Arab Nationalism,' *Journal of American History* 75 (September 1988): 501–27.

27. For more on Arsanjani, see Bill, *Eagle and the Lion,* 143–46. *Christian Science Monitor,* 28 May 1963.

28. One writer has speculated that the shah used Amini, forcing him to take the blame for his own decision to remove several generals who were becoming too powerful. Gholam Hossein Razi, 'The Press and Political Institutions in Iran,' *Middle East Journal* 22 (Autumn 1968): 465. Until his death in December 1992, Amini headed a coalition of exile groups in Paris.

29. Ramazani, *Iran's Foreign Policy, 1941–1975,* 299–303.

30. Ibid., 315–18; *Bamshad* (Tehran), 17 September 1962; Sorensen, *Kennedy,* 713. After lengthy negotiations the Iranian government informed the United States in late August that it would accept the military package offered in April.

31. William Gaud, Oral Interview Transcript, 41, JFKL. The peasants' congress may have been in part a response to the National Front congress held in Tehran in December 1962. See William Green, 'Political Organization in Iran: From Dowrah to Political Party,' *Middle East Journal,* 23 (Spring 1969): 348.

32. Shah Mohammed Riza Pahlavi, Oral Interview Transcript, 1964, 12–13, JFKL.

33. Bowling, letter to author, 28 March 1988.

34. Gaud oral interview, 41; *Khandaniha* (Tehran), 26 July 1962; K. Sagha, 'The 1962 Iranian Land Reform' (Ph.D. dissertation, Claremont Graduate School, 1983); George B. Baldwin, *Planning and Development in Iran* (Baltimore, 1967), 97; *Kayhan,* 12 and 13 March 1963. Alam may have been the only Iranian who could argue with the shah. But he was basically a courtier and was unlikely to oppose vigorously the general movement toward autocracy. Edward Bayne, interview with Alam, Tehran, 1 March 1966, Lilly Library, Indiana University, Bloomington.

35. Cottam, *Nationalism in Iran,* 316–17; Eric J. Hooglund, *Land and Revolution in Iran, 1960–1980,* Modern Middle East Series, no. 7. (Austin, 1982); also, Sagha '1962 Iranian Land Reform'; Baldwin, *Planning and Development,* 97.

36. William S. Gaud to Administrator US AID, 2 March 1963 (*Declassified Documents,* 1982), 000200; William Brubeck to McGeorge Bundy, 21 January 1963 (*Declassified Documents,* 1978–79), 80B; Dean Rusk to President, 20 April 1963, NSF: Meetings and Memoranda, NSAM 228, box 340. Brubeck was too optimistic. After Arsanjani's departure, the shah did not try energetically to win peasant support.

37. Hansen to Komer, 7 May 1963, NSF: M/M, NSAM 228, box 340.

38. Bundy to Members of Standing Group, 17 May 1963, NSF, M/M, NSAM 228, box 340.

39. 'U.S. Strategy for Iran,' 21 May 1963, NSF: M/M, NSAM 228, box 340.

40. Willem Floor, 'The Revolutionary Character of the Ulama: Wishful Thinking or Reality?' 88–92; and Azar Tabari, 'Shi'i Clergy in Iranian Politics,' in Keddie (ed.), *Religion and Politics in Iran: Shi'ism from Quietism to Revolution,* 66–70; Hossein Bashiriyeh, *The State and Revolution in*

Iran, 1962–82 (New York, 1984), 60–1, 79; Abrahamian, *Iran Between Two Revolutions*, 425.

41. Amir Taheri, *The Spirit of Allah: Khomeini and the Islamic Revolution* (Bethesda, MD, 1986), 139; Abrahamian, *Iran Between Two Revolutions*, 426. Khomaini was not set on destroying the monarchy – that came later.

42. Ibid., 424, 460–61; Cottam, *Nationalism in Iran*, 306–9.

43. Tabari, 'Shi'i Clergy,' 69; Richard Cottam, *Iran and the United States: A Cold War Case Study* (Pittsburgh, 1988), 130. This was the beginning of Bazargan's long association with Khomaini.

44. In the words of *Kayhan*, 'a minority of mullas, wedded to the delusion that they could reverse the trend of history, aligned themselves with filthy elements to plunge the country into anarchy.' 6 June 1963. See, for example, *New York Times*, 6 June 1963; *Newsweek*, 17 June 1963; *Time*, 14 June 1963. Even the *Christian Science Monitor* accepted this interpretation, although it also published a letter from Ali Shayegan, a cabinet minister under Musaddiq, refuting this 'orthodox' view of the riots. See *CSM*, 24 June 1963. Like the Americans, the Soviets accepted the official Iranian view of the demonstrations. See Ramazani, *Iran's Foreign Policy, 1941–1975*, 315.

45. When the Buddhists led massive protests against the regime of Ngo Dinh Diem, also in June 1963, US officials were surprised. They were unaware that Buddhist monks traditionally exercised leadership in time of crisis. The Buddhist mind remained 'terra incognita,' said one Kennedy adviser. The same could be said of the Shi'a mind and of the traditional leadership role of the ulama in modern Iran. Kennedy to shah, 15 July 1963 (*Declassified Documents*, 1982), 1765. The shah's leading courtiers, such as Husain Ala, Nasrollah Intizam, and even Prime Minister Alam, were counseling him to move slowly on reform and to avoid becoming too directly involved in the administration of reform programs so that no one could hold him responsible for the failings of those programs. White House officials recommended the opposite. Shortly after the riots Averell Harriman met with Ambassador Holmes in Washington to stress the importance of the shah's moving forward with reforms and doing all he could 'to revive and stimulate the economy.' See Memorandum for Governor Harriman, 18 June 1963, Memorandum for Ambassador Holmes, 20 June 1963, NSF, Country Files, Iran: General, box 116.

46. *New York Times*, 20 September 1963; *Kayhan*, 12 September 1963; *Asnad-i lanah-i jasusi-i Amrika* [Documents from the Nest of American Spies] (Tehran, n.d.), 5: 44–5 (These are documents seized at the US Embassy in Tehran); Andrew F. Westwood, 'Politics of Distrust in Iran,' *Annals of the American Academy* 358 (March 1965): 134.

47. See Martin F. Herz, *A View from Tehran: A Diplomatist Looks at the Shah's Regime in June 1964* (Institute for the Study of Diplomacy, Georgetown University, Washington, 1981), 11.

48. There are interesting parallels between US policy toward the shah and Iran and toward dictator Antonio Salazar and the Portugese empire in Africa. In both cases the Kennedy administration backed away from

early plans to press for political reform. See Whitney Schneidman, 'Divining an African Policy: The American Experience with Portugal, Angola and Mozambique, 1961–1974' (Paper delivered at the African Studies Association Conference, New Orleans, 22–26 November 1985), and Richard D. Mahoney, *JFK: Ordeal in Africa* (New York, 1983), 218–22.

14 As the Shah Goes

1. Bill, *Eagle and the Lion*, 156; February 1968, Walt Rostow to Lyndon Johnson (*Declassified Documents Reference System*, Washington, 1988), 000169.
2. Armin Meyer interview, 29 March 1985, 55, Foundation for Iranian Studies (FIS), Bethesda, MD.
3. 12 November 1964, CIA, (Dec. Docs., 1989), 001843. Colonel Gratian Yatsevitch, 59, FIS. 5 June 1967, CIA, (Dec. Docs., 1988), 3108, *Asnad*, 60: 41.
4. Alam, *The Shah and I*, 262.
5. Bill, *Eagle and the Lion*, 173; 28 November 1965, Meyer to Secretary of State, (*Dec. Docs.*, 1988), 000167; 21 May 1966, Rostow to LBJ (*Dec. Docs.*, 1989), 002327; LBJ to Muhammad Riza Pahlavi (*Dec. Docs.*, 1989), 000458.
6. Taheri, *Nest of Spies*, 54. Rubin, *Paved with Good Intentions*, 124.
7. Taheri, *Nest of Spies*, 66; Rubin, *Paved with Good Intentions*, 139; May 1975, Kissinger to Gerald R. Ford, Memorandum for President, box 3, Edward J. Savage papers, Gerald R. Ford Library (GRFL), Ann Arbor, Michigan.
8. Taheri, *Nest of Spies*, 265.
9. May 1975, Memo for President, box 3, Savage papers, GRFL.
10. Douglas MacArthur III interview, 29 May 1985, 45, FIS; George Lenczowski interview, 30 November 1984, 10, FIS; Richard Helms interview, Iran Oral History Project (IOHP), Harvard University. Gary Sick, NSC Middle East expert in the Carter administration, admits that this behavior continued on the Democrats' watch. He refers to the 'embarrassingly obsequious' tone adopted by Ambassador William Sullivan (1977–9) in a draft letter from the president to the shah. *All Fall Down: America's Tragic Encounter With Iran* (New York, 1987), 56.
11. 22 February 1976, Muhammad Riza Pahlavi to President Ford, box 25, White House Central files, GRFL.
12. *Asnad*, 60: 95; William Miller, IOHP.
13. *Asnad*, 60: 84–85; May 1975, Memo for President, box 3, Savage papers, GRFL; MacArthur interview, 7.
14. Sick, *All Fall Down*, 6, 8.
15. Herz, *Contacts with the Opposition*, 17, 26–27. Miller, IOHP.
16. 31 October 1958, 'US policy toward Iran,' Policy papers, NSC series, Off. Spec. Asst. NSA, WHO; 6 June 1960, OCB Memorandum, Briefing notes subseries, NSC series, Off. Spec. Asst. NSA, WHO, DDEL.
17. A.H.H. Abidi, ed., *The Tehran Documents* (New Delhi, 1988), 75.
18. 25 November 1978, William Sullivan to Secretary of State, *Iran: The*

Making of U.S. Policy, 1977–1980, National Security Archive (Alexandria, VA, 1990), 01801.

19.   Nikki R. Keddie, *Roots of Revolution: An Interpretive History of Modern Iran* (New Haven, 1981), 141; Said Amir Arjomand, *The Turban for the Crown: The Islamic Revolution in Iran* (New York, 1988), 140.

20.   Rajaee, 'Islam, Nationalism and Musaddiq's era,' in Bill and Louis (eds), *Musaddiq, Iranian Nationalism and Oil,* 129 ff. Ervand Abrahamian, *Khomeinism: Essays on the Islamic Republic* (Berkeley and Los Angeles, 1993), 104–10.

21.   Richard Helms interview, 1985, FIS.

Bibliography

UNPUBLISHED PRIMARY SOURCES

United States

Bennett Library, University of Michigan, Ann Arbor
  Francis W. Kelsey Papers
Declassified Documents Reference System
Dwight D. Eisenhower Library, Abilene, Kansas
  Christian A. Herter Papers
  C.D. Jackson Papers
  Dwight D. Eisenhower Papers (Ann Whitman File)
    Dulles–Herter Series
    International Meetings Series
    International Series
    National Security Council Series
  White House Office, National Security Council Staff Papers
    Operations Coordinating Board Central File Series
  White House Office, Office of Staff Secretary, Records of L. Arthur Minnich
    Cabinet Series
    Subject Series
  White House Office, Office of the Special Assistant for National Security
    Affairs
    National Security Council Series
    Special Assistant Series
  John Foster Dulles Papers
    Subject Series
    Chronological Series
    Minutes of Telephone Conversations
  Dwight D. Eisenhower Oral History Collection
    Clifford Matlock
Gerald R. Ford Library, Ann Arbor, Michigan
  Edward J. Savage Files
  White House Central Files
John F. Kennedy Library, Boston, Massachusetts
  National Security Files
  Robert F. Kennedy, Oral History Collection
    William Douglas
  John F. Kennedy Oral History Collection
    William Gaud
    Shah Mohammed Riza Pahlavi
Library of Congress, Washington, DC
  Averell Harriman Papers
Lilly Library, Indiana University, Bloomington

Edward Bayne (taped interviews with shah and Alam)
Burton Y. Berry Papers
Ezra Pound Papers
Seeley G. Mudd, Manuscript Library, Princeton University
    Allen W. Dulles Papers
National Archives, College Park, MD
    Foreign Broadcast Information Service (FBIS) [microfilm]
    Tehran Post Files (Record Group [RG] 84)
    General Records of the Departmnent of State (RG 59)
    Records of the Department of Agriculture (RG 166)
    Records of the National Security Council (RG 273)
    Records of the Joint Chiefs of Staff (RG 218)
    Records of the Office of the Secretary of Defense (RG 330)
    Records of the Office of the Secretary of the Interior, 1933–53 (RG 48)
National Archives Pacific Southwest, Laguna Niguel, CA
    Richard M. Nixon Pre-Presidential Papers
Navy Historical Center, Washington Naval Yard, Washington DC
    Review of the Office of Naval Intelligence
    Strategic Plans Division, Office of the Chief of Naval Operations
Franklin D. Roosevelt Library, Hyde Park, New York
    John Wiley Papers
Harry S. Truman Library, Independence, Missouri
    Dean Acheson Papers
    Robert Garner Papers
    Henry F. Grady Papers
    Francis F. Lincoln Papers
    Naval Aide to the President Papers
    Harry S. Truman Oral History Collection
        Henry Villard
        William Warne
    Harry S. Truman Papers (President's Secretary's File)
        General File
        Intelligence File
        Subject File
    Harry S. Truman Papers (White House Central File)
        Official File

Correspondence and Interviews with the Author

John Bowling
Henry Byroade
Richard Cottam
Robert W. Komer
George McGhee
George Middleton
Howard Page (conducted by Ben Wall)
Mehdi Samii
Dean Rusk
Phillips Talbot
Denis Wright

Oral Interviews

Columbia University Oral History Project
  Loy Henderson
Iranian Oral History Project, Houghton Library, Harvard University
  Richard Helms
  General Hasan Kia
  William Miller
  Dr. Gholam-Husain Musaddiq
Foundation for Iranian Studies, Bethesda, Maryland
  Oral Interview Collection
    Richard Helms
    Armin Meyer
    Colonel Gratian Yatsevitch
    Douglas MacArthur III

Great Britain

Bodleian Library, Oxford
  Clement Attlee Papers
  Richard Stokes Papers
Open University, Milton Keynes
  Kenneth Younger Diary
London School of Economics
  Hugh Dalton Diary
  Oral History Collection
    Lord Butler
    Sir Robert Scott
Public Record Office, Kew
  Records of the Cabinet Office (CAB 128, 130)
  Political Correspondence of the Foreign Office (FO 371)
  Tehran Post Files (FO 248)
  Records of the Treasury (T 236)
  Records of the Ministry of Fuel and Power (POWE 33)
  Records of the Chiefs of Staff Committee (DEFE 4)

Australia

Australian Archives, Belconnen, ACT
  Records of the Australian High Commissioner, London

PUBLISHED PRIMARY SOURCES

Official

British Petroleum. *History of British Petroleum in Iran.* 3 vols. Edited by Rose
  L. Greaves. London, 1970. [Privately published].
Great Britain, *Parliamentary Debates* (Commons), 5th ser., 489, 491 (1951).

International Labour Office. *Labour Conditions in the Oil Industry in Iran.* 1950.

Iran. *Muzakirat-i Majlis* [Parliamentary Proceedings]. Tehran.

Some Documents on the Nationalization of the Oil Industry in Iran. Washington, DC, 1951.

National Front. *Akhbar-i jabhay-i milli-i Iran.* [News of the Iranian National Front]. Tehran, 29 July, 7 September 1962.

United Nations. Security Council. *Official Records, 1951.* New York.

US Congress. House of Representatives. Committee on Foreign Affairs. *Selected Executive Session Hearings of the Committee, 1951–56 The Middle East, Africa, and Inter-American Affairs.* History series, vol. 16. Washington, 1980.

Senate, Armed Services Committee. *Military Situation in the Far East.* Washington, 1951.

Senate, *Congressional Record,* 82nd Cong., 1st sess., 10, pt. 8: 10564, pt. 10: 12978.

Senate, Subcommittee on Multinational Corporations and United States Foreign Policy. *Multinational Petroleum Companies and Foreign Policy.* 93d Cong., 2d sess., pt. 7.

US Department of State. *Foreign Relations of the United States.* Washington, DC, 1970–1993 (FRUS).

US Embassy. Iran. *Tehran Press Review, 1952–54.* Tehran.

Unofficial

Abidi, A.H.H., ed. *The Tehran Documents.* New Delhi, 1988.

Alam, Asadollah. *The Shah and I.* New York, 1992.

Alexander, Yonah and Allen Nanes, eds. *The United States and Iran: A Documentary History.* Frederick, Md., 1980.

Asnad-i lanah-i jasus-i Amrika. [Documents from the Nest of American Spies]. Tehran, n.d.

Breasted, James H. 'The University of Chicago Expedition to the Middle East, 1919–1920.' *The University Record* 7: 1–20.

Buzurgmihr, Jalil. *Taghrirat-i Musaddiq dar zindan.* [Musaddiq's Conversations in Prison]. Edited by Iraj Afshar. Tehran, 1980.

Grady, Henry F. 'What Went Wrong in Iran.' *Saturday Evening Post* 224: 28.

Hedayati, M.A. *Situation politique et sociale de l'Iran en 1950–1951: Année de la nationalisation du pétrole.* Neuchâtel, 1951.

Herz, Martin F., ed. *Contacts With the Opposition: A Symposium.* Lanham, Md., 1986.

A View from Tehran: A Diplomatist Looks at the Shah's Regime in June 1964. Washington, 1981.

Kennedy, John F. *Strategies of Peace.* Edited by Allan Nevins. New York, 1960.

Maleki, Khalil. *Niruy-i sivum piruz mishavad.* [The Third Force Will Win.] Tehran, 1951.

Mir-Ashrafi, Mihdi. *Qiyam dar rah-i sultanat, 19 Esfand-28 Mordad, 1332.* [Uprising on the Road to Monarchy, 10 March–19 August 1953]. Tehran, 1954.

Musaddiq, Muhammad. *Speech by Musaddiq to Representatives of the American Press, 18 March 1952.* Lima.

Murtazavi, Muhammad Ali. *Yak mah mamuriiyyat-i tarikhi dar Khuzistan barayi ijrayi qanun-i milli shudan-i san'at-i naft.* [One-Month's History-Making Assignment in Khuzistan to Implement Nationalization of the Oil Industry]. Tehran, n.d.

National Security Archive. *Iran: The Making of U.S. Policy, 1977–1980.* Alexandria, Va., 1990.

Sakha'i, Mahmud. *Musaddiq va Rastakhiz-i Millat.* [Musaddiq and the Resurrection of the Nation.] Tehran, 1953.

Shuckburgh, Evelyn. *Descent to Suez: Diaries, 1951–56.* New York, 1987.

Memoirs

Acheson, Dean. *Present at the Creation: My Years in the State Department.* New York, 1969.

Attlee, Clement. *Twilight of Empire.* London, 1960.

Bakhtiar, Shahpour. *Ma fidelité.* Paris, 1985.

Bowles, Chester. *Promises to Keep: My Years in Public Life, 1941–1969.* New York, 1971.

Colville, John. *The Fringes of Power: 10 Downing Street Diaries.* New York, 1985.

Eden, Anthony. *Full Circle: The Memoirs of Sir Anthony Eden.* London, 1960.

Farman Farmaian, Sattareh. *Daughter of Persia: A Woman's Journey From Her Father's Harem Through the Islamic Revolution.* New York, 1992.

Galbraith, Kenneth. *Ambassador's Journal: A Personal Account of the Kennedy Years.* Boston, 1969.

Ghani, Qasim. *Yaddashtha-yi Duktur Qasim Ghani.* [The Notebooks of Doctor Qasim Gahni]. Vol. 9. Edited by Cyrus Ghani. London, 1982.

Keshavarz, Fereidun. *Man motaham mikonam.* [I confess.] Tehran, 1977.

Krock, Arthur. *Memoirs: Sixty Years on the Firing Line.* New York, 1968.

Lilienthal, David E. *The Journals of David E. Lilienthal: The Harvest Years, 1959–1963.* Vol. 5. New York, 1971.

McGhee, George. *Envoy to the Middle World: Adventures in Diplomacy.* New York, 1983.

Millspaugh, Arthur. *Americans in Persia.* Washington, 1946.

Musaddiq, Mohammad. *Musaddiq's Memoirs.* Edited by Homa Katouzian. London, 1988.

Nixon, Richard M. *Memoirs.* New York, 1978.

Pahlavi, Mohammad Reza Shah. *Mission for My Country.* London, 1961.

Radji, Parviz. *In the Service of the Peacock Throne.* London, 1983.

Roosevelt, Kim. *Countercoup: The Struggle for Control of Iran.* New York, 1979.

Ross, Albion. *Journey of an American.* Indianapolis, 1957.

Ruhani, Fuad. *Tarikh-i milli shudan-i naft-i Iran.* [A History of the Nationalization of Oil in Iran]. Tehran, 1973.

Sulzberger, C.L. *A Long Row of Candles: Memoirs and Diaries, 1934–54.* Toronto, 1969.

Walters, Vernon. *Silent Missions.* New York, 1978.

Newspapers and Journals

Al-Ahram
Al-Akhbar
Al-Gomhouria
Azarin
Bakhtar-i Imruz
Bamshad
Cahier de l'orient contemporain
Central Asian Review
Christian Science Monitor
Current Digest of the Soviet Press
Dad
Daily Telegraph
Diplomat
Economist
Egyptian Gazette
Iradeh-yi Azarbaijan
Ittila'at
Journal de Tehran
Kayhan
Khandaniha
Khavar
Mard-i Imruz
Mardum
Mehr Iran
Melliyun
Nabard-i Millat
Newsweek
New York Times
Oil Forum
Parcham-i Islam
Peigham Imruz
The Reporter
Sada-yi Mardum
Setareh Islam
Shahid
Spectator
The Tehran Journal
The Times
Times of India
Tulu'
Washington Post

Books and Articles

Foreign Language
Alizadeh, Ahmad. *Shuhadayi Siyum-i Tir Mah 1331.* [The Martyrs of 21 July 1952]. Isfahan, 1952.

Bihniya, Husain. *Pardih-hay-i siyasat: Naft, nihzat, Musaddiq, Zahidi.* [Behind the Scenes: Oil, Resurgence, Musaddiq, Zahidi]. Tehran, n.d.

Kayustuvan, Husain. *Siyasat-i muvazinih-ye manfi dar majlis-i chahardahom.* [The Policy of Negative Equilibrium in the Fourteenth Majlis]. Tehran, 1951.

Lentz, Wolfgang. *Iran, 1951/52.* Heidelberg, 1952.

Ramtin, Husain. *Amrika'iha dar Iran.* [Americans in Iran]. Tehran, 1962.

Shayegan, Ali. 'Faja'i siyyom-i tir.' [The Tragedy of the Twenty-first of July]. *Yaghma* 5: 303–10.

English

Abrahamian, Ervand. *Iran Between Two Revolutions.* Princeton, 1982.
    Khomeinism: Essays on the Islamic Republic. New York, 1988.

Akhavi, Shahrough. 'The Role of the Clergy in Iranian Politics, 1949–1954.' In *Musaddiq, Iranian Nationalism and Oil,* James A. Bill and William Roger Louis, eds. Austin, 1988.

Ambrose, Stephen. *Eisenhower.* Vol 1., *Soldier, General of the Army, President Elect, 1890–1952.* New York, 1983.

Arjomand, Said Amir. *The Turban for the Crown: The Islamic Revolution in Iran.* New York, 1988.

Azimi, Fakhreddin. *Iran: The Crisis of Democracy, 1941–53.* New York, 1989.
    'The Reconciliation of Politics and Ethics, Nationalism and Democracy: An Overview of the Political Career of Dr. Muhammad Musaddiq.' In *Musaddiq, Iranian Nationalism and Oil,* James A. Bill and William Roger Louis, eds. Austin, 1988.

Baldwin, George B. *Planning and Development in Iran.* Baltimore, 1967.

Bamberg, J.H. *The History of the British Petroleum Company. The Anglo-Iranian Years, 1928–1954.* Cambridge, 1994.

Bashiriyeh, Hossein. *The State and Revolution in Iran, 1962–1982.* New York, 1984.

Bill, James A. 'America, Iran and the Politics of Intervention, 1951–1953.' In *Musaddiq, Iranian Nationalism and Oil,* James A. Bill and William Roger Louis, eds. Austin, 1988.
    The Eagle and the Lion: The Tragedy of American-Iranian Relations. New Haven, 1988.

Brands, H.W. *Inside the Cold War: Loy Henderson and the Rise of the American Empire, 1918–1961.* New York, 1991.

Brown, Seyom. *The Faces of Power: Constancy and Change in United States Foreign Policy from Truman to Reagan.* New York, 1983.

Butler, David. *British General Election of 1951.* London, 1952.

Carr, C.D. 'The United States-Iranian Relationship, 1948–78: A Study in Reverse Influence.' In *The Security of the Persian Gulf,* Hossein Amirsadeghi ed. New York, 1981.

Cottam, Richard. *Iran and the United States: A Cold War Case Study.* Pittsburgh, 1988.
    Nationalism in Iran. Pittsburgh, 1964.
    'Nationalism in Twentieth-Century Iran and Dr. Muhammad Musaddiq.' In *Musaddiq, Iranian Nationalism and Oil,* James A. Bill and William Roger Louis eds. Austin, 1988.

Decter, Midge. 'Kennedyism.' *Commentary* 49: 21.

Diba, Farhad. *Mohammed Mossadegh: A Political Biography*. London, 1986.

Divine, Robert A. 'The Education of John F. Kennedy.' In *Makers of American Diplomacy: From Benjamin Franklin to Henry Kissinger*, ed. Frank J. Merli and Theodore A. Wilson. New York, 1974.

Donoughue, Bernard and G.W. Jones. *Herbert Morrison: Portrait of a Politician*. London, 1973.

Dorman, William A. and Mansour Farhang. *The U.S. Press and Iran: Foreign Policy and the Journalism of Deference*. Berkeley, 1987.

Elm, Mostofa. *Oil, Power, and Principle: Iran's Oil Nationalization and Its Aftermath*. Syracuse, 1992.

Elwell-Sutton, L.P. *Persian Oil: A Study in Power Politics*. 1955. Reprint. Westport, Conn., 1975.

Floor, Willem. 'The Revolutionary Character of the Ulama: Wishful Thinking or Reality?' In *Religion and Politics in Iran: Shi'ism from Quietism to Revolution*. Nikki R. Keddie ed. New Haven, 1983.

Ford, Alan W. *The Anglo-Iranian Oil Dispute, 1951–52*. Berkeley and Los Angeles, 1954.

Gasiorowski, Mark. 'The 1953 Coup D'état in Iran.' *International Journal of Middle East Studies* 19: 261–86.

    U.S. Foreign Policy and the Shah: Building a Client State in Iran. Ithaca, 1991.

    'The Qarani Affair and Iranian Politics.' Paper read at Middle East Studies Association meeting, 23 November 1991, Washington, DC.

Gilbert, Martin. *Winston S. Churchill*. London, 1988.

Goode, James F. 'A Good Start: The First American Mission to Iran, 1883–1885.' *The Muslim World* 74: 100–19.

    'Reforming Iran During the Kennedy Years.' *Diplomatic History* 15 (Winter 1991): 13–29.

    The United States and Iran: The Diplomacy of Neglect, 1946–51. London, 1989.

Green, William. 'Political Organization in Iran: From Dowrah to Political Party.' *Middle East Journal* 23: 348.

Hamilton, Charles W. *Americans and Oil in the Middle East*. Houston, 1962.

Hahn, Peter J. *The United States, Great Britain and Egypt: Strategy and Diplomacy in the Early Cold War*. Chapel Hill, 1991.

Harter, John J. 'Mr. Foreign Service on Musaddiq and Wristonization.' *Foreign Service Journal* (November, 1980): 17–18.

Heath, Jim. *Decade of Disillusionment: The Kennedy-Johnson Years*. Bloomington, 1975.

Heiss, Maryann. 'The United States, Great Britain, and the Creation of the Iranian Oil Consortium, 1953–1954.' *International History Review* 16 (August, 1994): 511–35.

James, Robert Rhodes. *Anthony Eden: A Biography*. New York, 1987.

Katouzian, Homa. *Musaddiq and the Struggle for Power in Iran*. London, 1990.

    The Political Economy of Modern Iran: Despotism and Pseudo-Modernism, 1926–1979. New York, 1981.

    'Oil Boycott and the Political Economy: Musaddiq and the Strategy of Non-oil Economics.' In *Musaddiq, Iranian Nationalism, and Oil*, James Bill and William Roger Louis eds. Austin, 1988.

Kaufman, Burton I. *The Oil Cartel Case: A Documentary Study of Antitrust Activity in the Cold War Era*. Westport, Conn., 1978.

Keddie, Nikki R. *Roots of Revolution: An Interpretive History of Modern Iran.* New Haven, 1981.

Klebanoff, Shoshana. 'Oil for Europe: American Foreign Policy and Middle East Oil.' Ph.D. dissertation, Claremont Graduate School, 1974.

Krause, Walter W. *Soraya, Queen of Persia.* London, 1956.

Kuniholm, Bruce. *Origins of the Cold War in the Near East.* Princeton, 1980.

Ladjevardi, Habib. 'Constitutional Government and Reform under Musaddiq.' In *Musaddiq, Iranian Nationalism and Oil,* James Bill and William Roger Louis eds. Austin, 1988.

Labor Unions and Autocracy in Iran. Syracuse, 1985.

Lapping, Brian. *End of Empire.* New York, 1985.

Little, Douglas. 'From Even-Handed to Empty-Handed: Seeking Order in the Middle East.' In *Kennedy's Quest for Victory: American Foreign Policy, 1961–1963.* New York, 1989.

'JFK, Nasser and Arab Nationalism,' *Journal of American History* 75 (September 1988): 501–27.

Longrigg, Stephen H. *Oil in the Middle East: Its Discovery and Development.* New York, 1954.

Mahdavi, Hossein. 'Patterns and Problems of Economic Development in Rentier States: The Case of Iran.' In *Studies in the Economic History of the Middle East,* M.A. Cook ed. London, 1970.

Mahoney, Richard D. *JFK: Ordeal in Africa.* New York, 1983.

McClellan, David S. *Dean Acheson: The State Department Years.* New York, 1976.

Miyata, Osamu. 'Khalil Maleki During the Oil Nationalization Period in Iran.' *Jusur* 1: 51–3.

Mottahedeh, Roy. *The Mantle of the Prophet: Religion and Politics in Iran.* New York, 1985.

Painter, David S. *Oil and the American Century.* Baltimore, 1986.

Parmet, Herbert S. *JFK: The Presidency of John F. Kennedy.* New York, 1983.

Paterson, Thomas G., ed. 'Introduction: John F. Kennedy's Quest for Victory and Global Crisis.' In *Kennedy's Quest for Victory.* New York, 1989.

Pelling, Henry M. *The Labour Governments, 1946–51.* New York, 1984.

Qaimmaqami, Linda Wills. 'The Catalyst of Nationalization: Max Thornburg and the Failure of Private Sector Development in Iran, 1947–1951.' *Diplomatic History* 19 (Winter 1995): 1–31.

Rajaee, Farhang. 'Islam, Nationalism and Musaddiq's Era: Post-Revolutionary Historiography in Iran.' In *Musaddiq, Iranian Nationalism and Oil,* James A. Bill and William Roger Louis eds. Austin, 1988.

Ramazani, Ruhollah K. *Iran's Foreign Policy, 1941–1973: A Study of Foreign Policy in Modernizing Nations.* Charlottesville, 1975.

Razi, Gholam Hussein. 'The Press and Political Institutions in Iran.' *Middle East Journal* 22 (Autumn 1968).

Richard, Yann. 'Ayatollah Kashani.' In *Religion and Politics in Iran: Shi'ism from Quietism to Revolution.* Nikki R. Keddie ed. New Haven, 1983.

Rubin, Barry. *Paved With Good Intentions: The American Experience and Iran.* New York, 1980.

Said, Edward. *Orientalism.* New York, 1978.

Sagha, K. 'The 1962 Iranian Land Reform.' Ph.D. dissertation, Claremont Graduate School, 1983.

Schlesinger, Arthur M., Jr. *A Thousand Days: John F. Kennedy in the White House.* Boston, 1965.

Schneidman, Whitney. 'Divining an African Policy: The American Experience with Portugal, Angola and Mozambique, 1961–1974.' Paper read at the African Studies Association Conference, 22–26 November 1985 at New Orleans.

Siavoshi, Sussan. *Liberal Nationalism in Iran: The Failure of a Movement.* Boulder, CO, 1990.

Sick, Gary. *All Fall Down: America's Tragic Encounter with Iran.* New York, 1987.

Sorenson, Theodore. *Kennedy.* New York, 1965.

Tabari, Azar. 'Shi'i Clergy in Iranian Politics.' In *Religion and Politics in Iran: Shi'ism from Quietism to Revolution.* Nikki R. Keddie ed. New Haven, 1983.

Taheri, Amir. *Nest of Spies America's Journey to Disaster in Iran.* New York, 1988.
The Spirit of Allah: Khomeini and the Islamic Revolution. Bethesda, 1986.

Twain, Mark. *Notebook.* New York, 1935.
Innocents Abroad. Boston, 1895.

Walker, Franklin. *Irreverent Pilgrims: Melville, Browne and Mark Twain in the Holy Land.* Seattle, 1974.

Wall, Bennett H. *Growth in a Changing Environment: A History of Standard Oil Company (New Jersey) Exxon Corporation, 1950–1975.* New York, 1988.

Weintal, Edward and Charles Bartlett. *Facing the Brink: An Intimate Study of Crisis Diplomacy.* New York, 1967.

Westwood, Andrew F. 'Politics of Distrust in Iran.' *Annals of the American Academy* 358: 123–35.

Yapp, M.E. *The Making of the Modern Near East, 1792–1923.* A History of the Near East. New York, 1987.

Yergin, Daniel. *The Prize: The Epic Quest for Oil, Money and Power.* New York, 1991.
Shattered Peace: The Origins of the Cold War and the National Security State. Boston, 1978.

Index